RESPONDING TO AUTHORITARIAN POPULISM AT THE EUROPEAN COURT OF HUMAN RIGHTS

The book offers the first systematic account of the European Court of Human Rights' actual and potential response to the wave of authoritarian populism consolidating across Council of Europe states. It develops an original framework combining philosophical, social-scientific, and legal analysis. The book first argues that authoritarian populism is characterized by a severe distortion of democracy and a corrupt rule of law. Drawing on these insights, the book then points to the infrastructural erosion of Convention rights, highlighting the limits of the Court's 'democratic society' in the media, judicial, and electoral domains. Taking into account the Court's subsidiary position, the book finally demonstrates how the Court's proportionality test can and should be enhanced to better detect and respond to infrastructural erosion across these areas.

ALAIN ZYSSET specializes in the normative analysis of the practices of law with particular reference to international courts and tribunals. Trained in philosophy, history, and law, Alain is currently a reader at the School of Law, University of Glasgow, Scotland.

STUDIES ON INTERNATIONAL COURTS AND TRIBUNALS

General Editors
Andreas Føllesdal, University of Oslo
Geir Ulfstein, University of Oslo

Studies on International Courts and Tribunals contains theoretical and interdisciplinary scholarship on legal aspects as well as the legitimacy and effectiveness of international courts and tribunals.

Other books in the series:

Mads Andenas and Eirik Bjorge (eds.) *A Farewell to Fragmentation: Reassertion and Convergence in International Law*

Cecilia M. Bailliet and Nobuo Hayashi (eds.) *The Legitimacy of International Criminal Tribunals*

Amrei Müller with Hege Elisabeth Kjos (eds.) *Judicial Dialogue and Human Rights*

Nienke Grossman, Harlan Grant Cohen, Andreas Follesdal and Geir Ulfstein (eds.) *Legitimacy and International Courts*

Theresa Squatrito, Oran R. Young, Andreas Føllesdal and Geir Ulfstein (eds.) *The Performance of International Courts and Tribunals*

Robert Howse, Hélène Ruiz-Fabri, Geir Ulfstein and Michelle Q. Zang (eds.) *The Legitimacy of International Trade Courts and Tribunals*

Marlene Wind (ed.) *International Courts and Domestic Politics*

Christina Voigt (ed.) *International Judicial Practice on the Environment: Questions of Legitimacy*

Martin Scheinin (ed.) *Human Rights Norms in 'Other' International Courts*

Freya Baetens (ed.) *Legitimacy of Unseen Actors in International Adjudication*

Shai Dothan *International Judicial Review: When Should International Courts Intervene?*

Silje Langvatn, Mattias Kumm and Wojciech Sadurski (eds.) *Public Reason and Courts*

Daniel Behn, Szilárd Gáspár-Szilágyi and Malcolm Langford (eds.) *Adjudicating Trade and Investment Disputes: Convergence or Divergence?*

Sondre Torp Helmersen *The Application of Teachings by the International Court of Justice*

Daniel Behn, Ole Kristian Fauchald and Malcolm Langford (eds.) *The Legitimacy of Investment Arbitration: Empirical Perspectives*

Eric De Brabandere *International Procedure in Interstate Litigation and Arbitration: A Comparative Approach*

Chiara Giorgetti and Mark Pollack (eds.) *Beyond Fragmentation: Cross-Fertilization, Cooperation and Competition among International Courts and Tribunals*

Stavros Brekoulakis and Georgios Dimitropoulos (eds.) *International Commercial Courts: The Future of Transnational Adjudication*

Matthew Gillett *Prosecuting Environmental Harm before the International Criminal Court*

Sassan Gholiagha *The Humanisation of Global Politics: International Criminal Law, the Responsibility to Protect, and Drones*

Ezgi Yildiz *The European Court of Human Rights and the Norm against Torture: Between Forbearance and Audacity*

Christina Voigt and Caroline Foster (eds.) *International Courts versus Non-Compliance Mechanisms: Comparative Advantages in Strengthening Treaty Implementation*

Luise Müller *The Right to Punish: Political Authority and International Criminal Justice*

Theresa Squatrito *Judging under Constraint: The Politics of Deference by International Courts*

RESPONDING TO AUTHORITARIAN POPULISM AT THE EUROPEAN COURT OF HUMAN RIGHTS

A Calibrated Framework

ALAIN ZYSSET
University of Glasgow

CAMBRIDGE
UNIVERSITY PRESS

CAMBRIDGE
UNIVERSITY PRESS

Shaftesbury Road, Cambridge CB2 8EA, United Kingdom

One Liberty Plaza, 20th Floor, New York, NY 10006, USA

477 Williamstown Road, Port Melbourne, VIC 3207, Australia

314–321, 3rd Floor, Plot 3, Splendor Forum, Jasola District Centre, New Delhi – 110025, India

103 Penang Road, #05–06/07, Visioncrest Commercial, Singapore 238467

Cambridge University Press is part of Cambridge University Press & Assessment, a department of the University of Cambridge.

We share the University's mission to contribute to society through the pursuit of education, learning and research at the highest international levels of excellence.

www.cambridge.org
Information on this title: www.cambridge.org/9781009377966

DOI: 10.1017/9781009377935

When citing this work, please include a reference to the DOI 10.1017/9781009377935

First published 2026

Cover image: interior of the European Court of Human Rights. Image by Andia / Alamy Stock Photo.

A catalogue record for this publication is available from the British Library

Library of Congress Cataloging-in-Publication Data
Names: Zysset, Alain author
Title: Responding to authoritarian populism at the European Court of Human Rights : a calibrated framework / Alain Zysset, University of Glasgow.
Description: Cambridge, United Kingdom ; New York, NY : Cambridge University Press, 2026. | Series: Sict studies on international courts and tribunals | Includes bibliographical references and index.
Identifiers: LCCN 2025037155 | ISBN 9781009377966 hardback | ISBN 9781009377973 paperback | ISBN 9781009377935 ebook
Subjects: LCSH: European Court of Human Rights | European Court of Human Rights – Cases | Human rights – Europe | Rule of law – Europe | Authoritarianism | Populism | LCGFT: Law materials
Classification: LCC KJC5138 .Z97 2026 | DDC 341.4/8094–dc23/eng/20250808
LC record available at https://lccn.loc.gov/2025037155

ISBN 978-1-009-37796-6 Hardback

For Jacqueline

CONTENTS

ACKNOWLEDGEMENTS

The research leading to this publication was greatly facilitated by two fellowships that secured some precious time off from my position at the School of Law, University of Glasgow. Preliminary research was made possible thanks to a re:constitution fellowship funded by the Stiftung Mercator. I am thankful for the generous support offered by the fellowship scheme and express my gratitude to its coordinator, Dorit Modersitzki, for her thoughtful and continuous guidance.

The fellowship allowed me to visit the Centre for Fundamental Rights at the Hertie School in Berlin as a visiting fellow in the academic year 2019–20. I am very grateful to the Centre's co-director, Başak Çalı, for including me in the Centre's research activities, for inviting me to present my preliminary ideas at its research colloquium, and for discussing the formative ideas of the project. I further developed these ideas and presented an emerging analytical framework at the University of Dresden in the autumn of 2019 via a lecture at the Centre for International Studies. I thank Dominik Steiger for inviting me and the audience for providing much helpful feedback at this early stage.

As the pandemic shredded our social life throughout the year 2020, I was fortunate to form singular relationships that accompanied the solitary writing process in these troubled times. I thank Juan for the memorable days in the (otherwise-)empty but bright office space of Friedrichstraße, revisiting the power of ethereal indie music. To Katharina, a short note will not do justice to the generosity, love, and support received at that time and the joy of numerous (and often aimless) walks around Schöneberg. The first article manuscript of the project was submitted to the *International Journal of Constitutional Law* in early 2021 and published in early 2022 (Alain Zysset, 'Calibrating the Response to Populism at the European Court of Human Rights', *International Journal of Constitutional Law* 20, no. 3 (2022): 976–1005). I thank the journal editors for reusing some material from the piece in this monograph.

Expanding a journal article into a monograph project was greatly facilitated by a twenty-four-month research fellowship funded by the Norwegian Research Council under the auspices of PluriCourts, a Center for Excellence at the University of Oslo, throughout the academic years 2021–3. I thank Jane Mair, Dean of the School of Law at the University of Glasgow, for helping secure leave from my position to take up the fellowship. PluriCourts offered me unrivalled working conditions in a highly interdisciplinary environment. This monograph is also a testament to PluriCourts' ambition of learning from and overcoming disciplinary boundaries within a discrete piece of research.

I am particularly indebted to PluriCourts co-director, Andreas Føllesdal, for his continuous support and for inviting me to present work in progress at PluriCourts' lunch seminar. I am grateful to Andreas and to Steven Ratner for facilitating a greatly inspiring visit to the University of Michigan Law School, thanks to an International and Comparative Law Research Fellowship in the autumn of 2022. I remain grateful also for the company of colleagues and friends at PluriCourts during my various stays in Oslo, in particular, Laura Létourneau-Tremblay, Runar Lie, and last – but not least – Jonathan Kuyper for sharing both a flat in this beautiful city and the receipts of its extortionate beers.

I presented more advanced chapter drafts at a workshop, 'The European Court of Human Rights Facing Populism and Authoritarianism: Time for System Change?', in Oslo in the spring of 2023. I thank Joseph Finnerty for his incisive comments and for continuing conversations on the topic. A more advanced argument and framework was presented in a lecture at King's College London, also in early 2023. I thank Lorenzo Zucca and Massimo Renzo for inviting me and the audience for highly stimulating comments and questions. The final chapters were written in the first months of 2024, spent at the University of Hong Kong's Faculty of Law as a visiting fellow. I thank Cora Chan for facilitating the visit and organizing a lecture at the Centre for Comparative and Public Law. I am also grateful to Samantha Besson for inviting me to present the final iteration of the argument in Fribourg in the fall of 2024 and for her acute comments. I thank audiences at various events in Copenhagen, Edinburgh, Hanover, Gothenburg, and Madrid, and for questions and comments on the topic and associated themes.

At Cambridge University Press, I thank Tom Randall, Natasha Burton, and Edgar Mendez for their patience and superb editorial guidance, and

Kathleen Fearn for her fantastic copy-editing work. I am grateful to the three peer reviewers of the initial project for their constructive and insightful comments. I am also very grateful to Solly Mayers, research intern at the School of Law, for his world-class research assistance and attentive reading of the manuscript and to Michał Stambulski and Karolina Kocemba for offering thougthful comments on drafts of key chapters of the manuscript.

In Glasgow, and throughout the time of writing this book, I could count on the precious companionship and generosity of Marco Goldoni and Bosko Tripkovic. In the more recreational register, I thank Conal, Euan, Greg, Jamie, and Ian, my sparring partners and dear friends at the Western Tennis Club, for providing me with much-needed endorphins while mercilessly revealing the flaws of my backhand strokes. In Glasgow, I am also grateful to Yulia for her thoughtful support and feedback, a quiet but meaningful source of strength in approaching the finish line. In Switzerland, I thank Alex and Alexandra for the memorable away days and holidays over the course of the time of writing the book. I thank Alex B. for the most enjoyable (and always too short) times spent together over the last years. In Canada, I thank Kim for her friendship and generosity. In Greece, I thank Emmanuel and Eugenia for their friendship and for the reinvigorating visits to Athens. My deepest gratitude goes to my parents, Gabrielle and Frédy and to my brother, Thierry, my sister-in-law Caroline, and their beautiful children Benjamin, Romain, and Marine, for joyful familial moments. I dedicate this book to my aunt Jacqueline and pay tribute to her grace, presence, and generosity received throughout my life.

TABLE OF CASES

European Court of Human Rights

A., B. and C. *v.* Ireland (GC), 16 December 2010, Application No. 25579/05.
Advance Pharma SP. Z O.O *v.* Poland, 3 February 2022, Application No. 1469/20.
Alajos Kiss *v.* Hungary, 22 May 2010, Application No. 38832/06.
Animal Defenders International *v.* United Kingdom (GC), 22 April 2013, Application No. 48876/08.
Axel Springer AG *v.* Germany (No. 2), 10 July 2014, Application No. 48311/10.
Aziz *v.* Cyprus, 22 June 2004, Application No. 69949/01.
Baka *v.* Hungary (GC), 23 June 2016, Application No. 20261/12.
Bakirdzi *v.* Hungary, 10 November 2022, Application Nos. 49636/14 and 65678/14.
Bladet Tromsø and Stensaas *v.* Norway (GC), 20 May 1999, Application No. 21980/93.
Bochev *v.* Bulgaria, 13 November 2008, Application No. 73481/01.
Bowman *v.* United Kingdom (GC), 19 February 1998, Application No. 24839/94.
Călin Georgescu *v.* Romania, 11 February 2025, Application No. 37327/24.
Centro Europa 7 S.R.L. and Di Stefano *v.* Italy (GC), 7 June 2012, Application No. 38433/09.
Ciubotaru *v.* Moldova, 27 April 2010, Application No. 27138/04.
Communist Party of Russia and Others *v.* Russia, 19 June 2012, Application No. 29400/05.
Cumpănă and Mazăre *v.* Romania (GC), 17 December 2004, Application No. 33348/96.
Davydov *v.* Russia, 30 May 2017, Application No. 75947/11.
Demopoulos and Others *v.* Turkey (GC), 26 January 2010, Application Nos. 46113/99, 3843/02, 13751/02, 13466/03, 10200/04, 14163/04, 19993/04, and 21819/04.
Dolińska-Ficek and Ozimek *v.* Poland, 8 November 2021, Application Nos. 49868/19 and 57511/19.
Dupuis and Others *v.* France, 7 June 2007, Application No. 1914/02.
Dyuldin *v.* Russia, 31 July 2007, Application No. 25968/02.
E.G. and Others *v.* Hungary, 21 November 2024, Application No. 12918/19.
Emin Huseynov *v.* Azerbaijan, 7 May 2015, Application No. 59135/09.
Erdoğdu and İnce *v.* Turkey (GC), 8 July 1999, Application No. 25067/94.
Erményi *v.* Hungary, 22 November 2016, Application No. 22254/14.
Frodl *v.* Austria, 8 April 2010, Application No. 20201/04.
Georgian Labour Party *v.* Georgia, 8 July 2008, Application No. 9103/04.
Golder *v.* United Kingdom, 21 February 1975, Application No. 4451/70.

Grzęda *v.* Poland (GC), 13 March 2022, Application No. 43572/18.
Gündüz *v.* Turkey, 4 December 2003, Application No. 35071/97.
Guðmundur Andri Ástráðsson *v.* Iceland (GC), 1 December 2020, Application No. 26374/18.
Guðmundur Gunnarsson and Magnús Davíð Norðdahl *v.* Iceland, 16 April 2024, Application Nos. 24159/22 and 25751/22.
Handyside *v.* United Kingdom, 7 December 1976, Application No. 5493/72.
Harabin *v.* Slovakia, 20 November 2012, Application No. 58688/11.
Hirst *v.* United Kingdom (No. 2) (GC), 6 October 2005, Application No. 74025/01.
Hösl-Daum and Others *v.* Poland, 7 October 2014, Application No. 10613/17.
Ikotity and Others *v.* Hungary, 5 October 2023, Application No. 50012/17.
Informationsverein Lentia and Others *v.* Austria (GC), 24 November 1993, Application Nos. 13914/88, 15041/89, 15717/89, 15779/89, and 17207/90.
Ireland *v.* United Kingdom, 18 January 1978, Application No. 5310/71.
Jersild *v.* Denmark (GC), 23 September 1994, Application No. 15890/89.
Juszczyszyn *v.* Poland, 6 October 2022, Application No. 35599/20.
Kania and Kittel *v.* Poland, 21 June 2010, Application No. 35105/04.
Karácsony and Others *v.* Hungary (GC), 17 May 2016, Application Nos. 42461/13 and 44357/13.
Karajanov *v.* 'The Former Yugoslav Republic of Macedonia', 6 April 2017, Application No. 2229/15.
Khodorkovskiy *v.* Russia, 31 May 2011, Application No. 5829/04.
Kostadin Mihaylov *v.* Bulgaria, 27 March 2008, Application No. 17868/07.
Kövesi *v.* Romania, 5 May 2020, Application No. 3594/19.
Kyprianou *v.* Cyprus (GC), 15 December 2005, Application No. 73797/01.
Labita *v.* Italy (GC), 6 April 2000, Application No. 26772/95.
Lavents *v.* Latvia, 28 November 2002, Application No. 58442/00.
Lindheim and Others *v.* Norway, 12 June 2012, Application Nos. 13221/08 and 2139/10.
Lingens *v.* Austria, 8 July 1986, Application No. 9815/82.
Mándli and Others *v.* Hungary, 26 May 2020, Application No. 63164/16.
Manole and Others *v.* Moldova, 17 September 2009, Application No. 13936/02.
Maširević *v.* Serbia, 11 February 2014, Application No. 30671/08.
Mathieu-Mohin and Clerfayt *v.* Belgium, 2 March 1987, Application No. 9267/81.
Matthews *v.* United Kingdom (GC), 18 February 1999, Application No. 24833/94.
Matuz *v.* Hungary, 21 October 2014, Application No. 73571/10.
Melchynuk *v.* Ukraine, 5 July 2005, Application No. 28743/03.
Melnychenko *v.* Ukraine, 19 October 2004, Application No. 17707/02.
Merabishvili *v.* Georgia (GC), 28 November 2017, Application No. 72508/13.
Micallef *v.* Malta (GC), 15 October 2009, Application No. 17056/06.
Mihal *v.* Slovakia, 5 July 2011, Application No. 22006/07.
Mironescu *v.* Romania, 30 November 2021, Application No. 17504/18.
M.K. and Others *v.* Poland, 23 July 2020, Application Nos. 40503/17, 42902/17 and 43643/17.
M.L. *v.* Poland, 14 December 2023, Application No. 40119/21.

M.M. *v.* Hungary, 4 May 2023, Application No. 26819/15.
Moohan and Gillon *v.* United Kingdom, 6 July 2017, Application Nos. 22962/15 and 2334/15.
Mugemangango *v.* Belgium (GC), 10 July 2020, Application No. 310/15.
Namat Aliyev *v.* Azerbaijan, 8 April 2010, Application No. 18705/06.
NIT S.R.L. *v.* the Republic of Moldova (GC), 5 April 2022, Application No. 28470/12.
Objective Television and Radio Broadcasting Company and Others *v.* Azerbaijan, 18 February 2025, Application No. 257/12.
Pellegrin *v.* France (GC), 8 December 1999, Application No. 28541/95.
Perinçek *v.* Switzerland (GC), 15 October 2015, Application No. 27510/08.
Piermont *v.* France, 27 April 1995, Application Nos. 15773/89 and 15774/89.
Py *v.* France, 11 January 2005, Application No. 66289/01.
Radio Twist, A.S. *v.* Slovakia, 19 December 2006, Application No. 62202/00.
Razvozzhayev *v.* Russia and Ukraine and Udaltsov *v.* Russia, 19 November 2019, Application Nos. 75734/12, 2695/15, and 55325/15.
Reczkowicz *v.* Poland, 22 July 2021, Application No. 43447/19.
Refah Partisi (The Welfare Party) and Others *v.* Turkey (GC), 13 February 2003, Application Nos. 41340/98, 41342/98, and 41344/98.
Ringeisan *v.* Austria, 16 July 1971, Application No. 2614/65.
R.K. *v.* Hungary, 22 June 2023, Application No. 54006/20.
Sabuncu and Others *v.* Turkey, 10 November 2020, Application No. 23199/17.
S.A.S. *v.* France (GC), 1 July 2014, Application No. 43835/11.
Scoppola *v.* Italy (No. 3) (GC), 22 May 2012, Application No. 126/05.
Selahattin Demirtaş *v.* Turkey (GC), 22 December 2020, Application No. 14305/17.
Şik *v.* Turkey (No. 2), 24 November 2020, Application No. 36493/17.
Szurovecz *v.* Hungary, 8 October 2019, Application No. 15428/16.
Thorgeir Thorgeirson *v.* Iceland, 25 June 1992, Application No. 13778/88.
Tkachevy *v.* Russia, 14 February 2012, Application No. 35430/05.
Tuleya *v.* Poland, 6 July 2023, Application Nos. 21181/19 and 51751/20.
Tymoshenko *v.* Ukraine, 30 April 2013, Application No. 49872/11.
Udaltsov *v.* Russia, 6 October 2010, Application No. 76695/11.
Ukraine *v.* Russia (re Crimea) (GC), 25 June 2024, Application Nos. 20958/14 and 38334/18.
United Communist Party of Turkey and Others *v.* Turkey (GC), 19 June 2012, Application No. 29400/05.
Vajnai *v.* Hungary, 8 July 2008, Application No. 33629/06.
Vides Aizsardzības Klubs *v.* Latvia, 27 May 2004, Application No. 57829/00.
Vilho Eskelinen and Others *v.* Finland (GC), 19 April 2007, Application No. 63235/00.
Von Hannover *v.* Germany (No. 2) (GC), 7 February 2012, Application Nos. 40660/08 and 60641/08.
Vučković and Others *v.* Serbia (preliminary objection) (GC), 25 March 2014, Application Nos. 17153/11, 17157/11, 17160/11, 17163/11, 17168/11, 17173/11, 17178/11, 17181/11, 17182/11, 17186/11, 17343/11, 17344/11, 17362/11, 17364/11, 17367/11, 17370/11, 17372/11, 17377/11, 17380/11, 17382/11, 17386/11, 17421/11,

17424/11, 17428/11, 17431/11, 17435/11, 17438/11, 17439/11, 17440/11, and 17443/11.
Wałęsa *v.* Poland, 23 November 2023, Application No. 50849/21.
Wille *v.* Liechtenstein (GC), 28 October 1999, Application No. 28396/95.
Xhoxhaj *v.* Albania, 9 February 2021, Application No. 15227/19.
X *v.* Poland, 16 September 2021, Application No. 20741/10.
Young, James, and Webster *v.* United Kingdom, 13 August 1981, Application No. 7601/77.
Yumak and Sadak *v.* Turkey (GC), 8 July 2008, Application No. 10226/03.
Ždanoka *v.* Latvia (GC), 16 March 2006, Application No. 58278/00.
Żurek *v.* Poland, 16 June 2022, Application No. 39650/18.

European Court of Justice

Case C-123/22, Commission *v.* Hungary, ECLI:EU:C:2024:493.
Case C-204/21, Commission *v.* Poland, Order of the Vice-President of the Court of 27 October 2021, EU:C:2021: 878.

1

Introduction

1.1 The Court's Interpretive Equipment in the Populist Age

In a widely cited article published in 2018, the then-president of the European Court of Human Rights (hereafter, 'the Court' or 'the ECtHR') Róbert Spanó distinguished two main phases in the relation of the Court to the forty-seven (now forty-six) state parties to the European Convention on Human Rights (hereafter, 'the Convention' or 'the ECHR') to date.

The first, called the 'substantive embedding phase', spans a forty-year long period since the Court started operating in 1969 until the 2010s during which the Court 'gives substance to these norms for the primordial purpose of infusing them into the domestic legal systems'.[1] By 'giving substance', Spanó refers to the establishment of general principles defining the grounds, content, and scope of the Convention rights, considering the irremediably short and abstract wording of the document. This interpretive 'edifice of human rights',[2] however, was built with the indispensable premise lodged in Article 1 of the Convention that state parties are the primary interpreters of these rights, reflecting a central iteration of the principle of 'subsidiarity' organizing the allocation of jurisdictional authority in the system. The Court is and should remain a 'supervisory organ' for the domestic implementation of the Convention. Offering interpretive guidance to national authorities was therefore pivotal to the Court's task of embedding the Convention into the domestic legal landscape.

The second phase, described by Spanó as the 'procedural embedding phase', marks a significant recalibration of the Court's role vis-à-vis

[1] Róbert Spanó, 'The Future of the European Court of Human Rights: Subsidiarity, Process-Based Review and the Rule of Law', *Human Rights Law Review* 18, no. 3 (2018): 473–94.

[2] Ibid., 477.

national authorities since the 2010s. While the Court ensures that these authorities genuinely engage with the rights and associated obligations autonomously defined by the Court, it grants these authorities more discretion in how to fulfil these obligations, including in the requirement of proportionality assessment for alleged interferences. In so doing, the Court has reinforced another iteration of the principle of subsidiarity at the level of interpretation – to the point that we are still living, in Spanó's words, in the 'age of subsidiarity'. Reflecting this evolution, the so-called margin of appreciation doctrine found a place in the Preamble of the Convention as a result of Protocol 15 signed in 2018 and entered into force in 2021.

Three years later, Spanó published another article entitled 'The Rule of Law as the Lodestar of the European Convention on Human Rights',[3] signalling a change of tone and pinpointing the potential limits of the procedural embedding phase. The article highlights how the Court has strengthened its scrutiny of the separation of powers and judicial independence under Article 6. Spanó cites the recent case law pertaining to the dismissal of judges in Hungary and Poland, which 'will be subject to strict scrutiny by the Court on the basis of the principle of the irremovability of judges'.[4] Moreover, Spanó argues, 'judicial independence is only one of the prominent manifestations of a broader development towards a more robust enforcement of the rule of law which is now permeating the Court's jurisprudence', therefore pointing to a more attentive role of the Court in this domain.[5]

But attentive to what? Does the Court's renewed scrutiny in this domain respond to isolated and country-specific events, or is it speaking to a wider and patterned phenomenon both within the state party under scrutiny and across the European region?

The attack on judicial independence is not an isolated concern in at least two respects. First, it has wider consequences for the very machinery of the system of the Convention. When the guarantees of the independence and impartiality of domestic judges are compromised, the premises of the subsidiarity principle, and the very notion of 'shared responsibility' ardently promoted by both state parties and the Court, crumbles. Procedural and admissibility provisions, such as the requirement of

[3] Róbert Spanó, 'The Rule of Law as the Lodestar of the European Convention on Human Rights: The Strasbourg Court and the Independence of the Judiciary', *European Law Journal* 27, nos. 1–3 (2021): 211–27.

[4] Ibid., 218.

[5] Ibid., 218.

exhaustion of domestic remedies (Article 35 of the Convention), are particularly concerned. Indeed, one of the normative points of subsidiarity is that there is an effective and available remedy for domestic courts to examine compliance with the Convention (also reflected in Article 13 of the Convention) and enforce its substantive rights – a remedy that is closer to the circumstances of the alleged violation. When an apex court is effectively captured by the government of a state party, individuals cannot rely on that remedy any more – and this applies to all substantive provisions. This highlights the crucial role of the rule of law under Article 6 as the 'lodestar' of the Convention in the subsidiary constellation of the system.

Second, the attack on judicial independence is a particularly grave symptom of a wider and multifaceted erosion of the democratic process in Europe with significant implications for other central provisions of the Convention. The erosion affects different stages of the process in different ways: the deliberative stage may be distorted by a majority tightly controlling the informational and deliberative sphere, obstructing the circulation of opinions and facts and preventing democratic subjects from discussing and deliberating public affairs. Such distortion does not necessarily affect the very capacity of individuals to exercise democratic rights, such as freedom of expression (Article 10 of the Convention). It rather affects the background conditions that render the exercise of these rights meaningful and consequential. The same symptom appears when a parliamentary (super)majority marginalizes the opposition by expediting lawmaking procedures or subjecting it to enhanced disciplinary proceedings. If needed, electoral norms and institutions may in turn be altered or captured just enough to bend the verdict in favour of the incumbents. Here too, 'free' elections may formally be guaranteed when conceived as a mere equal entitlement to vote, but such a right loses much of its normative purpose if the democratic process is severely distorted as a matter of informational and deliberative infrastructure. On this view, rather than the rule of law only it is the value of democracy that is being stripped from its form. In fact, the attack on the rule of law paves the way for a much more comprehensive and insidious political project orchestrated by the incumbents, a project also reflected in a sweeping practice of constitutional amendment or replacement. Its manifestations – dressed in the terms of the Convention – are only slowly reaching the Strasbourg bench.

Two interrelated questions follow from this brief sketch. The first amounts to systematizing the aforementioned symptoms to establish whether one is witnessing a distinct attack on democracy and the rule of law, distinct from totalitarian or authoritarian variants in its ideational dimension and its mode of operation. The second is to return to the Court and its role in responding to this phenomenon, and whether it may call for inaugurating an age of 'post-' or 'selective subsidiarity', requiring the Court to revisit and amend the very substantive principles that the 'procedural embedding' phase took for granted. While the rule of law has already been 'upgraded' with reference to judicial independence, should the Court recalibrate its scrutiny to the wider symptoms just outlined?

The hypothetical answer to the first question is that the democratic process being concomitantly eroded at various stages is not a coincidence. It can be reconstructed as reflecting the core characteristics of authoritarian populism. While modern history has known notorious examples of left-wing and 'progressive' or 'democratic' populism from the Populist Party in the United States in the late nineteenth century to Peronism or Chavismo in Latin America in the mid and late twentieth century to the more recent experiences of Syriza in Greece or the Five Star movement in Italy, Europe has known an exponential spread of markedly right-wing populism in the last two decades. Indeed, it is today difficult not to find one or several political parties (in government or in opposition) in any of the Council of Europe (hereafter, 'the CoE') states whose discourse, manifesto, or record of policies is not described (by politicians, the media, NGOs, civil society, or academia) as populist, often if not always of an authoritarian kind. This goes in tandem with a massive increase of electoral support for these populist parties across all states in the region.[6] To quote just two remarkable numbers, from 2000 until 2017 populist parties in Europe almost doubled (from thirty-three to sixty-three), while the vote for populist parties reached 24.1 per cent (or 17.7 per cent if one considers right-wing populism only) while in 2000 it was only 8.5 per cent.[7] Central and Eastern European countries – with the clearest examples of Hungary (Fidesz) and Poland (PiS) but also the Western European examples of Italy (Fratelli d'Italia), the United Kingdom (the Conservatives and Reform), Germany (AfD), and the

[6] Rui Silva, 'Populist Parties Thrive on Discontent: The Data Proves It', The Conversation, 12 November 2024, http://theconversation.com/populist-parties-thrive-on-discontent-the-data-proves-it-242278.

[7] Martin Eiermann, Limor Gultchin, and Yascha Mounk, 'European Populism: Trends, Threats and Future Prospects', Tony Blair Institute for Global Change, 29 December 2017, https://institute.global/insights/geopolitics-and-security/european-populism-trends-threats-and-future-prospects.

Netherlands (PVV), following the earlier steps of Austria (FPÖ) and Switzerland (SVP) – have all experienced authoritarian populism in the last two decades, either in government or leading the opposition. The authoritarian kind of populism has earned its currency as the descriptor of a new age of democracy in Europe, and an impoverished one. Among other things, what brings all these countries all together is that they are signatories of the Convention.

At its ideational core, populism thrives on the antagonism that a 'corrupt elite' has concertedly neglected the 'true' or 'real people' and, correlatively, that only populists can legitimately represent them. The 'will of the people', populists claim, should be restored. To that end, the authoritarian variant of populism promotes a more direct representation of the people in the figure of a party, movement, or government leader and contends that only populists can represent the 'people'. It employs a distinct register of democracy, a plebiscitary one, that has little regard either for subjects and minorities deemed not to belong to or represent the 'people' (including the 'elite' politicians and parties), or for the democratic channels and procedures that mediate the will of the people, whether these are the core institutions of the state, such as the legislative and the judiciary, or generally the public sphere construed as formative of the democratic will in a pluralist polity. This is because the 'will of the people' in the populist iteration pre-exists any instance of mediation – and if any, the role of institutions and channels is to facilitate the enforcement of that will. In practice, the distinct operation of populism is not to dismantle institutions and channels of accountability, but to run them against their purpose and preserve only the facade of democracy. On this account, the assault on judicial independence clearly appears as only the tip of the iceberg; the erosion of the informational and deliberative sphere, or the alterations to the parliamentary and electoral processes, can be anchored in the same populist distortion of democracy – to which the rule of law (its violation) is instrumentally connected.

Returning to Spanó's point that the rule of law can operate as the 'lodestar' of the Convention, the above considerations lead to seriously questioning whether a single article of the Convention, namely Article 6, can by itself detect and counter the populist wave. While it crucially matters to the effective machinery of the system, as previously indicated, Article 6 may ultimately gloss over the wider erosion of democracy. This invites us to tackle the second key and wider question: is the Court more generally apt and equipped to respond to authoritarian populism considering its human rights-specific, supranational, and subsidiary jurisdiction? This investigation examines the implications of the populist predicament for the role and practice of the Court in its position of ultimate interpreter of the Convention. Conceived as an interdisciplinary project, it aims to bring in closer contact the new realities of the populist age with the Court's interpretive record of protecting democracy and the rule of law through the medium of rights – with a view to 'updating' the Court's interpretive equipment to better respond to this phenomenon. The values of democracy and the rule of law inform the Court's catalogue of rights and their attached principles of interpretation since the birth of the Convention system. They do not only derive specific rights and associated obligations that form the backbone of the democratic process, but they also have a particularly strong resonance in the history of the Convention system, first justifying an 'alarm bell' system that state parties could trigger to prevent the return of totalitarianism in Europe.[8]

Furthermore, the Court has also had many occasions to expand on the meaning of these values and derived principles in its interpretive practice. The protection of democratic debate (under Articles 10 and 11), for example, occupies a prime place in the Court's register of democracy. The Court's mantra that freedom of expression is 'applicable not only to "information" or "ideas" that are favourably received or regarded as inoffensive or as a matter of indifference, but also to those that offend, shock or disturb the State or any sector of the population'[9] is a case in point, or the position that 'democracy does not simply mean that the views of the majority must always prevail. A balance must be achieved which ensures the fair and proper treatment of minorities and avoids any abuse of a dominant position.'[10] In relying on these principles for its adjudicatory routine, the Court speaks not only to the parties to the case, but to one of the first measures that autocrats took in reaching power in the twentieth century, namely, to brutally silence opposition, oppress minorities, and pay lip service to the rule of law. One may be content that the Court has such a strong grips on these cardinal values and ensures

[8] Ed Bates, ' The Birth of the European Convention on Human Rights – and the European Court of Human Rights', in *The European Court of Human Rights between Law and Politics*, ed. Jonas Christoffersen and Mikael Rask Madsen (Oxford University Press, 2011); Ed Bates, *The Evolution of the European Convention on Human Rights: From Its Inception to the Creation of a Permanent Court of Human Rights* (Oxford University Press, 2010).

[9] *Handyside* v. *United Kingdom*, 7 December 1976, Application No. 5493/72.

[10] *Young, James, and Webster* v. *United Kingdom*, 18 October 1982, Application Nos. 7601/76 and 7806/77, para. 63.

that its scrutiny remains aligned with them. But if one agrees that the threat to democracy and the rule of law has changed in *how* democracy and the rule of law are eroded, the question remains as to whether the Court has tailored its interpretive apparatus.

1.2 Outline of the Analytical Framework and Chapter Summary

This project incorporates populism as an ideational construct and as a practice of government and strives to maintain them in a mutually informative relationship. Each insight, it must be borne in mind, belongs to a distinct disciplinary framing. The former predominates among political theorists assigning normative and explanatory value to ideology. The latter is more empirically informed and attends to the effects of populist rule without necessarily distinguishing populism from broader categories of (competitive or legalistic) authoritarianism or illiberalism. In this investigation, I combine elements from both approaches by explaining, as far as possible, how the main effects of populist rule can meaningfully reflect the ideational basis distinctive of authoritarian populism. This combination is also needed to evaluate the Court's available equipment in effectively responding to populism, as I explain in what follows.

On the one hand, the project endorses the ideational approach to populism understood as an ontology of politics and popularized by Mudde,[11] rather than as a strategy for mobilization and an emancipatory project associated with left-wing, inclusive, and 'democratic' populism in the tradition of Laclau.[12] On the ideational account, authoritarian (or right-wing) populism defines two antagonistic groups that co-exist within the same polity in moral terms, the people and the 'elite'. On this view, 'populism is in essence a form of *moral* politics: "the élite" and "the people" is first and foremost moral (i.e., pure vs. corrupt), not

[11] Cas Mudde, 'The Populist Zeitgeist', *Government and Opposition* 39, no. 4 (2004): 541–63; Cas Mudde and Cristóbal Rovira Kaltwasser, 'Studying Populism in Comparative Perspective: Reflections on the Contemporary and Future Research Agenda', *Comparative Political Studies* 51, no. 13 (2018): 1667–93; Cas Mudde, 'Populism: An Ideational Approach', in *The Oxford Handbook of Populism*, ed. Cristóbal Rovira Kaltwasser, Paul Taggart, Paulin Ochoa Espejo, and Pierre Ostiguy (Oxford University Press, 2017); Kirk A. Hawkins, 'The Ideational Approach', in *Routledge Handbook of Global Populism*, ed. Carlos de la Torre (Routledge, 2018).

[12] Ernesto Laclau, *On Populist Reason* (Verso, 2007); Enrique Peruzzotti, 'Laclau's Theory of Populism', in *Routledge Handbook of Global Populism*, ed. Carlos de la Torre (Routledge, 2018).

situational (e.g., position of power), socio-cultural (e.g., ethnicity, religion), or socio-economic (e.g., class)'.[13] On the other hand, the project employs the resources of normative political theory – in particular, democratic theory – to identify the democratic norms and value that populism specifically but insidiously erodes. Building on the recent and seminal work of Urbinati[14] and Nässtrom,[15] I argue in Chapter 3 that populism distorts democratic deliberation and representation and corrupts the rule of law.

This normative basis is needed to clarify how parasitic populism is to democracy and the rule of law. While populism reclaims the power of the people, I suggest that it in fact entrenches and exacerbates deliberative and representative inequalities and ravages even the thinnest account of the rule of law. The normative premise here, which I also discuss in Chapter 3, is that deliberation and representation and their equality-enhancing functions are necessary to the justifiability of the democratic process. Corrupting the rule of law shows how fierce the populist attack is on these core requirements. While this constitutes a thin, yet robust analytical framework centred on the cardinal values of democracy (the distortion thereof) and the rule of law (the corruption thereof), I believe it has sufficient normative pull to guide the evaluation of the Court's interpretive equipment given the resonance these values have in the Court's reasoning.

However, to link the normative and theoretical discussion of populism to the Court's context and practice, one requires an overview of how populist governments operate once in power. This is needed to identify, in more practical terms, which Convention rights are implicated in these populist practices, and which aspects of these rights may be vulnerable. Indeed, the discourse of populism may not necessarily coincide with how a populist government, in practice, reshapes the domestic legal landscape and how Convention rights are affected as a result. This is why, in Chapter 5, I survey key effects of populist rule in three ideal-typical domains in the domestic sphere: the media, the electoral, and the judicial

13 Cas Mudde and Cristóbal Rovira Kaltwasser, 'Populism and (Liberal) Democracy: A Framework for Analysis', in *Populism in Europe and the Americas: Threat or Corrective for Democracy?*, ed. Cas Mudde and Cristóbal Rovira Kaltwasser (Cambridge University Press, 2012): 7–8.

14 Nadia Urbinati, *Me the People: How Populism Transforms Democracy* (Harvard University Press, 2019).

15 Sofia Näsström, *The Spirit of Democracy: Corruption, Disintegration, Renewal* (Oxford University Press, 2021).

domains. I then link these effects to three corresponding portions of the Court's case law: freedom of expression and freedom of assembly and association (Articles 10–11); the right to free elections (Article 3 Protocol 1); the right to a fair trial (Article 6) and the 'bad faith' provision (Article 18), respectively. This selection establishes the point of departure for the subsequent assessment of the Court's equipment in responding to these effects that I conduct in Chapter 6, 7, and 8.

The populist mode of attack across these domains is strikingly similar, and I label it *infrastructural* rather than *coercive* in how they affect the exercise of democratic rights. If populist governments resort to coercion by curbing the freedoms of individuals directly, they risk losing the democratic facade that conferred legitimacy on them in the first place. A subtler approach centres on the infrastructural prerequisites that make the exercise of such rights meaningful and consequential. While infrastructural erosion may have direct agential consequences – for example, the dismissal of a judge, an opposition politician subject to disciplinary proceedings – it forecloses the normative horizon of the democratic process understood as the pursuit of mutual justifiability.[16] Regarding the informational and deliberative sphere, for example, dissenting journalists are not assassinated, arrested, surveilled, or even violently intimidated with the coercive and arbitrary force of the security apparatus typical of an authoritarian state. The function of the judiciary is not to systematically indict, sentence, and jail them on dubious grounds that are too familiar of the standard authoritarian playbook. Rather, populist governments subtly and indirectly incapacitate the media, both public and private, through a much less violent but equally effective vehicle: infrastructure. The specific form that such an attack takes, varies. Independent outlets find themselves ineligible for state funding. They find themselves subject to aggressive takeovers from powerful conglomerates closer to the government. Journalists may be intimidated and arbitrarily sanctioned, but only with the help of the softer instrument of oversight, regulatory and supervisory bodies conveniently packed with

[16] I elaborate on this point in Chapters 4 and 9. Rainer Forst, 'The Justification of Human Rights and the Basic Right to Justification: A Reflexive Approach', *Ethics* 120, no. 4 (2010): 711–40; Rainer Forst, *The Right to Justification: Elements of a Constructivist Theory of Justice*, trans. Jeffrey Flynn (Columbia University Press, 2011); Mattias Kumm, 'The Idea of Socratic Contestation and the Right to Justification: The Point of Rights-Based Proportionality Review', *Law & Ethics of Human Rights* 4, no. 2 (2010): 142–75; Alain Zysset, 'The Right to Justification in the Context of Proportionality: A Plea for Determinacy and Stability', in *Public Reason and Courts*, ed. Mattias Kumm, Silje Langvatn, and Wojciech Sadurski (Cambridge University Press, 2020).

government loyalists. Common to all these examples is the infrastructural rather than coercive mode of affecting these rights, an erosion that progresses under the veneer of legality. The infrastructure of democratic rights is the privileged target of authoritarian populists in power.

Now, this erosion has been identified by political scientists and constitutional scholars as applicable to a wider conceptual, institutional, and geographical spectrum than the one contemplated here. In a pioneering book spanning examples from the United States to Peru and Hungary, Levitsky and Zibblatt showed that 'the erosion of democracy takes place piecemeal, often in baby steps. Each individual step seems minor – none appears to truly threaten democracy'[17] and pointed out the capture of 'referees' across core and regulatory bodies of the state to bend the rules of the system to the incumbents' advantage. Varol coined to concept of 'stealth' to refer to the way incumbents 'protect and entrench power when direct repression is not a viable option'.[18] The literature in comparative constitutional law has also produced a plethora of concepts pointing to the erosive degradation of democracy and the rule of law orchestrated from within the constitutional framework: 'constitutional capture',[19] 'abusive constitutionalism',[20] 'autocratic legalism',[21] 'anti-constitutional populist backsliding',[22] 'democracy decay',[23] or 'constitutional chicanery'.[24] This investigation takes place within more defined parameters with the aim of adding a level of accuracy, rigour, and depth in more specific context. Conceptually, it relies on the normative elucidation of populism in its relation to democracy and the rule of law. Geographically, it is confined to the Convention membership and institutionally to the machinery of the Convention system and the strictures of the Court's practice of adjudication.

[17] Steven Levitsky and Daniel Ziblatt, *How Democracies Die* (Viking, 2018), 34.

[18] Ozan O. Varol, 'Stealth Authoritarianism', *Iowa Law Review* 100, no. 4 (2014), 1678.

[19] Jan-Werner Müller, 'Rising to the Challenge of Constitutional Capture', 21 March 2014, https://www.eurozine.com/rising-to-the-challenge-of-constitutional-capture/. See also Jan-Werner Müller, *What Is Populism?* (University of Pennsylvania Press, 2016).

[20] David Landau, 'Abusive Constitutionalism', *UC Davis Law Review* 47, no. 1 (2013): 189–260.

[21] Kim Lane Scheppele, 'Autocratic Legalism', *University of Chicago Law Review* 85 (2018): 545–83.

[22] Wojciech Sadurski, *Poland's Constitutional Breakdown* (Oxford University Press, 2019).

[23] Tom Gerald Daly, 'Democratic Decay: Conceptualising an Emerging Research Field', *Hague Journal on the Rule of Law* 11, no. 1 (2019): 9–36.

[24] Renata Uitz, 'The Rule of Law at Risk: What Is Next?', *Hague Journal on the Rule of Law* 11, no. 2 (2019): 473–8.

It also follows from this that the present investigation focuses on one supranational judicial actor, namely the Court, and does not specifically address the other actor in Europe, namely the Court of Justice of the European Union (hereafter, 'the CJEU'). This is not only because each court adjudicates a vastly different subject matter – the Convention and the European Union (EU) Treaties, respectively – or because the systems of which each court is a part do not necessarily interact, even though the CJEU relies on the Court with respect to its human rights jurisprudence. It is primarily because the CJEU, together with the European Commission and the European Parliament, has been engaging in a distinct, concerted, and treaty-based response by reference to the 'values' of the European Union (Article 2 of the Treaty on the European Union) and has resorted to infringement procedures (Article 7 of the Treaty on the European Union) against both Hungary and Poland resulting in the imposition of hefty daily penalties on both Member States.[25] Several mechanisms, such as the adoption of the Rule of Law Conditionality Regulation, have reinforced a previously modest arsenal against the deterioration of the rule of law within Member States.[26] This response is therefore centred on the EU institutional framework.

Rather, while this investigation extensively refers to the experiences of Hungary and Poland, its objective is to contribute to this wider field through the lens of the Convention and the Court, joining up the study of populism to the Court in a specific and rigorous manner. Indeed, my analytical framework of populism is not tied to the experience of specific European governments within the Convention system, but it will appear that only some manifestations of populism have reached the confines of the Court's adjudication and these manifestations predominantly reflect the right-wing, exclusive, and authoritarian variant of populism with an emphasis on the experiences of Hungary and Poland.

[25] For Poland see for example *Commission* v. *Poland*, Order of the Vice-President of the Court of 27 October 2021, EU:C:2021:878. For Hungary, see *Commission* v. *Hungary* ECLI:EU:C:2024:493.

[26] See in the contributions in Barbara Grabowska-Moroz, Joelle Grogan, Dimitry V. Kochenov, and Laurent Pech, 'Reconciling Theory and Practice of the Rule of Law in the European Union', *Hague Journal on the Rule of Law* 14, no. 2 (2022): 101–5; Laurent Pech and Dimitry Kochenov, 'Respect for the Rule of Law in the Case Law of the European Court of Justice: A Casebook Overview of Key Judgments since the Portuguese Judges Case', SIEPS Report no. 3, September 2021, https://sieps.se/en/publications/2021/respect-for-the-rule-of-law-in-the-case-law-of-the-european-court-of-justice/; Carlos Closa and Dimitry Kochenov, eds., *Reinforcing Rule of Law Oversight in the European Union* (Cambridge University Press, 2016).

However, these experiences and their reflection in the Court's case law remain illustrative rather than constitutive of the analysis. The core ambition is to utilize a theoretical account of populism complemented by the ideal-typical effects of populist rule for the purpose of analysing the Court's interpretive equipment in effectively responding to it. The emphasis on Hungary and Poland is contingent and premised on the fact that these populist governments have benefited – and, in the case of Poland, benefited until October 2023 – from a large majority in their respective parliament since the 2010s and have profoundly remodelled their domestic constitutional landscape under the infrastructural mode of attack previously outlined. This allows for observing how the effects of populist rule have filtered through the Convention catalogue of rights and the Court's case law, as we shall see in Chapters 6, 7, and 8. In this sense, this project has a generalizable and prospective ambition beyond the irremediably particular trajectory of certain states and regions in Europe.

The other important boundary of this project is the concentration on a specific bundle of rights in the Convention – the democratic ones, with the addition of rule of law provisions, and their principles of interpretation that the Court has developed over the years, together with the mode of resolution of conflicts of rights, in particular proportionality. However, and as already indicated, these rights and their principles of interpretation are not defined independently from each other – rather, the Court connects them conceptually via the notion of 'democratic society', which then offers a vantage point for the task of evaluating the Court's equipment in a condensed, yet comprehensive manner. As will appear through the analysis of the case law, the Court *derives* key principles and obligations – themselves composed of relatively clear normative criteria and thresholds – from that overarching notion. The implication here is that if one wants to evaluate the Court's 'anti-populist' equipment meaningfully, reconstructing the Court's 'democratic society' in this holistic fashion appears to be required. Indeed, the degree to which this notion is systematized by the Court itself is limited. Therefore, in Chapter 4, I offer a normative reconstruction of the Court's approach to democratic deliberation and representation, and how these tenets feed into the Court's understanding of specific rights and the resolution of cases. I also identify where, in the structure of the Court's review, 'democratic society' plays a decisive role, namely in proportionality analysis when the respondent state attempts to justify their right(s)-interfering measure. The practice of proportionality testing, then, appears as a particularly useful terrain to gain evidence as to how decisive the Court's 'democratic society' is to the actual resolution of cases – that is, to the finding of a (non-)violation.

Now, it is indisputable that authoritarian populists assault other rights, including other rights protected by the Convention, in a much more direct fashion. Think, for example, of the 'hierarchy of assemblies' created by the PiS government in Poland in 2016, making it impossible to organize a (counter-)demonstration where a recognized 'cyclical assembly' organized by the public authorities takes place.[27] Memory laws in Poland and Hungary since the rise of PiS and Fidesz to power, which legislate the correct interpretation of key historical events and simplify responsibilities for crimes of the past, also serve the populist logic of distorting democratic and scientific deliberation, including through the imposition of civil and penal sanctions.[28] But as far as freedom of expression (Article 10), freedom of assembly and association (Article 11), and the non-retroactivity of criminal punishment (Article 7) are concerned, the Court has a solid interpretive equipment and record of cases at its disposal to respond to these direct attacks,[29] as we shall also see in Chapter 6.

Furthermore, one finds in the Court's recent case law decisions that have seemingly countered direct assaults of populist governments on access to abortion in Poland[30] and on the rights of asylum seekers in the form of 'pushbacks' failing to offer them a domestic remedy and an individualized decision for their removal,[31] as well as on sexual minorities such as same-sex couples[32] and transgender people.[33] In most of these cases, the interpretive arsenal of the Court, in terms of negative and positive obligations as well as non-discrimination, appears apt. However, whether the Court has analogous equipment to detect and

[27] Wojciech Sadurski, 'Populism and Human Rights in Poland', in *Human Rights in a Time of Populism: Challenges and Responses*, ed. Gerald L. Neuman (Cambridge: Cambridge University Press, 2020).

[28] See in particular Uladzislau Belavusau and Aleksandra Gliszczyńska-Grabias, eds., *Law and Memory: Towards Legal Governance of History* (Cambridge University Press, 2017).

[29] *Vajnai* v. *Hungary*, 8 July 2008, Application No. 33629/06; *Hösl-Daum and Others* v. *Poland*, 7 October 2014, Application No. 10613/17; *Perinçek* v. *Switzerland* (GC), 15 October 2015, Application No. 27510/08.

[30] *M.L.* v. *Poland*, 14 December 2023, Application No. 40119/21.

[31] *M.K. and Others* v. *Poland*, Application Nos. 40503/17, 42902/17, and 43643/17, 23 July 2020.

[32] *X* v. *Poland*, 16 September 2021, Application No. 20741/10.

[33] *R.K.* v. *Hungary*, 22 June 2023, Application No. 54006/20.

counter the erosion of democratic and rule of law infrastructure is less clear and needs a more nuanced analysis. While the Court can be seen as having extended rule of law provisions to judicial infrastructure (e.g., disciplinary chambers[34] and national judicial councils[35] under the 'lodestar' of Article 6), this investigation zooms in on select domains of democratic infrastructure that are particularly at risk of populist erosion.

1.3 The Key Claims of the Book

The infrastructural dimension of the populist attack poses an acute challenge to the Court's canons of interpretation for protecting democratic rights, I argue. This is because the Court has been historically preoccupied with what I call *existential* threats to democracy along the totalitarian lines of Nazism, fascism, or simply fully-fledged authoritarianism. The Court has constructed an account of democratic minimalism based on protecting the rights of political opposition and the place that pluralism and dissent ought to occupy in the democratic arena, which is best illustrated by what I define as the principle of 'deliberative pluralism' underlying the Court's interpretive repertoire under Articles 10–11 (freedom of expression and freedom of assembly and association), as we shall see in Chapter 6. Under this framework, democracy is protected by a free and pluralistic debate on issues of public interest – and the Court is extremely attentive to finding whether there is any public interest justifying the exercise of expression within the scope of Articles 10–11, as we shall see. On this view, the 'watchdogs of a democratic society' predominantly patrol outside of the boundaries and in fact against the institutions of the state.

But conversely, the infrastructure of democratic rights has not been at the centre of the Court's attention – and this constitutes the weak point of its interpretive equipment. Also in Chapter 6, I show how the Court has persistently fallen short of uncovering the interdependence between the stage of deliberation and the stage of elections despite celebrating their complementarity in principle. Indeed, I explain in Chapter 8 how the Court's commitment to free elections, for example, has centred around the basic protection of the right to vote and the right to stand for

34 *Reczkowicz* v. *Poland*, 22 July 2021, Application No. 43447/19. For an in-depth analysis of this and similar cases, see Chapter 7.

35 *Grzęda* v. *Poland* (GC), 13 March 2022, Application No. 43572/18. For an in-depth analysis of this and similar cases, see Chapter 7.

elections, which the Court overarchingly defines as 'the conditions which will ensure the free expression of the opinion of the people in the choice of the legislature' (Article 3 Protocol 1). Yet, in practice, these conditions essentially consist of protecting individuals against isolated instances of arbitrary disenfranchisement – again, a requirement without which there is no democracy to speak of. By the time individuals reach the voting booth, the populist capture of democratic deliberation through the informational and deliberative pathway has already been achieved – and the Court hardly examines whether the former justifies a much more robust scrutiny of the latter. This minimal and compartmentalized approach, I argue, does not suffice to grasp the piecemeal process of erosion – and, as a result, the Court's 'democratic society' loses much of its relevance effectiveness.

It would be short-sighted, however, to claim that the Court is inherently ill equipped to address infrastructural erosion. For example, as I illustrate in Chapters 6, 7, and 8, the Court has reinforced its catalogue of 'procedural guarantees' attached to substantive rights of the Convention, which allows for protecting individuals from the arbitrary abuse of governments in precisely those institutional fora within the state that are vulnerable to populist capture. Take the example of a disciplinary procedure against an opposition member of parliament (MP) for having disrupted parliamentary proceedings (by using a placard, banners, and megaphone) in *Karácsony and Others* v. *Hungary*.[36] The Court will be very attentive to the inclusion of the individual in the disciplinary procedure and require the government to offer reasons for the measures taken. But equally it will fall short of addressing the applicant's contention that the government had transferred the disciplinary authority from an independent and pluralist committee to the parliamentary supermajority. All together, these procedural guarantees appear so minimal that the Court's control risks turning a blind eye to the populist technique of maintaining the facade of a procedure while running it against its very purpose. More broadly, the Court does not delve into how the erosion of safeguards points to a distinct mode of attacking democracy and the rule of law, which challenges the adequacy of its 'democratic society' in principled terms. But equally, the Court is in principle open to consider, at the level of interpretation, that the meaningful exercise of democratic

[36] *Karácsony and Others* v. *Hungary* (GC), 17 May 2016, Application Nos. 42461/13 and 44357/13. For an in-depth analysis of this and similar cases, see Chapter 6.

rights can be attacked from a variety of angles, one of which is distinctively infrastructural. This is more encouraging – but is it enough?

How can the Court better detect and respond to the distinct attack of populism in more principled terms? Throughout the book, and in a more systematic form in Chapter 9, I develop the argument that proportionality analysis is an appropriate and effective framework at the disposal of the Court to better detect and calibrate its response to authoritarian populism. In fact, a response only based on enhanced procedural guarantees seems irremediably insufficient since these guarantees will be themselves subject to proportionality analysis as part of the Court's review process. We therefore need a more principled, systematic, and comprehensive approach. I believe that the Court could utilize the space that the various steps of the proportionality test afford it to inquire about the infrastructural erosion of democracy.

This argument has several layers and claims that are detailed in the concluding Chapter 9 and are only summarized here. When a respondent state party is asked to substantiate the purpose of the interference, its rationality and necessity, or when it must conduct a balancing exercise as to the impact of the interference on the alleged victim, the Court is not only mobilizing democratic and rule of law values that populists precisely attempt to subvert. Indeed, as much as democracy involves a vacuum as to the locus of political power, proportionality involves a vacuum as to the justifiability of interferences with rights. All the stages of proportionality assessment introduce elements of contingency, uncertainty, opposability, and fallibility that are all equally toxic to the ontological, exclusive, and antagonistic logic of authoritarian populism. As a result, the Court could develop the criteria informing these various steps accordingly and tailor them to the populist playbook. In Chapter 9, I suggest more specifically that the Court build a more robust account of 'legitimate aim' that precisely tracks infrastructural erosion. The Court has not been totally foreign to this idea: in its parsimonious case law on Article 18, which prohibits governments from using restriction grounds other than the ones set by the Convention, the Court resorts to a wider spectrum of (infrastructural) variables pertaining to the broader legal and political context – and infers the predominant aim of the restriction on that basis. I argue that the Court should systematize its infrastructural inquiry across the three domains of populist distortion and calibrate its evaluation of the purpose of the interference under the regular proportionality assessment accordingly. The key premise here is that the Court has not utilized its normatively loaded account of 'democratic society' (developed in understanding the substantive rights themselves) to inform the evaluation of the government's presented aim(s).

1.4 The Investigation in a Broader Scholarly Context

This book offers to study the nexus between authoritarian populism qua practice and concept, on the one hand, and the Court via the Court's overarching notion of 'democratic society' and the interpretive principles that derive from it for understand rights, on the other hand. By taking democracy as the unit of analysis throughout the book – both descriptively and normatively – it aims to offer an original angle for interrogating the Court's role in responding to the threat posed by authoritarian populism defined as a distinct threat to the Court's democratic ethos.

Generally, this approach builds on my prior research on the foundations, content, and limits of the Court's understanding of democracy, which have sustainably informed its resolution of cases.[37] This body of research aims at systematizing and critically examining the Court's approach to democracy through the lens of democratic and human rights theory and drawing implications for the very legitimacy of the Court's authority in adjudicating rights over and above domestic democracies.[38] Central to this broader project is the attempt both to move beyond a case-based approach to adjudication by reconstructing the overarching principles used by the Court, and to offer critical leverage as to whether its 'democratic society' is normatively sound and valuable. Because democracy inherently is a normative, open, and disputable concept, the Court's

[37] Alain Zysset, 'Searching for the Legitimacy of the European Court of Human Rights: The Neglected Role of "Democratic Society"', *Global Constitutionalism* 5, no. 1 (2016): 16–47; Alain Zysset, 'Freedom of Expression, the Right to Vote, and Proportionality at the European Court of Human Rights: An Internal Critique', *International Journal of Constitutional Law* 17, no. 1 (2019): 230–51; Alain Zysset, 'The Right to Justification in the Context of Proportionality: A Plea for Determinacy and Stability', 256–80, Alain Zysset, 'Calibrating the Response to Populism at the European Court of Human Rights', *International Journal of Constitutional Law* 20, no. 3 (2022): 976–1005; Alain Zysset, 'A Culture of Justification or a Culture of Presumption? The Turn to Procedural Review and the Normative Function of Proportionality at the European Court of Human Rights', in *Theory and Practice of the ECHR*, ed. Stephanie Schiedermair, Alexander Schwarz, and Dominik Steiger (Nomos/Hart Publishing, 2021).

[38] Richard Bellamy, 'The Democratic Legitimacy of International Human Rights Conventions: Political Constitutionalism and the European Convention on Human Rights', *European Journal of International Law* 25, no. 4 (2014): 1019–42. For a critique, see Zysset, 'Searching for the Legitimacy of the European Court of Human Rights'.

'democratic society' can be subject to robust normative scrutiny that bridges the Court's interpretive equipment and the resources of normative political theory and political science. In this sense, this wider project aims to be simultaneously practice- and theory-responsive.

There exist two objections to this broader project that also have implications for studying the Court's response to populism. First, it has been argued that the value of Court's 'democratic society' as operating in its reasoning is mostly rhetorical. Sadurski for instance argues that 'the "democratic society" clause is used to "soften" the audience, as it were, and to prepare it for the conclusion on the issue of breach'.[39] In this investigation and in the previous work just mentioned, I showed that 'democratic society' not only operates as a restriction clause in the proportionality test (at the balancing stage or proportionality *stricto sensu*) but also informs its principles of interpretation and derived obligations, helping the Court to identify prominent rights-holders and 'watchdogs' that are essential to preserving such a society in the Court's eyes.[40] The notion therefore feeds into both the rights and their grounds of restriction in a more consistent and normative manner than assumed, as I also show in Chapter 4. In systematizing such dialectic, I show that there is enough of a concept of democracy – if not a conception – that can serve the present investigation if populism primarily amounts, as I purport to show, to a severe distortion of democracy requiring an 'update' of the Court's approach.

Second, one could raise the more general objection that by requiring the Court to 'update' its account of democracy in this manner, the project stretches into a realm reserved for the constitutional and 'democratic' arrangements of state parties – a critique that the subsidiary role of the Court would typically support. Indeed, by emphasizing the infrastructural dimension of the populist erosion – and by tailoring the Court's response to this dimension, the project challenges its international and individual jurisdiction. This objection is reminiscent of the debate on the

[39] Wojciech Sadurski, 'European Court of Human Rights in Pursuit of Public Reason? A Study of Lost Opportunities', in *Public Reason and Courts*, ed. Mattias Kumm, Silje A. Langvatn, and Wojciech Sadurski (Cambridge University Press, 2020), 350.

[40] Zysset, 'Searching for the Legitimacy of the European Court of Human Rights'; Zysset, 'Freedom of Expression, the Right to Vote, and Proportionality at the European Court of Human Rights'; Susan Marks, 'The European Convention on Human Rights and Its "Democratic Society"', *British Yearbook of International Law* 66, no. 1 (1996): 209–38.

constitutional significance of the Convention system[41] and the constitutional role of the Court. It is worth recasting the main pieces of the debate here and moving forward.

On the one hand, the international character of the Convention system is foundational in the way each signatory state incorporates the Convention based on its own constitutional specificities, reflecting the contractual model of international law based on state consent. In terms of their obligations, and following Article 46 of the Convention, state parties and all their public authorities (legislative, executive, and judicial) must abide by the final judgment of the Court to which they are a party (*inter partes*). While Article 32(1) of the Convention grants the Court final jurisdiction over 'all matters concerning the interpretation and petition of the Convention' and gives the Court the competence to determine the limits of its own jurisdiction, the Court remains an international organ established by an international convention. Further, the subsidiary relation between the Court and state parties makes the former a 'supervisory' organ only – the Court often says that the implementation of the Convention is a 'shared responsibility'.

As a result, state parties remain the primary interpreters of the Convention and the only enforcers of the Court's judgments, and the Court affords considerable weight to the democratic process and to the interpretation of domestic bodies in its own findings, including by ultimately allocating a margin of appreciation to the respondent state in specific cases. Subsidiarity also shapes the jurisdictional and remedial dimensions of the system, as we shall see in Chapter 4.

On the other hand, the individual character of the system is inherent in the Court adjudicating a dispute between the right(s) of an individual (or of a group of individuals) and a government law or policy, which does neither necessarily nor directly require examining the wider infrastructure of the respondent state party in question, depriving the Court of the reach of apex courts domestically.[42] While the Court's authoritative role is having the ultimate say over the interpretation of the Convention, that

41 Luzius Wildhaber, 'The European Convention on Human Rights and International Law', *International and Comparative Law Quarterly* 56 (2007): 217–32; Steven Greer and Luzius Wildhaber, 'Revisiting the Debate about "Constitutionalising" the European Court of Human Rights', *Human Rights Law Review* 12, no. 4 (2012): 655–87.

42 See Stephen Gardbaum, 'Comparative Political Process Theory', *International Journal of Constitutional Law* 18, no. 4 (2020): 1429–57; Stephen Gardbaum, 'Comparative Political Process Theory II', *Global Constitutionalism* 14, no. 2 (2024): 219–37; Rosalind Dixon, *Responsive Judicial Review: Democracy and Dysfunction in the Modern Age* (Oxford University Press, 2023). In the context of the ECtHR, see Michaela Hailbronner and

same role is limited, in general, to *declaring* whether there was a violation of the Convention or not.

Yet this rather formal picture needs considerable nuances, and the relevant literature often employs the qualifier 'constitutional' to capture these nuances. What, however, is exactly the explanatory and/or normative value of the 'constitutional' qualifier in the Court's context? In addition to the Court's own contention that the Convention constitutes 'the constitutional instrument of European public order in the field of human rights',[43] there are several aspects of the Convention system that have been qualified as 'constitutional'. In the most abstract sense, the basic function of limiting what governments can do to their subjects invariably qualifies as constitutional.[44] Having the authority to do so in the superior capacity of reviewing national legislation also qualifies as constitutional.[45] Correlatively, the superior, constitutional, or sub-constitutional status of the Convention in the domestic hierarchy and the direct effect granted to the Court's judgments have also been deemed constitutional.[46] The judgments have in addition been deemed as having an *erga omnes* effect, which implies that a judgment against one state party equally binds all the other state parties to the Convention. As a result, individuals not parties to a case but in an identical situation to the victim of a violation can also claim a violation of the right in question.[47] Several steps in the evolution of the system were instrumental here, such as the full judicialization of the Court following Protocol 11 (1998) and the direct access to the Court for applicants. In addition, the so-called pilot procedure, which allows the Court to tackle repetitive

Lisa Kujus, 'Representation Reinforcement in the European Court of Human Rights', *Global Constitutionalism* 1 (2025): 1–23.

43 *Ireland* v. *United Kingdom*, 18 January 1978, Application No. 5310/71, para. 239. On this notion, see Kanstantsin Dzehtsiarou, *Can the European Court of Human Rights Shape European Public Order?* (Cambridge University Press, 2021).

44 Stephen Gardbaum, 'Human Rights as International Constitutional Rights', *The European Journal of International Law* 19, no. 4 (2008): 749–68.

45 Geir Ulfstein, 'Transnational Constitutional Aspects of the European Court of Human Rights', *Global Constitutionalism* 10, no. 1 (2021): 151–74.

46 Alec Stone Sweet, 'A Cosmopolitan Legal Order: Constitutional Pluralism and Rights Adjudication in Europe', *Global Constitutionalism* 1, no. 1 (2012): 53–90.

47 Oddný Mjöll Arnardóttir, 'Res Interpretata, Erga Omnes Effect and the Role of the Margin of Appreciation in Giving Domestic Effect to the Judgments of the European Court of Human Rights', *European Journal of International Law* 28, no. 3 (2017): 819–43; Christos Giannopoulos, 'The Reception by Domestic Courts of the Res Interpretata Effect of Jurisprudence of the European Court of Human Rights', *Human Rights Law Review* 19, no. 3 (2019): 537–59.

cases and reduce its chronic backlog by specifying remedial action, was also seen as making the Court akin to 'constitutional justice'.[48]

Still, it is one thing to depict constitutional aspects in these predominantly formal and descriptive terms, and yet another to claim that the Court adjudicates a constitutional subject matter in normative terms, that it has or should have the power or legitimacy of constitutional review. While scholars have pointed to the relevance of the Convention to the relationship between constitutional organs of the state,[49] as we shall see in Chapter 6, this relationship derives from specific Convention articles, rather than by anything indicative of an and overarching account of constitutionalism. This investigation suggests that (right-based) democracy – and to some extent the rule of law – generally have more descriptive and normative value than constitutionalism in the Court's context. This value operates at both the procedural and substantive stages. As we shall see in Chapter 4, the primacy accorded to state parties in interpreting the Convention and the exhaustion of remedies principles are notably, but non-exclusively, premised on democratic grounds. More importantly, in resolving cases the Court refers to 'democratic society' in a far more relevant and decisive manner than to anything deemed 'constitutional' along the senses previously outlined.

It does not follow, however, that the Court's 'democratic society' does not ramify into domains that are usually defined as belonging to the constitutional realm – but these incursions have a non-derivative basis in the Court's own references to 'democratic society'. This is pertinent, for example, for evaluating the current responses to populism offered by constitutional scholars: for example, heightened threshold for constitutional amendments or even eternity clauses do not map onto the Court's jurisdiction, as we shall see in Chapter 3. Designing a response from within the Court's subsidiary jurisdiction is therefore key. This is also pertinent to populism itself: constitutional theorists have indeed debated whether populism itself could reflect a distinct, and potentially desirable, account of

[48] Stone Sweet, 'A Cosmopolitan Legal Order'; Dilek Kurban, 'Forsaking Individual Justice: The Implications of the European Court of Human Rights' Pilot Judgment Procedure for Victims of Gross and Systematic Violations', *Human Rights Law Review* 16, no. 4 (2016): 731–69.

[49] See Mathieu Leloup, 'The Concept of Structural Human Rights in the European Convention on Human Rights', *Human Rights Law Review* 20, no. 3 (2020): 480–501.

constitutionalism.[50] As previously outlined, the authoritarian variant of populism is contemplated in this investigation as a serious distortion, rather than a corrective, to one of the core values of constitutionalism, namely democracy. The book postulates that populism has a principled, albeit profoundly distorted, relation to democracy, while it relates to another constitutional value, namely the rule of law, in instrumental terms.

[50] Cristóbal Rovira Kaltwasser, 'The Ambivalence of Populism: Threat and Corrective for Democracy', *Democratization* 19, no. 2 (2012): 184–208; Paul Blokker, 'Populism as a Constitutional Project', *International Journal of Constitutional Law* 17, no. 2 (2019): 536–53; Mark Tushnet and Bojan Bugarič, *Power to the People: Constitutionalism in the Age of Populism* (Oxford University Press, 2022).

2

Authoritarian Populism

An Insidious Threat to the Court's 'Democratic Society'

One does not necessarily need a sophisticated theory to imagine what authoritarian populists could say against the Court's supranational judicial authority. They could reclaim the 'will of the people' against any finding of a (non-)violation of the Convention by the Court that does not align with that will. They could, in principle or in passing, denounce the Court's very existence and the intergovernmental institution that created it (the Council of Europe, hereafter, 'the CoE'). From a populist standpoint, the Court constitutes an optimal object of vilification: it benefits from compulsory jurisdiction; it represents a highly institutionalized and international club of 'corrupt elites'; and its overarching function is precisely to review and sanction the majoritarian abuses of states.

More insidiously, however, populist governments also may very well rely on the interpretive discretion granted to them by the Court – typically, in the context of the proportionality test and the margin of appreciation that they can benefit from under certain conditions. This applies when the domestic right-interfering norm has gone through proper democratic channels, as we shall see in later chapters. Indeed, state parties remain the primary interpreters of the Convention under the subsidiary regime, and the case reaching Strasbourg implies that multiple domestic authorities have legally validated governmental action from the Convention standpoint. Furthermore, in their plea to the Court, populist governments may subtly pick up on the Court's own register of democracy to dress their political project as precisely reinforcing democracy. This risk highlights the question of whether the interpretive equipment of the Court is apt to detect and respond to populism in its supranational position.

One therefore needs to link the discourse and the practice of populist governments, on the one hand, to the Court's role and practice, on the other. How does one go about doing that conceptually and methodologically? In this chapter, I argue that research in (European) human rights law has not sufficiently identified, measured, and evaluated the risk that authoritarian populism poses to the Court's adjudicatory record. Moreover, while the literature on the response of constitutional law – including constitutional or apex courts – to populism has grown rapidly in recent years, the question remains whether these are relevant and applicable to the supranational and human rights context of the Court. In what follows, I survey important contributions to this area of research before presenting the analytical and methodological framework that will help to build the bridge between populism as an ideational construct and the Court as a supranational judicial institution.

2.1 Mapping the Research Gap

In this section, I explain and illustrate the lack of a Court-centred account of the response to populism in the predominant literature. I show that while the literature on the legal response to populism is vibrant, it leaves out the question of whether there exists a specific nexus between the Convention and the Court, on the one hand, and authoritarian populism, on the other hand – a nexus that would help craft the Court's response to it.

When one reviews the exponential literature on the legal response to populism, one is struck by two recurrent features. One is that it remains difficult to delineate a response that would distinctively address populism without equally applying to other more established and direct threats to democracy. In what follows, I illustrate this risk of overdetermination by surveying the growing literature on constitutional amendment and replacement, as well as the longer tradition of 'militant democracy', to illustrate this difficulty. If this book's objective is to craft the response to authoritarian populism specifically, it is crucial to rationally link, as much as possible, the discourse and the manifestations of populism to a specific ideational basis. Only then will we be able to devise an appropriate response to this novel threat to democracy.

The second feature is that the predominant constitutionalist response is rather difficult to replicate in the Court's jurisdiction as an international and subsidiary organ. This feature may partially explain why there has not been a theoretically informed study of the role of the Court in responding to populism thus far. This gap remains surprising, as the constitutional order of CoE states is shaped, informed, or even structured by the Convention and the effects of the Court's judgments. But it does not follow that the Convention and the Court's function can be portrayed as constitutional for the purpose of crafting the response. And while constitutional scholars almost always mention some relevant Convention provisions or Court cases in their analysis of populism,[1] they do not systematically engage with the question of whether a closer nexus exists between the Court as a supranational guarantor of basic democratic and rule of law guarantees, on the one hand, and populism as a distinct threat to these guarantees, on the other hand.

In a nutshell, the risk here is to assume that the Court enjoys the same jurisdiction as (apex) courts domestically (or the CJEU) and more generally that the Court is portrayed as the ultimate guardian of a constitutional terrain that populists aim to excavate. The international and subsidiary role of the Court adds significant complexity to this portrayal and calls for further analysis that incorporates the conditions of its adjudicatory role. The same caution applies, as we shall see, to the burgeoning human rights scholarship on the response to populism, which often proceeds on an assumption of continuity, as I explain in the next section.[2] If the constitutionalist lens is not adequate, which theoretical and methodological framework ought to be used?

2.1.1 The Constitutionalist Response and Its Limits

In domestic jurisdictions, one of the salient effects of authoritarian populists in power is constitutional amendment or, in some cases, constitutional replacement. Among the CoE states that have distinguished themselves in such a process is Hungary. As is well known, the ruling Fidesz party in Hungary made use of its two-thirds supermajority in parliament to enact a new constitution in 2011 after spending its first year in power making no fewer than fifty-three constitutional amendments to the old constitution. One of these was the process of appointing judges to

[1] Gábor Halmai, 'Populism, Authoritarianism and Constitutionalism', *German Law Journal* 20, no. 3 (2019): 296–313; Gábor Halmai, 'The Making of "Illiberal Constitutionalism" with or without a New Constitution: The Case of Hungary and Poland', in *Comparative Constitution Making*, ed. David Landau and Hanna Lerner (Edward Elgar Publishing, 2019): 302–23; Gábor Halmai, 'Illiberalism in East Central Europe', in *Routledge Handbook of Illiberalism*, ed. András Sajó, Renáta Uitz, and Stephen Holmes (Routledge, 2021): 813–21; Landau, 'Abusive Constitutionalism'; András Sajó, Renáta Uitz, and Stephen Holmes, eds., *Routledge Handbook of Illiberalism* (Routledge, 2021); Svetlana Tyulkina, *Militant Democracy: Undemocratic Political Parties and Beyond* (Routledge, 2015).

[2] Jure Vidmar, *European Populism and Human Rights* (Brill Nijhoff, 2020); Lawrence Helfer, 'Populism and International Human Rights Law Institutions: A Survival Guide', in *Human Rights in a Time of Populism: Challenges and Responses*, ed. Gerald Neuman (Cambridge University Press, 2021): 218–49.

the Constitutional Court: while electing nominees used to require the majority of parties and parliamentary members to agree, the new rule allows the Fidesz party to nominate candidates to be then elected by its governing parliamentary majority.[3]

The new Fundamental Law in Hungary has also enabled the prime minister to directly appoint the head of oversight agencies, which effectively allows them 'to choose among those who are loyal to them, and therefore raises serious questions of political independence'.[4] This is quintessentially the case for media regulation, which became a 'centralized, pyramid-shaped, institutional structure with the Media Council's Chair on top, herself appointed by the Prime Minister'.[5] This capture also concerned content monitoring, the distribution of frequency, and the allocation of public media funding, as we shall see in Chapter 5. Another domain severely affected by constitutional replacement is elections and their ecosystem. In Hungary, the seats on the electoral commission that were supposed to be filled through political negotiation and compromise between the government and opposition parties are filled by members of Fidesz. As Halmai et al. explain, 'thus the Commission could thwart attempts by civil society groups to use referendums to derail aspects of the government's program'.[6]

Constitutional scholars have suggested that to curtail these forms of 'constitutional dismemberment',[7] amendment should be rendered more difficult to achieve. Targeted measures such as heightened parliamentary thresholds for amendment have been put forward: 'the lower the amendment threshold, the more vulnerable a system would be to abusive constitutional amendments. The stock solution in modern constitutional theory is to use tiered amendment thresholds.'[8] Hungary passing a new constitution within existing amendment rules provides an example of the limits of that approach, however. This raises the questions of which response would be the most effective, and when the response should be effectuated. Democracy-reinforcing measures,

[3] Miklós Bánkuti, Gábor Halmai, and Kim Lane Scheppele, 'Disabling the Constitution', *Journal of Democracy* 23, no. 3 (2012): 138–46.

[4] Attila Vincze, 'Hungary: Regulatory Bodies in an Illiberal Democracy', in *Governance and Constitutionalism*, ed. Bogdan Iancu and Elena Simina Tănăsescu (Routledge, 2018), 127.

[5] Péter Bajomi-Lázár, 'The Party Colonisation of the Media: The Case of Hungary', *East European Politics and Societies* 27, no. 1 (2012): 86.

[6] Bánkuti, Halmai, and Scheppele, 'Disabling the Constitution', 140.

[7] Richard Albert, 'Constitutional Amendment and Dismemberment', *The Yale Journal of International Law* 43, no. 1 (2017): 84.

[8] Landau, 'Abusive Constitutionalism', 226.

such as having popular consultation at spaced intervals, for example, could 'reduce the possibility that incumbent politicians and parties can take advantage of temporary spikes in their popularity to push through amendments that are harmful to democracy'.[9] The latter point echoes the more general idea of regular elections to ensure that the government's agenda receives continual support.[10] All together, these measures could fall under the wider umbrella of the doctrine of 'unconstitutional constitutional amendments'.[11] But whether these measures are effective remains largely an empirical, rather than a principled or conceptual, question.

Furthermore, one may readily ask whether a constitutionalist response alone is adequately and sufficiently tailored to populism specifically – and therefore whether only populists go for constitutional dismemberment. In his article on 'populist constitutions', Landau argues that constitutional overhaul can be tracked back to populism's ideational core, which is to view populists as the only legitimate representatives of the people's will: 'unilateral, rather than negotiated, constitution-making or constitutional change fits populist ideology because it avoids negotiation with members of a corrupted elite'.[12] Yet, in this second article, for example, Landau does not articulate a response that targets (authoritarian) populism specifically – rather, his focus remains 'the functions that constitutions play in populist regimes'.[13] It seems that the responses of heightened parliamentary thresholds or popular consultations, for example, could equally apply to preventing the rise of potentially any non-democratic regime. That is not necessarily the case for populism, which does incorporate the vocabulary and the forms – if not the substance – of democracy. In the words of Sajó, 'the democratic power-grab has not centred on taking over the armed forces or secret service as

[9] Ibid., 228.

[10] Samuel Issacharoff, 'The Corruption of Popular Sovereignty', *International Journal of Constitutional Law* 18, no. 4 (2020): 1109–35; Samuel Issacharoff, 'Fragile Democracies', *Harvard Law Review* 120, no. 6 (2007): 1405–67; Tushnet and Bugarič, *Power to the People*, 32.

[11] Yaniv Roznai, *Unconstitutional Constitutional Amendments: The Limits of Amendment Powers* (Oxford University Press, 2019); Yaniv Roznai and Tamar Hostovsky Brandes, 'Democratic Erosion, Populist Constitutionalism, and the Unconstitutional Constitutional Amendments Doctrine', *Law & Ethics of Human Rights* 14, no. 1 (2020): 19–48.

[12] David Landau, 'Populist Constitutions', *The University of Chicago Law Review* 85, no. 2 (2018): 528.

[13] Ibid., 541.

tools of violent oppression or total domination'.[14] Populism rather thrives on a distorted register of democracy, as we shall see in Chapter 3.

Similarly, Dixon and Landau in a recent book articulate the value-based framework of 'responsive judicial review', which identifies the risks of 'antidemocratic monopoly', 'democratic blind spots', and 'burdens of inertia' as the grounds for stronger scrutiny by constitutional courts.[15] The framework aims to build a third way between the established positions of 'strong' and 'weak' review in justifying the extent and depth of judicial intervention in the broad tradition of John Hart Ely,[16] which was also recently revived through the 'political process theory' approach.[17] As will appear throughout this investigation of the Court, I share the diagnosis but not the remedy advanced in these important works. For example, Dixon and Landau understand 'legislative blind spots' when legislators fall short of considering the impact of policies – something that the framework of proportionality testing is apt to detect. As I explain in Chapters 4 and 9, the populist project, when carried out through law, is prone to proportionality failure. Further, while Dixon and Landau's account centres upon a 'democratic minimum core', they explicitly limit the framework's applicability to domestic judiciaries across the constitutional realm: 'there may be some differences between specialized and generalized courts when it comes to their ability to counter certain forms of democratic blockage. But, in principle, all courts with constitutional jurisdiction have the capacity to perform the forms of democratic protection and promotion.'[18] A responsive framework applicable to the Court requires first discussing the role and practice of that Court with reference to its international and subsidiary jurisdiction, as well as its specific human rights subject matter. This is why I shall suggest the methodological shift of normative reconstruction in lieu of applying an abstract and generically constitutionalist framework.

[14] Andras Sajó, *Ruling by Cheating: Governance in Illiberal Democracy* (Cambridge University Press, 2021), 19.

[15] Rosalind Dixon and David Landau, *Abusive Constitutional Borrowing* (Oxford University Press, 2021); Rosalind Dixon and David Landau, '1989–2019: From Democratic to Abusive Constitutional Borrowing', *International Journal of Constitutional Law* 17, no. 2 (2019): 489–96.

[16] John Hart Ely, *Democracy and Distrust: A Theory of Judicial Review* (Harvard University Press, 1980).

[17] Gardbaum, 'Human Rights as International Constitutional Rights'; Gardbaum, 'Comparative Political Process Theory II'; Gardbaum, 'Comparative Political Process Theory'.

[18] Dixon and Landau, *Abusive Constitutional Borrowing*, 18.

Andras Sajó's recent contribution also provides an example of a refined constitutionalist lens specifically tailored to trace the constitutional effects of populist rule, in particular in Hungary.[19] Under the title of 'militant constitutionalism', Sajó proposes a vast programme of constitutional entrenchment that matches the three domains previously examined in this book (judicial independence, media freedom, and elections): 'super-entrenchment' should ensure 'that constitutional courts can be the effective guardians of the constitution' against the attempt to pack the judiciary; the requirement that independent agencies 'should be led by non-partisan leadership, appointed by processes driven by political consensus' to avoid executive control of the media, for example; and the rules pertaining to the electoral system, 'including rules on how parties and procedures are funded and how candidates access the media' to avoid the manipulation of electoral competition.[20] As we shall see in Chapter 3, Sajó's account is based on an account of Caesarism in which the leader is directly emanating from – and can abuse – the will of the people: 'this extremism makes the totalitarian potential of democracy manifest, since a directly elected president can claim uniquely to incarnate the "will of the people"; as a result, a president is prone to assume a "super legitimacy" which he or she will be tempted to deploy against any countervailing institution, including the courts and the press'.[21]

It appears that while Sajó's account aims to address the specific effects of populism within the constitutional order, it employs a thick normative account of constitutionalism too, which in turn widens the scope of the (super-)entrenchment response quite significantly. Further, Sajó's Caesarist account presents populism as tied to the risk of turning totalitarian, which further justifies the scale of entrenchment. These two premises deserve further scrutiny in the context of the ECtHR. On the one hand, the question again remains whether a thick constitutionalist account can be replicated in the international and subsidiary context of the Court. On the other hand, it is not obvious whether the totalitarian risk should lie at the centre of the response, as we shall see in the next chapter.

[19] Sajó, *Ruling by Cheating*; Sajó, Uitz, and Holmes, *Routledge Handbook of Illiberalism*.
[20] Sajó, *Ruling by Cheating*, 199.
[21] Ibid., 30.

2.1.2 Beyond the Constitutionalist Lens

The predominant constitutionalist lens does not only highlight the challenge of designing a response that closely matches the coordinates of the populist attack. Indeed, while intending to target populism, the response may ultimately apply to a variety of other (existential) threats to democracy. It also raises the deeper and methodological question of which theoretical perspective(s) should be privileged to evaluate authoritarian populism for the purpose of crafting the response. As I further explain in Chapter 3, I believe that, while constitutionalism may help reconstruct and evaluate some features of authoritarian populism, democracy is significantly more insightful from an analytical and normative perspective. Furthermore, democracy is significantly more relevant in the context of the Court's adjudication and its potential response to populism. As I explain in Chapter 4, democracy (the protection thereof) does not only inform the historical role of the Court and underpin key provisions of the Convention, but it is also embedded in the subsidiary regime of the system in structuring the allocation of authority between the national and the supranational levels.

The latter point is perhaps the most straightforward at this juncture: reviewing the constitutionalist response helps to better grasp that what may be unfolding in terms of constitutional alteration or dismemberment within CoE states simply does not apply to the Court itself. In terms of effects on the Court specifically, the Court remains relatively immune to the typical populist manoeuvres of court packing, jurisdiction stripping, or budget reduction.[22] A similar dismantling process would indeed require the majority of state parties of the CoE to consent to amending – and potentially dismembering – the Convention system itself. In the absence of a similar process at the supranational level, how does one problematize the relationship between the Court and populism? Can one readily employ the lens of (abusive) constitutionalism?[23] One can doubt that the nature, jurisdiction, and practice of the Court's system can be idealized the way constitutionalism idealizes the constitutional order. While it can be argued that the Court performs a constitutional function of reviewing compliance of all public authorities within state parties with

[22] Jan Petrov, 'The Populist Challenge to the European Court of Human Rights', *International Journal of Constitutional Law* 18, no. 2 (2020): 476–508.

[23] David Kosař and Katarína Šipulová, 'The Strasbourg Court Meets Abusive Constitutionalism: Baka v. Hungary and the Rule of Law', *Hague Journal on the Rule of Law* 10, no. 1 (2018): 83–110.

(Convention) rights, the Court simply does not enjoy the powers of a constitutional court and does not, and by far, enjoy jurisdiction over the prototypical matters that define the constitutional framework. It is limited by its international and subsidiary nature, as I further explain in Chapter 4.

This calls for a resolutely Court- and practice-centred approach to the response to populism – that is, how the Court itself may relate to populism in its jurisdictional position and established case law. Both a solid account of authoritarian populism – conceptually defined and empirically informed – and a thorough reconstruction of the Court's position and practice are prerequisites to this investigation. Now, there are contributions engaging with the nexus between populism and the Court from a predominantly sociological rather than normative angle and without engaging with the Court's practice and reasoning at great length. Petrov, for instance, adopts a sociological account of legitimacy – in particular, the perception of state parties of the Convention – and concludes that populism 'has clear implications for how democracy should work and explains why challenging the ECtHR is justified or even necessary',[24] without however addressing the Court's practice in detail. Pin connects the rise of populism at the domestic (political) level to the notorious 'living instrument' doctrine of the Court at the supranational (judicial) level.[25] Pin intimates that the Court overusing this dynamic approach to interpretation has strengthened a 'progressive' approach that has exacerbated the populist frustration. However, the level of argument remains descriptive and explanatory. Those studies examining human rights courts generally have not explored the Court's practice in any significant depth either.[26]

Before getting to the Court specifically, one may object that constitutional law and human rights law are not the only disciplines with a track record of critically examining populism in relation to the Court. The absence of a critical mass of research does not imply an absence of conceptual tools and empirical measures to investigate the issue. One approach is to examine the growing wave of criticism(s) raised against the Court and try to situate the populist among them, an approach popularized in recent years by the 'backlash against international courts' literature in political science and international relations. However, it

24 Petrov, 'The Populist Challenge to the European Court of Human Rights', 505.

25 Andrea Pin, 'The Transnational Drivers of Populist Backlash in Europe: The Role of Courts', *German Law Journal* 20, no. 2 (2019), 225.

26 Helfer, 'Populism and International Human Rights Law Institutions: A Survival Guide'.

quickly appears that the conceptual perimeter distinctive of the backlash literature appears excessively broad to capture what is distinctively populist about the backlash and, further, what is populist about the backlash against the Court specifically. Indeed, 'backlash' refers to the idea of 'the action of the reactionary: a reaction to a development that is sought to be blocked or reversed'.[27] The definition remains therefore neutral vis-à-vis the level of reaction (national, regional, international) and regarding its ideational basis (populist, authoritarian, or else).

A connected approach consists in correlating populist rule with the state criticisms against the Court. In his study of twenty-eight 'backlash episodes' emanating from (right-wing and left-wing) populist leaders against international courts, Voeten indicates that none specifically and directly concerns the Court. His argument remains insightful in illustrating the different and perhaps distinctive kind of instrumentality that populist governments entertain with international courts, which is voicing criticisms when criticizing an international court's judgment further lends support a 'pre-existing narrative' at the domestic level – in particular, a narrative that concerns mega-identity politics.[28] The backlash literature here helps depict the kind of instrumental and opportunistic relationship that populist governments entertain with international courts in general and with the Court in particular: rather than placing friendly judges on their apex court, for example, they selectively criticize those judgments that conveniently fit the narratives that populists promote and nurture domestically – and here again, the populist ambition is not necessarily to overturn the (supranational) institutional system in place.

To fill the gap of a specifically normative examination, this investigation focuses on the response to populism that the ECtHR *should* offer but also the extent to which it *can* do so given its nature, jurisdiction, and established practice. Of course, populism as an analytical concept is foreign to the Court's terminological apparatus. Populism may however already be present in the facts and the arguments presented by an applicant, by a respondent state, or in the Court's adjudication without being qualified as such. To give just one clear example, in *Baka v. Hungary* the Court examined the question of access to a court

[27] Mikael Rask Madsen, Pola Cebulak, and Micha Wiebusch, 'Backlash against International Courts: Explaining the Forms and Patterns of Resistance to International Courts', *International Journal of Law in Context* 14, no. 2 (2018): 197–220.

[28] Erik Voeten, 'Populism and Backlashes against International Courts', *Perspectives on Politics* 18, no. 2 (2020), 409.

(under Article 6) in the context of the dismissal of the former president of the Hungarian Supreme Court, which intuitively resonates with the well-known populist trend of court packing, as we shall see in Chapter 7.[29]

2.2 Identifying the Tension between Populism and the Court

The previous section pointed to the absence of a Court- and practice-focused analysis – descriptively or normatively oriented – of the response to populism. This book undertakes to fill this gap at the normative level (the 'should') constrained by the Court's specific nature, jurisdiction, and practice (the 'is' and the 'can'). Now, what kind of conceptual and methodological equipment does this project need? Two premises form the foundations of the book in this respect. The first and obvious one has to do with the proper definition of authoritarian populism as an ideational construct. I tackle this premise in Chapter 3, where I articulate a working and selective definition that centres upon the attacks on deliberation and representation as cardinal democratic values. While both democracy and populism appeal to the people, they radically diverge over how the popular will ought to be formed and enacted and, consequently, over how the (normative) legitimacy of the political order obtains. Building on the fervent theoretical literature of populism, I build the claim that deliberation and representation are two constitutive requirements of democratic legitimacy that populism cannot accommodate in its attempt to employ the register of democracy. As such, populism distorts the core ideal of democracy as a pursuit for political equality: while celebrating the people and denouncing the elite, populism in fact perpetuates and entrenches existing participatory and deliberative inequalities. The same distortion explains how populism can virtually ignore the requirements of the rule of law. In the same exclusive fashion in which populism represses the values of deliberation and representation, it also denies the constraint(s) that the rule of law poses on democratically adopted norms. The exclusion proceeds via the same reference to a projected people whose will requires a quasi-direct enforcement, as we shall see. More on this in Chapter 3.

Now, focusing on deliberation, representation, and the rule of law not only helps to diagnose the pathologies of populism, but it also helps to identify a thicker tension between populism on the one hand and the Court's role and practice on the other hand – a nexus that motivates this

[29] *Baka* v. *Hungary* (GC), 23 June 2016, Application No. 20261/12.

study through and through: the values of deliberation, representation, and the rule of law are embodied in key provisions of the Convention. As we shall see in detail, the process of deliberation is primarily protected by Articles 10 (expression) and 11 (assembly and association); the process of representation is primarily protected by Article 3 Protocol 1 (free elections); and the rule of law is primarily protected by Article 6 (fair trial) and Article 14 (non-discrimination), as well as Articles 17–18 (abuse of rights). As I shall explain in Chapter 4, the Court does not view these rights in isolation but through the unifying notion of 'democratic society'. There is consensus in the literature that the predominant models of democracy underlying the Court's practice are deliberative and representative, while rule of law provisions apply across the Convention.[30] Therefore, these selected provisions are principally relevant to the democratic distortion of populism in the context of analysing the Court's actual and potential response.

2.3 The Puzzle of the Book

Now, the specific puzzle that this book addresses is whether having these provisions enshrined in the Convention can detect and respond to the distinctively populist threat to rights at the level of the Court's adjudication. The answer depends on conducting further investigations, and that is for two related reasons, one conceptual and the other institutional. Conceptually, whether the Court is equipped to respond to populism depends on how the Court understands its right-based 'democratic society', and how such a normative construct can effectively detect and counter the distinctive effects of populism. Having general and abstract rights enshrined in the Convention is certainly not enough. This is one reason for scrutinizing the case law of the Court in the relevant domains of populist erosion. And to effectively run this analysis, one needs a clear and comprehensive understanding of how populist rule may affect and erode rights. Indeed, it is one thing to claim that, at the ideational level, populism undermines the values of deliberation, representation and the rule of law. It is yet another thing to show *how* populists, once in power, effectively operate such a manoeuvre, and how Convention rights are implicated. To accurately calibrate the Court's response to populism,

[30] Paulien de Morree, *Rights and Wrongs under the ECHR: The Prohibition of Abuse of Rights in Article 17 of the European Convention on Human Rights* (Intersentia, 2016).

one needs an up-to-date template of the kinds of attack that populist governments orchestrate. In relying on recent research by political scientists and constitutional scholars, I show in Chapter 5 that the effects of populist rule are primarily infrastructural, posing, I suggest, a serious challenge to the Court's approach to democracy and the rule of law.

As already mentioned, the second, institutional reason for exploring the Court's practice in depth is that it remains – unlike the CJEU or an apex court domestically – an international and subsidiary court. By being subsidiary, the Court does not substitute itself for the primary role of domestic authorities in interpreting the Convention but only 'supervises' – the favourite wording of the Court – the domestic implementation of that Convention. At the level of interpretation, this deference is quintessentially reflected in the doctrine of the margin of appreciation: state parties are often allocated an interpretive discretion by the Court. This allocation, we shall see, specifically takes place in the proportionality test where rights are 'balanced' against public interests and justifications offered by the respondent government. That is where the Court's institutional position – a subsidiary and international one – has important implications for the project of designing the response to populism: such deference may limit the ability of the Court to detect the populist erosion developing domestically. In repeatedly qualifying state authorities as 'better placed' (as epistemic justification) and benefiting from 'democratic legitimation' (as normative justification) when it accords the margin to a respondent state, the Court may in fact turn a blind eye to the insidious capture of democratic institutions and values by populist rulers. Since the margin of appreciation is allocated on a case-by-case basis (and remains, one should recall, a creation of the Court), here again one needs to delve into its case-based reasoning to measure this risk to optimally frame the response, which further justifies investigating the relevant domains. Chapters 6 to 8 will therefore zoom in on each of the aforementioned rights with particular attention paid to the practice of proportionality and the margin of appreciation.

2.4 The Court's Foundational Purpose and the Relevance of Authoritarian Populism

Before engaging with the other pieces of the puzzle (the concept of populism, the jurisdictional position of the Court, and its case law), an important premise should be discussed – a discussion that will occupy the rest of this preliminary chapter and form part of the background to the next steps of our investigation. The premise is the following: when one engages with the notion of (right-based) democracy in the context of the Court, one is also engaging with the chief and foundational purpose of the Convention system, which was to prevent the return of totalitarian regimes (e.g., Nazism, fascism, communism) in the aftermath of the Second World War. Unlike other human rights conventions and treaties emerging at the time, which refer to thick and aspirational notions – in particular, the Universal Declaration of 1945 and its grounding in 'dignity' – the initial Convention is primarily (but not only) preoccupied with some foundational aspects of democracy and, in terms of rights, with those of political participation and opposition. Approaching the Court from this broad historical angle helps clarify that what makes this court relatively distinct in contrast to other judicial fora (domestic or international) is the external protection of distinctively democratic and rule of law rights. This also further strengthens the case for an investigation specific to the Court: it is not only that populism may erode the right-based foundations of democracy. It is also that these foundations form a core part of the legal edifice that the European Movement, and then the CoE, sought to institutionalize back in the late 1940s, which then raises the issue of adequacy: is this edifice, as interpreted by the Court, solid enough to address and counter populism?

In what follows, I expand on these historical and conceptual points and claim that, while the Court's foundational purpose was to contain and existential threats to democracy, the rise of populism may require the Court to adjust its interpretive apparatus to populism's insidious and endogenous nature. I believe that the Court's value-based mandate – the triad of democratic deliberation, representation, and the rule of law – needs to be reviewed in this light. As I shall argue throughout the following chapters, the margin of appreciation accorded to domestic authorities is a legacy of this historically limited role of preserving the necessary conditions of democracy.

2.5 Democracy and the Rule of Law in the Founding Moments of the Convention System

As far as the burgeoning history of the Convention system is concerned, the protection of democracy and the rule of law via an international oversight mechanism appears central when one reviews the key steps – informal and formal – leading to the adoption of the Convention on 4 November 1949 by the Committee of Ministers of the CoE. One may go back as far as the opening speech by Winston Churchill at the Hague Congress in May 1948 (at which the so-called European Movement was inaugurated). It emphasized the project of a permanent union or federation of distinctively democratic states with a human rights charter at its centre: 'it is a dynamic expression of democratic faith based upon moral conceptions and inspired by a sense of mission. In the center of our movement stands the idea of a Charter of Human Rights, guarded by freedom and sustained by law.'[31] Equally, membership in the imagined European system would require democratic credentials domestically: 'the admission of a nation to membership of a European Union must therefore be conditional upon its acceptance of democratic principles and its assurance to its citizens of the fundamental rights of the individual'.[32] This applies equally today to membership in the CoE. Furthermore, the 'Message to the Europeans', in which the Hague Congress culminates, specifically mentions the right to political opposition as the cornerstone of the imagined charter – 'a Charter of Human Rights guaranteeing liberty of thought, assembly and expression as the right to form a political opposition'.[33]

Similar solemn references to democracy are found in the statute of the CoE – the international organization that went on to adopt the European Movement proposal and ultimately the Convention as we know it – and in particular 'the spiritual and moral values which are the common heritage of their peoples and the true source of individual freedom, political liberty and the rule of law, principles which form the basis for all genuine democracy' found in the Preamble to the Council of Europe.[34] Now, Duranti has well explained how the emphasis on 'heritage' justifies labelling the Convention as a 'conservative revolution': 'rather than equate human rights with natural rights, it presented human rights as a product of the historical development of European legal and political

[31] Address given by Winston Churchill at the Congress of Europe in The Hague (7 May 1948) quoted in Alfred William Brian Simpson, *Human Rights and the End of Empire: Britain and the Genesis of the European Convention* (Oxford University Press, 2004), 605.

[32] Ibid., 605.

[33] *Congress of Europe: The Hague, 7–11 May 1948 / Congrés de l'Europe: La Haye, 7–11 Mai 1948* (Council of Europe, 1999), https://book.coe.int/en/books-on-europe/8118-congress-of-europe-the-hague-7-11-may-1948.html.

[34] Statute of the Council of Europe, Preamble, https://rm.coe.int/1680306052.

norms',[35] which also explains why the Convention has been notably deprived of any self-standing social, economic, or cultural right. In the words of Bates, 'at this stage at least the proposed Convention was not about creating a new set of rules and standards; it was concerned with making sure standards remained in place and that democratic security was safeguarded'.[36]

Another point on the historical continuum is the discussion over the specific provisions to be included in the draft of the European Movement Convention – and that is where the minimalism built into its democratic provisions emerges clearly: it mentions 'those fundamental, personal and political rights which it is practicable to enforce through the process of a court of law' ... 'to protect the minimum essential, rather than the maximum desirable, leaving it to the Signatory States to extend the scope of the agreement'.[37] This is particularly relevant, again, to the rights of political opposition. Although suppressed in the final version of the Convention, Article 2 of the draft Convention for instance required each state 'faithfully to respect the fundamental principles of democracy' and to proscribe any action 'which would interfere with the right of political criticism and the right to organise a political opposition'.[38]

A later historical point is the *travaux préparatoires* of the Convention to be submitted to the Consultative Assembly of the CoE (based on the European Movement Convention) in September 1949. Here, the role of the imagined Court is apprehended through explicitly naming the kind of the threat it would address: 'we are less concerned to set up a European judicial authority capable of righting isolated wrongs, isolated illegal acts committed in our countries, than to prevent, from the onset, the setup up in one or other of these countries of a regime of the fascist or Nazi type'.[39] This system's function was minimal in that sense. As Bates coined the

[35] Marco Duranti, *The Conservative Human Rights Revolution: European Identity, Transnational Politics, and the Origins of the European Convention* (Oxford University Press, 2017), 325.

[36] Bates, 'The Birth of the European Convention on Human Rights – and the European Court of Human Rights', 54.

[37] European Movement, *The European Movement and the Council of Europe* (Hutchinson and Co. Ltd., 1949) chapter VII and appendix II, quoted in Bates, 'The Birth of the European Convention on Human Rights – and the European Court of Human Rights', 51–2.

[38] Ibid., 54.

[39] Council of Europe, *Collected Edition of the 'Travaux préparatoires' of the European Convention on Human Rights / Council of Europe / Recueil des travaux préparatoires de la Convention européenne des droits de l'homme* (Martinus Nijhoff, 1975), Vol. 1, 90.

term, 'as to the Court, it would be the conscience of the free Europe, acting like an "alarm bell" warning the other nations of democratic Europe that one of their number was going "totalitarian". At this stage, then, the human rights guarantee was minimalist in its ambition.'[40] Duranti also suggests that while preventing the return of totalitarian regimes was not the only motive for establishing the system, it 'served as a point of consensus to rally support around the proposals of the European unity movements'.[41] A final point on the continuum is the famous Teitgen report, which was drafted by the Committee on Legal and Administrative Questions and presented to the Assembly of the CoE. It made clear that 'the Committee unanimously agreed that for the moment, only those essential rights and freedoms could be guaranteed which are, today, defined and accepted after a long usage, by democratic regimes'.[42]

Now, while minimal democracy and the rule of law are central to the nascent system, it is noteworthy that ultimately the ministers of the Council of Europe did not include the right to free and fair elections in the text of the initial Convention. Disagreement over the content of this right proved impossible to overcome then – for example, the United Kingdom was worried about including universal suffrage in the text of the right, as this would have serious implications for enfranchisement in their colonies and protectorates. However, the right was later lodged in Article 3 of Protocol 1 signed on 4 March 1952. Important to the text of this Article is the explicit reference to parliamentary democracy: 'the High Contracting Parties undertake to hold free elections at reasonable intervals by secret ballot, under conditions which will ensure the free expression of the opinion of the people in the choice of the legislature' (Article 3 Protocol 1). This adds a positive element to the Convention's approach to democracy. Kovács puts the point succinctly: 'the core concept of Article 3 is associated negatively with anti-totalitarianism and positively with parliamentary democracy'.[43] Importantly, this commitment to parliamentary democracy remains neutral with respect to the

40 Bates, 'The Birth of the European Convention on Human Rights – and the European Court of Human Rights', 21.

41 Marco Duranti, *The Conservative Human Rights Revolution*, 338.

42 Council of Europe, *Collected Edition of the 'Travaux préparatoires' of the European Convention on Human Rights*, Vol. 1, 218.

43 Kriszta Kovács, 'Parliamentary Democracy by Default: Applying the European Convention on Human Rights to Presidential Elections and Referendums', *Jus Cogens* 2 (2020), 242.

specific forms that it takes, as we shall see in Chapter 8. This embodiment was left to the state parties' constitutional arrangements. And this has not been without contention until today. In the famous case of *Hirst* v. *United Kingdom*, a joint dissenting opinion held that 'the lack of precision in the wording of that Article (3 of the First Protocol) and the sensitive political assessments involved call for caution'.[44] As we shall further see in Chapters 4 and 6, the firm protection of the basic rights of political opposition, on the one hand, and the thinly defined right to political participation, on the other, permeate the Court's practice until today. In the next section, I suggest that this tension exemplifies the Court's minimal understanding of democracy.

2.6 Existential Threats to Democracy

Moving from historical to theoretical frameworks, securing minimal democracy (and the rule of law) domestically is also found in the literature aiming to explain the initial delegation of authority to supranational human rights bodies such as the nascent Court. Adopting a liberal-republican framework of international relations theory, Moravscik made the seminal point that 'creating a quasi-independent judicial body is a tactic used by governments to "lock in" and consolidate democratic institutions, thereby enhancing their credibility and stability vis-a-vis non-democratic political threat'.[45] Central to this argument is the assumption that sovereign states binding themselves to an international human rights body – with potentially more extensive implications for their constitutional arrangements than domestic courts – enhances political stability domestically. Such benefit overrides the sovereignty costs involved: 'in the language of international relations theory, this "two-level" commitment "ties the hands" of future governments, thereby enhancing the credibility of current domestic policies and institutions'.[46] Note that historians have questioned the concentration on governments and their domestic interests at the expense of civil and transnational dynamics (echoing constructivist theorizing) as explanatory variables.[47]

However, such a theoretical account says relatively little about which account of democracy is getting locked in. In the context of the Court,

[44] *Hirst* v. *United Kingdom (No. 2)* (GC), 6 October 2005, Application No. 74025/01, para. 5, Joint Dissenting Opinion of Judges Wildhaber, Costa, Lorenzen, Kovler, and Jebens.

[45] Andrew Moravcsik, 'The Origins of Human Rights Regimes: Democratic Delegation in Postwar Europe', *International Organization* 54, no. 2 (2000), 228.

[46] Ibid., 228.

[47] Duranti, *The Conservative Human Rights Revolution*.

both the 'alarm bell' (Bates) and the 'democracy lock-in' (Moravscik) notions are tied to a minimalist account of democracy (and the rule of law), one designed only to prevent existential threats. This claim not only reflects the historical continuum just reviewed, but it is also consistent with the liberal-republican account of international relations in which the goal of securing democracy and the rule of law via international agreements is pursued at the lowest cost to the sovereign state. More importantly for our purposes, one judicial expression of this minimalism is that the Court restricts the exercise of democratic rights (e.g., freedom of expression (Article 10), freedom of assembly and association (Article 11)) if and only if there is a foreseeable risk of the dismantling of democracy within the respondent state party as a result, as will be illustrated (in Chapter 6). But can such minimalism respond effectively to the insidious threat of populism?

The claim that the Court's foundational purpose is to contain existential threats also allows one to start conceptualizing the Court's predominant understanding of democratic rights and their limits. In that sense, the Court's initial minimalism still appears when one pays closer attention to the practice of the Court and the detailed content adduced to these rights. As the next chapters will show in detail, minimal democracy is exemplified in two seemingly contrasting forms in that practice. One pertains to the principled limits adduced to these rights, which apply to all state parties, while the other concerns the breadth of the margin of appreciation that a respondent state may benefit from in interpreting these rights in given circumstances. To give just one example, the former form is found in the famous case of *Refah Partisi and Others* v. *Turkey* in which the Turkish constitutional tribunal banned the Islamist party Refah Partisi on grounds of anti-secularism, which forms the cornerstone of the Turkish modern constitution. The Court's decision as to the limits of Article 11, however, centred upon whether the party in question would seize power and implement its anti-democratic agenda:

> The Court accordingly considers that at the time of its dissolution Refah had the real potential to seize political power without being restricted by the compromises inherent in a coalition. If Refah had proposed a programme contrary to democratic principles, its monopoly of political power would have enabled it to establish the model of society envisaged in that programme.[48]

[48] *Refah Partisi and Others (The Welfare Party)* v. *Turkey* (GC), 13 February 2003, Application Nos. 41340/98, 41342/98, and 41344/98, para. 108.

The Court hence established as a matter of principle that holding and defending anti-democratic views (under Article 10 or 11) is certainly not sufficient for these views to be banned from the public arena – what rather draws the line is the likelihood of these views being translated into law and policy. As we shall see in Chapter 4, posing such limits to Article 11 complements the Court's generous approach to Article 10 according to which freedom of expression 'is applicable not only to "information" or "ideas" that are favourably received or regarded as inoffensive or as a matter of indifference, but also to those that offend, shock or disturb the State or any sector of the population'.[49] The Court has for a long time extended protection to the expression of political extremism as long as the threat is not existential (to democracy).

The latter form of minimalism is best exemplified in the Court's approach to the right to free and fair elections (Article 3 Protocol 1). As we shall see in more detail in Chapter 6, the latitude accorded by the Court to domestic authorities significantly increases – to the point where the specific requirements of a democratic society in the electoral domain are simply left to domestic authorities to determine. The margin of appreciation is the vehicle of that deference. For example, *Ždanoka* v. *Latvia* concerned to the right to stand for election of a candidate on behalf of the Community Party of Latvia (CPL):

> The Court therefore accepts in the present case that the national authorities of Latvia, both legislative and judicial, are better placed to assess the difficulties faced in establishing and safeguarding the democratic order. Those authorities should therefore be left sufficient latitude to assess the needs of their society in building confidence in the new democratic institutions, including the national parliament, and to answer the question whether the impugned measure is still needed for these purposes, provided that the Court has found nothing arbitrary or disproportionate in such an assessment.[50]

This self-limitation in the electoral domain is far from new in the Court's practice. In its very first case involving this right, the Court held that:

> There are numerous ways of organising and running electoral systems and a wealth of differences, inter alia, in historical development, cultural diversity and political thought in Europe, which it is for each Contracting State to mould into its own democratic vision.[51]

[49] *Handyside* v. *United Kingdom*, para. 49.
[50] *Ždanoka* v. *Latvia* (GC), 16 March 2006, Application No. 58278/00, para. 102.
[51] *Mathieu-Mohin and Clerfayt* v. *Belgium*, 2 March 1987, Application No. 9267/81, paras. 103–4.

It will be crucial to reconstruct the grounds invoked by the Court to justify discretion in this type of case (epistemic and/or normative) and what the implications for the Court's level of scrutiny are. For now, these passages only aim to illustrate the Court's multifaceted minimalism: either in banning parties only when they are on the brink of dismantling democracy or in excluding itself from examining electoral arrangements in any real depth, the Court reasserts the historical posture according to which it concentrates on the necessary conditions of democracy. Is this posture enough to address and respond to authoritarian populism?

2.7 Militant Democracy and Its Limits

To transition to conceptual analysis and problematize our investigation further, here I start by looking at one concept intuitively suited to approaching the Court's minimalist democracy. We briefly saw that the Court's foundational role can be apprehended via the liberal-republican view of international relations, which remains a descriptive one. I here turn to a concept that has more of a normative pull, that of militant democracy. I argue that while the concept helps measure and problematize the Court's minimal democracy, it highlights two important issues. First, it cannot explain the Court's active stance in extending rather than restricting some of the Convention's democratic rights. Second, in its primary concern of containing a categorical and existential threat to democracy, one wonders about militant democracy's merit in the context of a rising threat that does not disavow the form of democracy, namely populism.

The literature on militant democracy addresses the question of whether a democratically elected government should erect legal barriers against anti-democratic threats.[52] While tied to the domestic context, this approach has intuitive appeal regarding the Court's assigned function of 'locking in' democracy via an international 'alarm bell' system. Yet, while the concept of militant democracy has been used to examine portions and provisions of the Court's practice,[53] it remains to be seen whether it is

52 Karl Loewenstein, 'Militant Democracy and Fundamental Rights', *The American Political Science Review* 31, no. 3 (1937): 417–32; Karl Loewenstein, 'Militant Democracy and Fundamental Rights, II', *The American Political Science Review* 31, no. 4 (1937): 638–58.

53 Gregory H. Fox and Georg Nolte, 'Intolerant Democracies', in *Democratic Governance and International Law*, ed. Gregory H. Fox and Brad R. Roth (Cambridge University Press, 2000); Jan-Werner Müller, 'Militant Democracy', in *The Oxford Handbook of Comparative Constitutional Law*, ed. Michel Rosenfeld and András Sajó (Oxford:

a valid framework for responding to populism. Indeed, the primary purpose of militant democracy as a concept has not been to establish and discuss an independent account of democracy. Rather, the concept has been predominantly functional in that it discusses the measures (that should be) taken by established democracies to defend themselves against an existential threat. In the context in which Loewenstein coined the term, 'a closer study of fascist technique led to discovery of the vulnerable spots in the democratic system, and of how to protect them'. Löwenstein believed that one could undertake such a study based on 'the uniformity of the fascist technique in undermining the democratic state'.[54] A concept being functional requires examining its effect(s) – in the case of militant democracy, the effect(s) of the anti-extremist measures: 'the value of militant democracy lies in its capacity to quickly react and effectively contain extremists in the short term'.[55] In that sense, the concept of militant democracy presumes a threat that is existential. This primarily applies to the Nazi and fascist threats. In the succinct words of Löwenstein, 'fascism has declared war on democracy'.[56]

In other words, the value of the concept for linking up an existential threat to democracy to the effects sought to counter it – in the words of Capoccia, between the tasks of identifying 'how to identify the enemies of democracy' and determining 'what type of legal measures are legitimate and how to assess their proportionality'.[57] These temporary measures typically take the form of rights-restricting legislation pertaining to political participation – from banning political parties to disenfranchising particular individuals. However, there is significant heterogeneity within these parameters. The measures may be enshrined in the constitution – Article 18 of the German Basic law is usually taken as the most explicit and far-reaching militant democracy provision among CoE states – but they also may have effects at the levels of administrative, criminal, and private law. They may be informed and shaped by that state's particular history.[58] Conversely, the insidious and endogenous

Oxford University Press, 2012); de Morree, *Rights and Wrongs under the ECHR*, 147–84; Tyulkina, *Militant Democracy*.

54 Loewenstein, 'Militant Democracy and Fundamental Rights, II', 644.

55 Anthoula Malkopoulou and Ludvig Norman, 'Three Models of Democratic Self-Defence: Militant Democracy and Its Alternatives', *Political Studies* 66, no. 2 (2017): 446.

56 Loewenstein, 'Militant Democracy and Fundamental Rights', 432.

57 Giovanni Capoccia, 'Militant Democracy: The Institutional Bases of Democratic Self-Preservation', *The Annual Review of Law and Social Science* 9 (2013): 214.

58 Peter Niesen, 'Anti-Extremism, Negative Republicanism, Civic Society: Three Paradigms for Banning Political Parties', *German Law Journal* 3, no. 7 (2002): 32.

threat may mutate – as a result, the concept has been employed in the context of the fight against terrorism[59] or religious extremism.[60]

The concept of militant democracy can certainly help interpret various trends of the ECtHR's practice previously outlined, but it also reveals an intriguing ambiguity. On the one hand, the Convention's historical purpose can be seen as militant, in particular the notions of 'democracy lock-in' and 'alarm bell', albeit translated onto a regional and supranational plane. Militant democracy can also make sense of the Court's adducing limits to the Convention as in the case of Article 11: the likelihood that an anti-democratic party may actually seize power and implement its ideology can be framed as militant. This speaks to militant democracy's focus on restricting rights for the sake of democracy's survival. In that militant direction, however, the Court has remained very timid when compared to the catalogue of restricting measures taken domestically, which may very well call for protecting an entire constitutional framework from capture.[61] That is not applicable to the Court's right-based practice. In the words of de Moree, 'support for modification of the legal and constitutional order of a state is in itself not incompatible with the principles of democracy'.[62]

On the other hand, militant democracy cannot explain the vast practice of the Court aiming to enhance democracy via an extension of some of the Convention's democratic provisions. Indeed, in the domain of Article 10 the Court has firmly taken the opposite direction to what the concept of militant democracy would explain, namely, not to restrict but to allow even extremist views to be 'find a place in the public arena' in the name of its 'democratic society'. As we shall see in Chapter 4, states must demonstrate that there is 'pressing need' to interfere with this right via proportionality analysis. In this vein, the denial of the Armenian massacre as 'genocide' for example still falls within the scope of the Convention.[63] As we shall see in Chapter 8, the right to free elections also illustrates the gap: while militant democracy measures extend to limiting referenda called by the (populist) government,[64] the Court has consistently refused to rule on whether Article 3 Protocol 1 includes the

[59] Sajó, *Ruling by Cheating.*
[60] Tyulkina, *Militant Democracy.*
[61] Ibid.
[62] de Morree, *Rights and Wrongs under the ECHR*, 242.
[63] *Perinçek v. Switzerland.*
[64] Sajó, *Ruling by Cheating*, 200; Sajó, Uitz, and Holmes, *Routledge Handbook of Illiberalism*, 200.

right to a referendum. The margin of appreciation and the subsidiary position of the Court play an important role in explaining this.

Now, central to the account of militant democracy is the point at which these extraordinary measures are deemed actionable – that is, when an 'enemy of democracy' is identified. Since the measures aimed at systematically restricting rights to the point of discriminating against individuals and groups, the threat must be correspondingly acute and endanger a democratic core. That is an inherently normative premise recently debated in the literature.[65] This normative indeterminacy explains why the range of applicable measures may extend just to one's view of what counts as a existential threat to democracy. And since defending an independent theory of democracy has not been the initial purpose of militant democracy, this indeterminacy may loom large. In the words of Rovira Kaltwasser, 'militant democracy can work under the condition that there is (almost) no disagreement when it comes to determining who should be seen as an internal enemy of democracy'.[66] The literature on militant democracy has conventionally presumed a threat that is categorical – that is, a threat that is ideologically antithetical to democracy and may, if materialized, dismantle it. While this existential threat was relatively easy to establish in the context of totalitarian regimes (Nazism, fascism, and communism) and more recently terrorism and religious fundamentalism, it is more difficult to achieve in the context of populism, as we shall see in Chapter 3. This diminishes the explanatory value of militant democracy considerably. As Landau explains, 'the strategy is unlikely to work well when dealing with ideologically ambiguous political

[65] Stefan Rummens, 'Populism as a Threat to Liberal Democracy', in *The Oxford Handbook of Populism*, ed. Cristóbal Rovira Kaltwasser, Paul Taggart, Paulin Ochoa Espejo, and Pierre Ostiguy (Oxford University Press, 2017); Alexander Kirshner and Anthoula Malkopoulou, *Militant Democracy and Its Critics: Populism, Parties, Extremism* (Edinburgh University Press, 2021); Jan-Werner Müller 'Stronger Together? Populist (and Non-populist) Politics of Peoplehood', in *Rule of Law vs Majoritarian Democracy*, ed. Giuliano Amato, Benedetta Barbisan, and Cesare Pinelli, Bloomsbury Collections (Hart Publishing, 2021); Jan-Werner Müller, 'Protecting the Rule of Law (and Democracy!) in the EU', in *Reinforcing Rule of Law Oversight in the European Union*, ed. Carlos Closa and Dimitry Kochenov (Cambridge University Press, 2016); Jan-Werner Müller, '"The People Must Be Extracted from within the People": Reflections on Populism', *Constellations* 21, no. 4 (2014): 483–93; Jan-Werner Müller, 'Should the EU Protect Democracy and the Rule of Law inside Member States?', *European Law Journal* 21, no. 2 (2015): 141–60; Müller, 'Militant Democracy'.

[66] Cristóbal Rovira Kaltwasser, 'Militant Democracy versus Populism', in *Militant Democracy and Its Critics Populism, Parties, Extremism*, ed. Anthoula Malkopoulou and Alexandra Kirshner (Edinburgh University Press, 2019), 87.

forces, rather than those that are clearly anti-democratic'.[67] The boundary between fascism and populism exemplifies this problem: in the words of Finchelstein, 'this centrality of repressive violence marks a key boundary, an epistemic wall, between populism and fascism'.[68] Consequently, the extent to which authoritarian populism can be deemed a categorical enemy of democracy is a question that requires more analysis.

2.8 Moving Forward

The lens of militant democracy helps us reach two intermediate points relevant to setting the conceptual parameters of our investigation. The first is that on the spectrum of rights-restricting measures, the Court's account of democracy outlined earlier seems undeniably modest. This modesty speaks to the Court's historical foundations – namely, to 'lock in' democracy – but it is also firmly built into the definition of the rights as the Court understands them. The minimal right to free elections is a clear case in point. Yet the Court's relation to democracy cannot be confined to this militant role. Indeed, the Court's 'democratic society' has justified the extension, rather than the restriction, of the Convention's democratic provisions. As such, the Court's account of democracy and militant democracy may be viewed as two intersecting circles with a limited overlap and pulling in opposite directions. This ambiguity needs further exploration. The second point concerns the conceptual difficulty of employing the concept of militant democracy in the populist context – and that has to do with the concept's fragile boundaries. Populism further complicates the setting of these boundaries precisely because it preserves the formal and procedural basis of democracy. Now, bridging these two points helps refine the puzzle of the book: if the overarching justification for setting up the Court's system was to 'lock in' basic democratic credentials in a militant fashion, on the one hand, and if militant democracy cannot easily identify populism as a categorical and existential threat, on the other, how are we to situate the Court's role in responding to populism?

[67] Landau, 'Populist Constitutions', 137.

[68] Federico Finchelstein, *From Fascism to Populism in History* (University of California Press, 2019), 181.

3

Populism

Distorting Democracy and Corrupting the Rule of Law

In the last chapter, I argued that while the literature on crafting the legal response to populism is growing at a fast pace, a response that incorporates the Court's specific role and practice is lacking. Central to filling this gap is the preliminary question of whether a close nexus between the ideational basis of populism and the nature and function of the Court exists – one that would justify embarking on a specific study.

Importantly, we saw that the predominant constitutionalist response for example via the constitutional amendment paradigm does not fit into the international and subsidiary context of the Convention and the Court. I claimed that this limitation calls for a response informed by the Court's specific jurisdiction and established practice. We also saw that the concept of militant democracy is not optimal to reconstruct and evaluate the Court's relation to populism. This is because populism is not a existential threat to democracy and the rule of law along the totalitarian lines of Nazism, fascism, or communism. This raises an issue for the Court, whose foundational purpose was to 'lock in' minimal democracy via an 'alarm bell' system. The question I raised is whether the Court's minimal democracy is sufficient to detect the populist attack on democracy and the rule of law, which also calls for examining the Court's practice in much more detail.

In this chapter, I elaborate on the first limb of this nexus, namely why and how authoritarian populism undermines these foundational values as a matter of principle. The next chapter examines the relevance of these values to the Convention and Court's system. These two chapters therefore constitute both the justification and the analytical grid for investigating the Court's practice in the chapters thereafter. Building on the rich theoretical literature of populism, I argue that deliberation and representation are two constitutive criteria of democratic legitimacy that populism cannot principally account for in appealing to democracy. As such, and this is the most important point, populism distorts the normative horizon of democracy as an egalitarian endeavour. While vocally celebrating the 'real' people and decrying the 'elite', populism in fact entrenches rather than attenuates political inequality in deliberative and representative terms. Furthermore, in the same exclusive fashion that populism denies the value and function of deliberation and representation in the political process, it also denies the constraint that the rule of law poses on democratically adopted norms.

3.1 The Ideational Core of Populism

The theoretical literature on the concept of populism is overwhelmingly rich. The field has been nourished by contributions from most social sciences and humanities – and it is beyond the scope of the chapter to even offer an overview of the field. I only draw on two areas of research that have sustainably engaged with the concept of populism in recent years: constitutional theory and democratic theory. While I believe that both are relevant components of the analysis, I argue that democratic theory is analytically and normatively more valuable for evaluating populism, and also more relevant in the context of the ECtHR.

3.2 Populism and the Constitution

It is today almost common parlance that authoritarian populism and constitutionalism are necessarily in tension with one another, or even in a relation of mutual exclusion. Not only the discourse but also the records of populist governments suggest a salient aversion for a shared and balanced framework of political authority distinctive of liberal constitutionalism, thin or thick. The erosion of judicial independence through court-packing has perhaps been the clearest example. To quickly illustrate this manoeuvre in the context of the Court's record, the case of *Reczkowicz* v. *Poland* illustrates the populist rejection of constraint(s) on majoritarian rule. The applicant, a district judge, complained that her case was not examined by a 'tribunal established by law' under Article 6 and the guarantees of independence and impartiality because of the government's control over the National Council of the Judiciary in charge of appointing judges,[1] as we shall see in Chapter 7.

However, a closer reading of the populist discourse suggests that it may be reconstructed as having affinities with some (radical) constitutional ideas, on the one hand, and has been deemed compatible with a thin

[1] *Reczkowicz* v. *Poland*, 22 July 2021, Application No. 43447/19.

account of constitutionalism, on the other hand. Such close reading will help, I argue, not only to indicate what is principally problematic about populism in its appeal and exaltation of the 'people' but should also highlight the limits of constitutionalism as the chief analytical and evaluative framework of populism. I argue that focusing on some constitutive value(s) of constitutionalism, and in particular democracy, will prove more helpful.

How can constitutionalism help to make sense of the ideational core of populism? 'Constituent power' and 'popular sovereignty' have been employed to characterize its principled relation to the constitutional order, and to the place of the 'people' within it. Constituent power portrays the people as the source of legitimate political authority. As such, the 'people' exist independently from (and prior to) any constituted power and remain unbound by any formally enacted constitution since only they can confer legitimacy to its authority, either substantive or procedural. As Kalyvas puts it, 'the various names used to designate it – "the multitude", "the Community", "the People", "the Nation" – suggest, in the last instance, the utter limit of any politics, a politics that survives the dissolution of governments, the disruption of legal systems, and the collapse of instituted powers'.[2] The ontological existence and normative power of the 'people' should however be kept distinct from 'will of the people' and its formation, as we shall see later. Constituent power presupposes the existence, identity, and capacity of the 'people' – persisting through time – and its exclusive entitlement to exercise power, including by enacting a new constitutional order. In his seminal analysis of populism as an implicit constitutional discourse, Corrias puts the point as follows: populism 'can be understood as defending a specific version of the revolutionary approach in which the constituent power of the people is (almost) absolute and can be exercised directly in the polity'.[3] In the words of Blokker, 'this understanding of the people as a homogenous unity that stands at the basis of the constitutional order implies a specific understanding of constitutionalism, in which the latter is ultimately to guarantee the existence and survival of a homogenous people'.[4] These ideas echo the revolutionary tradition of constituent power

2 Andreas Kalyvas, 'Popular Sovereignty, Democracy, and the Constituent Power', *Constellations* 12, no. 2 (2005), 227.

3 Luigi Corrias, 'Populism in a Constitutional Key: Constituent Power, Popular Sovereignty and Constitutional Identity', *European Constitutional Law Review* 12, no. 1 (2016), 15.

4 Paul Blokker, 'Populist Constitutionalism', in Carlos de la Torre, ed. 'Global Populism Histories, Trajectories, Problems, and Challenges', in *Routledge Handbook of Global Populism* (Routledge, 2018), 121–2.

and, in particular, the thought of Sieyiès according to which the 'nation' is the source of all legitimate authority.[5] However, the discourse of populism, we shall see later, does not necessarily operate with a thick normative basis like 'nationhood' or 'nationalism'.

In turn, and complementarily, 'popular sovereignty' can be used to make sense of the populists' deeply rooted distrust and dismissive attitude towards representative democracy and established political parties, posing the question of whether such a system is inherently defective or only dysfunctional according to them, considering the populists' embrace of immediacy and directness as modes of relating to political authority,[6] and the premise that only populists can legitimately represent the people.[7] The populist approach to democratic representation therefore needs more analysis, which I believe can be achieved through the means of normative democratic theory, as I purport to do in the next sections. The key issues concern the constitutive elements of the 'people', its implied ontology as a social and political subject, and its derived normative account of political legitimacy. To what extent the populist distrust and defiance of the 'elite' aligns with the much longer and distinguished tradition attached to the people's sovereignty vis-à-vis the Monarch since the early iterations of liberalism and democracy in the veins of Hobbes and Rousseau remains unclear. It remains unclear whether populism, and in particular authoritarian populism, entertains any principled relation to the institutional framework of shared and balanced authority distinctive of modern constitutionalism. The fact that populists in power tend not to abolish the institutional framework they inherit requires further analysis, too.

To gain further insights into that point, one may proceed empirically rather than just conceptually. In their important book, Bugarič and Tushnet argue that, upon inspecting a variety of populist phenomena, populists do not necessarily reject what the authors call 'thin constitutionalism', which includes the requirements of majority rule, the entrenchment of rights and structures of decision-making, judicial independence, and politicians and political parties (officeholders and office seekers seeking popular support).[8] It follows that populists overall do not necessarily break away from *any* constraint upon governmental power

[5] Corrias, 'Populism in a Constitutional Key', 12.
[6] Ibid., 12.
[7] Müller, 'Stronger Together? Populist (and Non-Populist) Politics of Peoplehood'; Müller, 'What Is Populism'.
[8] Tushnet and Bugarič, *Power to the People.*

and unleash pure majoritarianism. To specify one of these requirements, the entrenchment of structures for example refers to 'veto gates' and 'speed bumps' as the required approvals for advancing a policy proposal to the next stage of the lawmaking process, which echoes our discussion in Chapter 2 with respect to the constitutionalist paradigm of the response (e.g., heightened parliamentary thresholds for amendment). But do 'veto gates' and 'speed bumps' have normative value in and of themselves? As Bugarič and Tushnet acknowledge, it is arduous to evaluate, say, the form of constitutional amendment away from its substance – 'the focus should be on the substance of the amendments and their actual effect in the circumstances at hand rather on the fact of amendment itself'.[9] In fact, the same can be said of the ordinary lawmaking process: whether populists operate within the inherited framework of rules and institutions, including thin constitutionalism, seems independent of *how* these institutions are run and *how* these rules applied – and whether thin constitutionalism is enough to evaluate these modalities. As this investigation will show, the same conundrum applies to rights: populists hardly break away from the requirement of respecting rights in and of themselves – but they will grapple with the conditions under which rights are interpreted and how they may be restricted, as Chapters 6, 7, and 8 will show. This granular approach requires that one finds a more fundamental normative basis to depict the populism's principledness (or the lack thereof). As the next section suggests, I believe that democracy can offer such insights.

Another risk associated with focusing on (thin) constitutionalism is that it is secondary rather than primary to the discursive structure of populism. As we shall see (in Chapter 3), the discourse of populism and first and foremost about the 'people', and its will should be restored at the expense of a 'corrupt elite', invites the adoption of an evaluative framework neatly tied to this primary focus. Importantly, populists do not put forward a clear and distinct institutional pathway, or even a procedure, for their political project. For these reasons, I doubt that constitutionalism – in particular, an institutional account of it – can reliably provide insight into the principledness of populism (or the lack thereof). It is not just because constitutionalism remains internally malleable and contestable, but it is also because while it may have important constitutional implications and expressions, no populist discourse would confine itself to a 'constitutional' project. This does not dismiss the constitutionalist approach to populism – rather, it

[9] Ibid., 21.

suggests an order of conceptual priority. As I explain later, I find it crucial to operate with a normative basis that does not supervene on more fundamental concepts that may form part of one's account of constitutionalism, such as democracy, the rule of law, or human rights.

I therefore return to the 'people' in the populist discourse. At its core, populism indeed expresses an appeal to, and often an exaltation of, the 'people' portrayed as 'real', 'pure' or 'authentic'. The literature on the idea of populism conventionally starts with Mudde's standard: 'a thin-centered ideology that considers society to be ultimately separated into two homogeneous and antagonistic groups, the "pure people" versus the "corrupt elite"'.[10] Müller also speaks of a 'single, homogeneous, authentic people'[11] to characterize this ontology. On this basic account, populism is a Manichean concept to the extent that it morally defines two antagonistic groups that co-exist within the same polity, the people and the 'elite', in moral terms: 'populism is in essence a form of *moral* politics, as the distinction between "the élite" and "the people" is first and foremost moral (i.e., pure vs. corrupt), not situational (e.g., position of power), socio-cultural (e.g., ethnicity, religion), or socio-economic (e.g., class)'.[12]

Defining the 'people' morally and antagonistically is axiomatic to the ideational basis of populism. It is an ontological axiom because it posits the fundamental and ultimate constituents of social and political reality. Yet it should be emphasized that the contours of the antagonism – the defining criteria of the 'people' and the 'elite' – vary depending on which ends of the spectrum one looks at. On the right end of the spectrum, the existence of the 'people' flows from a naturalized and immanent moral order fuelled with (ethno)nationalism or (ethno)nativism. This is prevalent on the right side of the populist spectrum that typically predominates in Central and Eastern Europe,[13] built on a nationalist ground that pre-dates the rise of populism itself. Suteu for instance emphasizes 'the fact that ethnic nationalism has taken on populist garb and is being espoused by parties and politicians in power is therefore an exacerbation of an ailment that was already there'.[14] However, one also finds, across a distinct and intellectual

[10] Mudde, 'The Populist Zeitgeist', 543.

[11] Müller, *What Is Populism?*, 3.

[12] Mudde and Rovira Kaltwasser, 'Populism and (Liberal) Democracy', 7–8.

[13] Halmai, 'Populism, Authoritarianism and Constitutionalism'; Halmai, 'The Making of "Illiberal Constitutionalism" with or without a New Constitution'; Silvia Suteu, 'The Populist Turn in Central and Eastern Europe: Is Deliberative Democracy Part of the Solution?', *European Constitutional Law Review* 15, no. 3 (2019): 488–518.

[14] Suteu, 'The Populist Turn in Central and Eastern Europe', 492.

tradition with resonance in modern Latin American history, a social, inclusive, and aggregative ideal type that clearly rejects both nationalism and authoritarianism. According to the seminal work of Canovan,[15] this variant defends populism as a corrective of democracy: 'from this point of view, populism's broad appeal gave their parties heterogeneous followings that were unwieldy but also very effective in both reaching newly enfranchised voters and mobilizing different social strata'.[16]

Furthermore, when it comes to the populist parties' discourse, Bugarič argues how a 'democratic' form of populism is not necessarily anti-pluralist but rather inclusive and aggregative in contexts such as Greece (e.g., Syriza),[17] Italy (Five Star Movement),[18] and Spain (e.g., Podemos):[19] 'these examples of democratic, liberal, socially inclusive forms of populism quite clearly show that authoritarianism and anti-pluralism are not necessarily the key elements of populism'.[20] Urbinati explains that Podemos, for example, 'argues for the overcoming of traditional divides between old right and old left, with an eye to a more progressive politics than traditional leftism'.[21] This again speaks to the malleable definition of the people as a 'heterogeneous collective subject, as it is made up of a plurality of social categories'.[22] In a similar vein, Howse argues that one should carefully distinguish anti-pluralism from anti-elitism and emphasizes how the latter may be more intrinsic to populism than the former. In a provocative article, Howse asks why the populist qualifier applies to the exclusive

[15] Margaret Canovan, 'Populism for Political Theorists?', *Journal of Political Ideologies* 9, no. 3 (2006): 241–52. Margaret Canovan, 'Trust the People! Populism and the Two Faces of Democracy', *Political Studies* 47, no. 1 (1999): 2–16.

[16] Rovira Kaltwasser, 'The Ambivalence of Populism', 187.

[17] As Damiani puts, 'the "people" called upon by Syriza to participate in the new democratic process of transformation is an inclusive and plural subject, not limited by ethnical, racial, sexual or gender restrictions'. Marco Damiani, 'Radical Left-Wing Populism and Democracy in Europe', in *Routledge Handbook of Global Populism*, ed. Carlos de la Torre (Routledge, 2018), 304.

[18] As Urbinati writes, the Five Star Movement 'wants to be a movement of ordinary citizens (*gentismo*) that is aligned with what the indistinctive many – la *gente*, or the many – feel and claim. It aims to be much more inclusive and generalist than a traditional ideological party'. Urbinati, *Me the People*, 159.

[19] As Blokker explains, the 'people' of Podemos extends to foreigners, for example: 'for Podemos, foreigners are not the "enemy within", and its construction of the People is rather one which groups together those citizens (and non-citizens) that are victims of globalization and neoliberal capitalism'. Blokker, 'Populist Constitutionalism', 118.

[20] Bojan Bugarič, 'Could Populism Be Good for Constitutional Democracy?', *The Annual Review of Law and Social Science* 15, no. 1 (2019), 46.

[21] Urbinati, *Me the People*, 159.

[22] Damiani, 'Radical Left-Wing Populism and Democracy in Europe', 199.

kind and not to the inclusive one: 'why label the authoritarians "populists" in places like Hungary, rather than the thousands who have engaged in street protests against attacks on the judiciary and other independent institutions?'.[23]

These nuances are connected to another feature of populism, namely its 'thin-centredness': it can lodge itself within a variety of more comprehensive ideologies[24] – and serves a multiplicity of causes. Marxism and nationalism, for example, also operate with a founding distinction between the 'people' and an 'elite' and can display populist traits to that extent, but these doctrines however have a deeper layer of conceptual grounding, respectively 'social class' and 'the nation', which diverge from populism's core emphasis on the people as 'authentic' and 'real'. Equally, populism can also serve a variety of causes: 'greater redistribution, control over immigration, traditional moral values, and rejection of expertise and technocratic approaches to governance'.[25] What matters, as far as the conceptual overlap is concerned, is the antagonistic articulation of the 'people' and the 'elite' in moral terms. As Mudde recalls, 'determining the main opposition to be between the pure people and the corrupt elite, populism presupposes that the elite comes from the same group as the people, but have willingly chosen to betray them, by putting the special interests and inauthentic morals of the elite over of the people'.[26] In that sense, populism has a thin conceptual structure but does not collapse into an 'empty signifier' in the sense of Laclau.[27]

Now, as will become clear in turning to the object of this investigation, namely the role and practice of the Court in responding to populism, the relevant cases that have reached the ECtHR rather predominantly reflect the right-wing, exclusionary, and authoritarian variant of populism, in particular (but not limited to) Hungary (under the Fidesz government, 2010–present) and Poland (under the PiS government, 2012–23). This is because these governments benefited from a large majority in parliament in the 2010s and later, which allows for observing the practical effects of populists in power, as we shall see in Chapter 5. This does not mean that

[23] Robert Howse, 'Epilogue: In Defense of Disruptive Democracy. A Critique of Anti-Populism', *International Journal of Constitutional Law* 17, no. 2 (2019), 647.

[24] Michael Freeden, 'Ideology and Political Theory', *Journal of Political Ideologies* 11, no. 1 (2006): 3–22.

[25] Oran Doyle, 'Populist Constitutionalism and Constituent Power', *German Law Journal* 20, no. 2 (2019), 165.

[26] Mudde, 'Populism', 30.

[27] Laclau, *On Populist Reason*; Peruzzotti, 'Laclau's Theory of Populism'.

a study of how the Court relates to the left-wing, inclusive, and mobilizing variant is not relevant – only that, as far this investigation is concerned, the effects of the authoritarian variant are more relevant for the purpose of crafting the response by the Court. While it is worth repeating that authoritarian populism in Central and Eastern Europe has a rich and complex regional history and, again, responds to dynamics inherited from the fall of the Soviet Union,[28] it is also crucial to specify in conceptual and normative terms what authoritarian populism could be said to be a distortion of. Having explained why constitutionalism remains in my view suboptimal, I now turn to the values of democracy, in particular deliberative democracy.

3.3 Populism and Democracy

While the precise definition of the populist 'people' may be porous its antagonistic structure between the 'elite' or the 'establishment' is taken as indispensable for populism to minimally count as a distinct political discourse. What cements the authoritarian variant of populism is both the homogeneous character of the 'people' and the denunciation of an 'elite' or 'establishment' as morally corrupt. How problematic is this thin account normatively speaking, and how should we proceed in posing the non-derivative evaluative terms of our analysis? In this section and the next, I suggest taking the perspective of democratic theory and examine how the 'people' in this authoritarian variant are precisely construed. The central claim is that populism can hardly be reconciled with any democratic procedure that would be formative of the 'people' or mediating the various claims made on its behalf. This is particularly true of democratic deliberation. I then derive the proposition that authoritarian populism cannot accommodate the pursuit of political equality as the normative horizon of democracy. Equally, populism cannot account for the independent role of democratic representation and its contribution to this pursuit in institutional terms. I understand these two aspects – deliberation and representation – as the two chief distortions of populism.

Discursively, populism resembles democracy in its obsessive appeal to the people as the bearer of exclusive legitimate authority. However,

[28] Paul Taggart, 'Populism in Western Europe', in *The Oxford Handbook of Populism*, ed. Cristóbal Rovira Kaltwasser, Paul Taggart, Paulin Ochoa Espejo, and Pierre Ostiguy (Oxford University Press, 2017).

neither 'constituent power' nor 'popular sovereignty' alone is necessarily sufficient to count as democratic. The clearest implication of authoritarian populism is that it has very little to say about how the 'will of the people' is – and should – be formed and the role of procedures and institutions in this formation. On the one hand, the populist account of the 'people' denotes the aversion of deliberation as the procedure through which individuals aim for a collective basis of justification for the norms they live under. The mediating role of the constitution in serving such procedure is thereby dismissed. Similarly, populism evades deliberation as the mediating procedure for defining – through justification based on reasons that everyone can accept – the terms of political settlement. This constitutes the first distortion of democracy: populism denies that individuals situated outside of the 'people' are equally owed reasons and justification for the terms under which they must live. Deliberation precisely aims at an equally recognizable, sharable, and acceptable basis for defining these terms. In that respect, populism restricts the perimeter of democratic agency and its associated rights. This is more important to our subsequent examination of the Court's practice in later chapters, in particular freedom of expression (Article 10) and freedom of assembly and association (Article 11), as deliberation heavily informs the Court's understanding of these rights (Chapter 6).

On the other hand, populist representation compresses the space that representative democracy carves up between individuals and executive authority. While it does not necessarily favour direct democracy, authoritarian populism indeed leans towards direct democratic representation. This is often effectuated by personification in an acclaimed leader. In that sense, 'populism competes for political power in order to merge the representative and the represented'.[29] Crucially, what is lost is the additional democratic room that representation creates for collectively defining, contesting, justifying, and revising the terms of the political settlement, which the electoral verdict solidifies but never cements. This constitutes the second populist distortion of democracy. It exacerbates political inequality in evading the process of deliberation, on the one hand, and carves out a dangerous and slippery slope towards authoritarianism in representative terms, on the other hand. Indeed, the populist leader, once in power, may ultimately claim immunity from accountability and turn against, or simply fail to address, the demands of their own people. Representation as embodiment is not only anti-democratic and anti-

[29] Urbinati, *Me the People*, 90.

egalitarian, therefore, it is also proto-authoritarian. Here again, the discussion of representation is relevant to our assessment of the Court's understanding of Article 3 Protocol 1 (the right to free elections) in later chapters. The goal is to offer an assessment of populism that is relevant to interpreting and evaluation the Court's actual and potential response to it.

3.3.1 Populism and Deliberation

Why should one care about deliberation in evaluating the core of populism? I believe that focusing on deliberation helps measure the populist distortion of democracy. This is best appreciated by reviewing the evolution from social contract theories to more recent theories of deliberative democracy. Rather than rehearsing classical standards in the history of political thought, I selectively zoom in on the conceptual transition from 'interests' to 'reasons' for explaining the egalitarian attraction of deliberation and the populist distortion thereof.

The social contract tradition emphasizes the derivation of legitimate political authority from the will or consent of its subjects. On the view of Rousseau, for example, legitimate political authority can only derive from the general will unifying all individual wills. A legitimate institution, on this view, can only result from an act of the general will. The unification of these wills explains Rousseau's rejection of representative democracy – as Urbinati explains, institutions can only exist 'by electing law-redactors or lawmakers with instructions or by voting on the laws directly'.[30] Equally, for an act of the general will to be legitimate, it should constrain or favour everyone equally: 'the social pact establishes among the Citizens an equality such that all commit themselves under the same conditions and must all enjoy the same rights. Thus, by the very nature of the pact every act of sovereignty, that is to say every genuine act of the general will, either obligates or favors all Citizens equally.'[31] There is surely an affinity between the Rousseauian unification of the individual will with the collective will, on the one hand, and the populist appeal to a unitary 'people', as scholars have noted, on the other hand. However, this affinity is highly deceptive – and zooming in on both deliberation and representation can further clarify that point.

[30] Nadia Urbinati, 'Continuity and Rupture: The Power of Judgment in Democratic Representation', *Constellations* 12, no. 2 (2005): 202.

[31] Jean-Jacques Rousseau, *The Social Contract and Other Later Political Writings*, vol. 2, ed. Victor Gourevitch (Cambridge University Press, 2019), 64–5.

Indeed, scholars of Rousseau have highlighted how the concept of the general will is little preoccupied with the formative process of said will, individual or collective. In fact, the framework of the general will assumes that individuals have already formed their will and determined their interest(s). In the words of Manin, 'for Rousseau, the basis for legitimacy lies not in the free individual capable of making up his mind by weighing reasons, but rather in the individual whose will is already entirely determined, one who has made his choice'.[32] As a result, the role of uncertainty and disagreement – for example, when the individual is uncertain and/or when the individual and the general wills do not coincide – is not given serious consideration. This is best seen when Rousseau explains what happens to individuals in disagreement with the general will: 'if then there are opponents when the social compact is made, their opposition does not invalidate the contract, but merely prevents them from being included in it. They are foreigners among citizens. When the State is instituted, residence constitutes consent; to dwell within its territory is to submit to the Sovereign.'[33] This is where one may appreciate the transition, in conceptual and normative terms, from interest(s) to reason(s) and appreciate the appeal to the latter.

Indeed, deliberation implies relying on reasons, rather than predetermined wills or interests, as the relevant currency for defining the shared terms under which free and equal individuals ought to live. In the canonical terms of Cohen, 'the deliberative conception requires more than the interests of others be given equal consideration; it demands, too, that we offer politically acceptable reasons – reasons that are acceptable to others, given a background of differences of conscientious conviction'.[34] If they are to treat others as equals, individuals engaging in deliberation are required to offer reasons for their views as to what counts as being in the common interest – 'they give reasons with the expectation that those reasons (and not, for example, their power) will settle the fate of their proposal'.[35] Deliberation creates an arena for

[32] Bernard Manin, 'On Legitimacy and Political Deliberation', *Political Theory* 15, no. 3 (1987): 347.

[33] Jean-Jacques Rousseau, *The Social Contract and Other Later Political Writings*, 127. See also Joshua Cohen, *Rousseau: A Free Community of Equals* (Oxford University Press, 2010).

[34] Joshua Cohen 'Deliberation and Democratic Legitimacy', in *Deliberative Democracy – Essays on Reason & Politics: Essays on Reason and Politics*, ed. James Bohman and William Rehg (MIT Press, 1998), 417.

[35] Joshua Cohen, 'Procedure and Substance in Deliberative Democracy', in *Deliberative Democracy: Essays on Reason and Politics*, ed. James Bohman and William Rehg (MIT Press, 1998), 74.

forming, advancing, sharing, contesting, revising, and accepting reasons in a joint, public, and equal endeavour. Unlike will(s) or interest(s), the currency of reasons is genuinely sharable.

A core premise of the case for deliberation is undoubtedly one of agnosticism about moral truth and the prevalence of disagreement in modern politics considering what is commonly called 'the fact of pluralism'[36] or the 'fact of disagreement'.[37] In the absence of convergence on a comprehensive (and metaphysical) understanding of moral truth, the common good is only the substratum of reasons that survives the deliberative process among equals. Rather than the unanimity required by Rousseau's general will, deliberative democracy aspires to reach the consensus of all parties via collective and public reasoning – and short of that, majority voting should prevail. On the deliberative view, in other words, the standards of correctness are set by the procedure and are strictly independent from standards of truth, whether these are analytic or empirical: 'respecting people's liberty or autonomy therefore means that they cannot be made subject to others even in the name of true, or the best reasoned, claims'.[38]

One should note here that the emphasis on consensus does not necessarily exclude the epistemic appeal of deliberation. As the recent 'epistemic turn' has suggested, deliberation does not presuppose relativism or nihilism about moral truth. In fact, it has been argued that the search for truth is intrinsic to belief formation – even in the moral sphere – and motivates deliberation in the first place.[39] In this vein, scholars of epistemic democracy have attempted to delineate which deliberative arrangements lead to epistemic performance.[40] While epistemic considerations introduce consequentialist criteria of evaluation at odds with the deontological underpinnings of deliberation, 'it seems impossible to resist that there is something of an objective, epistemic nature that we aim to figure out when we vote or deliberate with each other about politics'.[41] What matters for us is the egalitarian

36 John Rawls, *Political Liberalism* (Columbia University Press, 1993).

37 Jeremy Waldron, *Law and Disagreement* (Oxford University Press, 1999).

38 Assaf Sharon, 'Populism and Democracy: The Challenge for Deliberative Democracy', *European Journal of Philosophy* 27, no. 2 (2019): 366.

39 Cheryl Misak and Robert B. Talisse, 'Debate: Pragmatist Epistemology and Democratic Theory. A Reply to Eric Macgilvray', *Journal of Political Philosophy* 22, no. 3 (2014): 366–76.

40 Nadia Urbinati and Maria Paula Saffon, 'Procedural Democracy, the Bulwark of Equal Liberty', *Political Theory* 41, no. 3 (2013): 442.

41 Ibid., 442.

performance of deliberation: if the outcome of the deliberative process links back to reasons that everyone can accept, therefore, then the terms of political association also are manifestly equal to the participating individuals. In that respect, deliberative democracy constitutes an alternative framework to pursue the ideal of self-government in the condition of disagreement.

Now, one may note that a basic proceduralist account is enough to view democracy as the best device to respect political equality. One may also use a thinner concept such as compromise to highlight the same deficit of deliberation, as Rostbøll suggests: 'the ethos of compromise is to deliberate with opponents about their and our own values and explore solutions to our disagreements that realize the values of everyone to an acceptable degree'.[42] In making shared reasons the premium of democratic legitimacy, however, the deliberative account explains how equality can be made manifest to individuals. In that sense, the ideal of deliberation aims higher – 'not simply to ensure that democratic politics proceed under fair conditions, not only to encourage just legislation, but also to ensure that the equality of citizens is manifest'.[43] It is also important to emphasize that deliberative democracy offers an ideal procedure of justification – an idealism that can here serve to measure the distance that populism entertains with the concern for political equality.

The literature has heavily emphasized the anti-pluralism of populism's ideational core – with the caveat already pointed out earlier. Müller, in particular, makes it a necessary and distinctive feature of populism's core claim that only populists properly represent the authentic people.[44] I believe that one way of specifying this feature in distinctively democratic terms is to note the populist aversion for deliberation. Since deliberation aims to publicly and manifestly treat individuals as equals, one may infer that populism blatantly denies outsiders access to the arena of democratic reason. As such, populism amounts to repudiating the equal status of individuals as agents of reasons and justification.[45] To return to the point made at the start of section, the antagonistic horizon of populism equally

[42] Christian Rostbøll, 'Second-Order Political Thinking: Compromise versus Populism', *Political Studies* 69, no. 3 (2021): 569. See also Christian Rostbøll, *Democratic Respect: Populism, Resentment, and the Struggle for Recognition* (Cambridge University Press, 2023).

[43] Cohen, *The Arc of the Moral Universe and Other Essays*, 343.

[44] Müller, *What Is Populism?*

[45] Forst, 'The Justification of Human Rights and the Basic Right to Justification'; Forst, *The Right to Justification*.

disables the role of the constitution and deliberation as the mediating devices for justifying political authority. In other words, as much as 'there is no need for a higher law that mediates between and integrates different social forces that compete for political power',[46] there is no need for deliberation to alleviate the irremediably heterogeneous nature of modern politics.

Surely, the inclusive ideal-type of populism reviewed earlier may very well appeal to deliberative channels in mobilizing and helping to form a wider umbrella of the 'people', but whether it retains an independent normative value remains unclear. Rather than Rousseau, therefore, populism and its ontological antagonism are closer to the Schmittian dichotomy of the 'friend' versus 'enemy'. It not just that, as for Schmitt, antagonism constitutes the horizon of the political. One may also say that populists assign an unsurpassable value to the descriptive analysis of Schmitt.[47] There is, as a result, no room for overcoming or mitigating that antagonism through an independent (democratic) procedure such as deliberation. As Urbinati aptly puts it, 'only the populists understand and practice "the partiality of the universal" or make the people in a constitutive part that refuses to speak in the name of the whole as [it] makes itself "a part that *is* the whole"'.[48] This explains why the antagonism of populism is both foundational and final. Where does this antagonism come from, and why is it so strong? This requires delving into the related issue of representation.

It may be useful to succinctly recast the claims made in this section. Methodologically, I argued that deliberation can help to see that (the theory of) democracy is better suited than (the theory of) constitutionalism to the task of evaluating the ideational core of populism. While populism may entertain apparent affinities with self-government qua constituent power or popular sovereignty, the latter says relatively little about how people are to self-govern as a people in the first place – and that question notably raises the issue of political equality. Conceiving individuals as agents of reasons and justification devises deliberation as the optimal (and constituted) framework for the pursuit of political equality. The populists' 'people' being both antecedent and ulterior to any constituted procedure cannot accommodate this demand. While it is not strictly necessary to use deliberation – as opposed to mere procedural

46 Blokker, 'Populism as a Constitutional Project', 542.
47 Carl Schmitt, *The Concept of the Political*, trans. George Schwab (University of Chicago Press, 2007 [1932]).
48 Urbinati, *Me the People*, 142.

democracy – to make this point, deliberation helps measure the extent to which populism constitutes an affront to specific democratic-procedural values.

3.3.2 Populism and Representation

One may object that the dismissal of deliberation – or of any democratic proceduralism, for that matter – equally applies to other anti-democratic ideologies, such as fascism. As we established in the last chapter, it remains crucial to offer an evaluation of populism that matches its distinctive coordinates, whether these are ideational or empirical. At the ideational level, I argue that such a diagnostic needs to be completed by adding a representative distortion to the deliberative distortion. Unlike fascism, for example, populism does confer value on the electoral process and, therefore, on democratic representation. However, the antagonism of populism equally affects the meaning and function of representation in a democratic society. This requires zooming in on the theory of democratic representation.

On a first inspection, one could say that populists view any representative process as captured by the 'elite'. The antagonism reviewed earlier seems to place the people in fierce opposition to any formal or informal incarnation of the 'elite'. It is hence tempting to portray the will of the people as unconditionally and directly enforceable (e.g., through directly voting on the law). Yet, as scholars of democracy have recently argued, this view is deceptive: populism distorts rather than bars representation. This distortion concerns the object of representation: while (the quest for) political equality requires the grounding of legitimacy in acceptable and justifiable reasons, which gives representation further room for finding and mediating these reasons, for populism the representative – a person, the leader – is formed through mythification: 'the actual people are transformed into an imaginary entity'.[49] On the populist view, as a result, the usual mediation offered by the fora of the party or the parliament in channelling claims and reasons are unnecessary and superfluous. The encompassing claim of this section is therefore that the joint distortion of deliberation and representation can sufficiently define the profoundly fraught relationship of populism with democracy. While representation has clear ideational and institutional parameters that deliberation does not have, it is political equality

[49] Ibid., 165.

in deliberation and representation that populism distinctively erodes in both.

I suggested above that populism – more specifically, its ontological antagonism – can only inhabit a quasi-absolutist notion of constituent power. That is because, formally speaking, the attraction of constituent power is primarily to denounce any legitimate authority over and above the people and, as such, to mark a complete rupture with an idea of political authority where only a few dominate. The revolutionary tradition of constituent power of eighteenth-century liberalism can lend support and historical continuity to this formal affinity. It is in that formal respect, and only in that respect, that one may confer on populism a genuinely democratic appeal. Yet this formalism is evidently not sufficiently democratic on any deontological account of it – specifically, on any account of democratic proceduralism. This point is well explained by Rostbøll and his emphasis on the kind of democratic recognition that populists seek: 'the main form of recognition promised by populism is not really procedural but rather substantive or outcome based. That is, populists promise to implement the popular will understood as a substantive and procedure-independent standard, rather than respecting anything that goes on in or is produced by a democratic procedure.'[50]

Exploring both deliberation and representation can substantiate this claim. In the case of representation, one may explain this by extending the analytical frame to the composition of this 'elite'. Indeed, it is a distinctively political elite – one whose primary platform is the party – that populism places at the centre of its denunciation. As Mansbridge and Macedo succinctly put it, 'in most populist movements, the elites have a clearer identity than the people'.[51] As populism cannot accommodate deliberation in its attempt to use to the register of democracy, it equally cannot accommodate the party as the platform that initially channels and organizes the claims and demands of the citizens. Elections remain essential to populist representation, but their normative role is peripheral if not epiphenomenal: elections confirm and celebrate a pre-existing and evident embodiment of the people in a person, the leader.

To better grasp how the populist antagonism erodes representation specifically, therefore, one should first reconstruct the normative point of

[50] Rostbøll, *Democratic Respect*, 121.

[51] Jane Mansbridge and Stephen Macedo, 'Populism and Democratic Theory', *Annual Review of Law and Social Science* 15, no. 1 (2019): 61.

democratic representation. Mansbridge classically wrote that 'representation is something more than a defective substitute for direct democracy'.[52] What does democratic representation specifically add to democracy? To answer that question, one can distinguish between three ideal-types of representation as political mandate; representation as contractual delegation; and representation as embodiment. Rousseau's framework of the general will epitomizes the contractual delegation model in which the representatives' role is to enforce a fiduciary contract. This hardly fits the populist reliance on an imaginary 'real people'. The model of a political mandate combines the formality of the act of authorization (via the election) with the informality of democratic openness (via deliberation). This combination hardly squares the populist dismissal of deliberation, which firmly puts populist representation in the category of embodiment. Yet it is not that the three models are conceptually independent from each other – rather, they supervene on democratic values themselves. This is where populist representation exits the register of democracy, as I will explain.

Based on the seminal views of Urbinati and Nässtrom, I submit that the normative function of representation qua political mandate is to create additional space – via the party, the parliament, but also via the constituted power of the judiciary – for the people and their representatives to define, contest, justify, and finalize the terms of their political settlement. This goes to the etymology of representation: rather than the people being present to deliberate, it is their claims that form the object of (equal) representation sanctioned by the election. Surely, representation may be conferred with the teleological value of 'constructing claims and constituencies'[53] required by the finality of politics – via the party or the election. Elections via majority rule are 'needed to figure out the purpose and direction of society'.[54] Yet representation should be continuous with the democratic process that precedes and survives the election – and this is where deliberation matters, again. Representation is therefore situated at the intersection of the informal and the formal: while requiring authorization and delegation via the electoral outcome, democratic representation does not mirror a contract whose clauses bring finality to the terms of a relationship. Representation is not a defective substitute but an ameliorative

[52] Jane Mansbridge, 'Rethinking Representation', *The American Political Science Review* 97, no. 4 (2003): 515.
[53] Urbinati, 'The Populist Substantialization of Popular Sovereignty', 35.
[54] Nässtrӧm, *The Spirit of Democracy*, 134.

alternative to direct democracy – 'it has shown itself to be able to unify claims without closing the game of claim making'.[55]

What guides the democratic view of representation is undoubtedly the aspirational value of political equality. Democratic representation requires a continuous and strenuous effort of emptying the object of representation of myth, symbol, or personality. Based on the seminal ideas of Lefort,[56] Nässtrom identifies the necessary vacuum of democratic representation: 'the locus of power becomes linked to an empty place, by which is meant that who it is that has power, and therefore counts as the appropriate incarnation of the people'.[57] This vacuum of representation is the correlate of an open democratic deliberation. And this is where the populist antagonism strikes with full power: 'populist leaders see impersonality as a stratagem that the minority of the population (the establishment or the political elite) devises in order to dominate politics with the acquiescence of the majority'.[58] It is the vacuum distinctive of the democratic ethos that is compromised in this process – in a democracy, Nässtrom explains, 'power is disincorporated, or classless. It serves to make sure that while everyone has an equal say on the purpose and direction of society, no one has the *final* say. There is always room for yet another debate on who "we, the people" are.'[59]

One implication of this antagonism is the superfluous mediation offered by the party: 'it breeds hostility not simply to the existing parties but more radically to partisan divisions and the party form of representation'.[60] Populists do not only contend that the democratic party system as the vehicle for advancing, discussing, and mediating the people's claims is currently dysfunctional, but they also assert that there is inherent fault: 'it is deeply affected by partisanship and invisible interest groups behind the scenes that operate for reasons of self-interest, rather than the common good of the ordinary citizens'.[61] The democratic quality of populist representation is its dependence on elections. This is because elections offer the formal insurance that the representation is channelled to the people's sanctioning votes and sheltered from the elite,

[55] Urbinati, 'Me the People', 114.
[56] Claude Lefort, *Democracy and Political Theory* (University of Minnesota Press, 1989).
[57] Sofia Näsström, 'Democratic Representation beyond Election', *Constellations* 22, no. 1 (2015), 3.
[58] Urbinati, 'Me the People', 33.
[59] Näsström, *The Spirit of Democracy*, 122.
[60] Urbinati, 'Me the People', 78.
[61] Blokker, 'Populism as a Constitutional Project', 120.

which is concomitant with its quasi-absolutist relation to constituent power. Beyond this formality, however, populism represses the agency that democratic representation creates and organizes.

Moreover, rather than the claims of individuals, the object of representation is personified and, as such, representation becomes an embodiment – or an incarnation – of the people in a leader. It is crucial to note how embodiment in a person differs from democratic representation in relation to political equality. I have argued that deliberation allows for channelling the terms of the political settlement to reasons that everyone can accept. Deliberation and consensus render these reasons manifest. Parties, most importantly, and then the electoral process, provide the platform for channelling reasons and cohering them into an ideological project. Crucially, 'the party is never merely "inside" the institution, but always has a strong base in society, among militants and sympathizers'.[62] While the party and the election instil stability in the form of a container, the content of democratic reason needs to remain ferociously open. Elections, on this view, prolong this process of containment but never close if off: 'together, voting and counting reflect a deeper insight, namely that the end of democracy is open. It does not have a predetermined purpose or goal.'[63]

Populist representation qua embodiment ravages this ecosystem entirely. It is trust and faith in a symbolic someone, rather than reasons or claims for or against a law or policy, that cements the people's understanding of legitimate authority. Urbinati explains that 'the engine of populist representation is *trust through faith*, rather than trust through free and open debate (which would entail contestation and dissent) among followers, and between followed and their representative'.[64] It is therefore a symbol, rather than set of reasons or claims, that enables the process of populist identification. This process is what Sajó and Urbinati term *plebiscitary* democracy – a variant of the Weberian charisma – 'which hides behind a legitimacy that is formally derived from the will of the people'.[65] The embodiment of the people in the person of the leader renders the electoral process instrumental – this procedure is only there to affirm and acclaim the embodying leader. As a result,

62 Urbinati, 'Me the People', 170.
63 Näsström, *The Spirit of Democracy*, 134.
64 Urbinati, 'Me the People', 164.
65 Sajó, *Ruling by Cheating*, 27.

'deliberation and participation are circumvented while the followers are mobilized'.[66]

To sum up, while the populist discourse starts with an obsessive appeal to the people – an appeal that may have democratic impetus – it ultimately conflates into a process of capture by the embodiment of the 'people' into a single, and potentially arbitrary, 'leader' as a matter of representation. This clarifies the extent to which populism significantly departs from the basic criteria of democratic legitimacy. This capture implies that democratic deliberation and representation, in particular, are left totally unaccounted for. The rights, processes, and institutions associated with and justified by these core values are rendered redundant. The ideal of self-government built into constituent power – and, more largely, into democracy – cannot be reconciled with representation as embodiment in a leader. Populism profoundly distorts democracy here too.

3.4 Populism and the Rule of Law

The rule of law has a strong, if not inherent, link to constitutionalism. In the words of Krygier, the two concepts overlap: 'constitutionalism has to do with the frame and architecture of governance, always formal and often substantive. The rule of law is less architectonically focussed, more process-oriented, than constitutionalism.'[67] Yet, as argued throughout this chapter, populism's distortions are primarily distortions of democracy – and, consequently, one can articulate these distortions without necessarily appealing to the broader concept of constitutionalism. This, however, does not imply that populism does not affect other values as a matter of consequence – and the rule of law is one of these, I suggest. This matters to the enterprise of evaluating how the response of the Court to populism through specific articles, but also cross-conventional criteria, distinctively protects the rule of law. Before getting to these specific provisions as the Court defines them in Chapter 7, it is important to understand precisely if and how populism erodes this value. This section therefore enlarges the

[66] Paula Diehl, 'Twisting Representation', in *Routledge Handbook of Global Populism*, ed. Carlos de la Torre (Routledge, 2018), 135.

[67] Martin Krygier, 'Tempering Power', in *Constitutionalism and the Rule of Law: Bridging Idealism and Realism*, ed. Maurice Adams, Anne Meuwese, and Ernst Hirsch Ballin (Cambridge University Press, 2017), 39.

conceptual and normative basis that will guide our critical interpretation of the Court's relevant practice.

I claim that populism corrupts rather than distorts the rule of law. It is corruption rather than distortion because populism goes as far as disregarding the thinnest criteria of the rule of law while still claiming to be operating within legal boundaries. Key to this grave departure is the normative power adduced to the 'will of the people'. As is well established, there exist thinner[68] and thicker[69] accounts of the rule of law – ranging from the formal to the procedural and the substantive. One may think of the democratic criteria previously discussed or the generic category of human rights – if one normatively assumes that these criteria ought to form part of the rule of law. The well-regarded Venice Commission, for example, considers that 'legality' in turn includes the requirement of a democratic process for enacting legislation.[70] In these cases, the distortions of the democratic process discussed earlier remain central. Certainly, populists in power may corrupt it for a wide range of reasons, including mere self-interest, and as such not all are linked to the ideational basis of populism discussed in this chapter.

Consequently, our task here is to explain if and how the distortions of democracy are linked to a thin account of the rule of law (its corruption) – and in this exercise disentangle, as Lacey recommends, the analytic from the contingent. On that point, it is helpful to start with the premise that the rule of law, thin or thick, enables and limits the exercise of public authority. In the thin case, where criteria are limited to, for example, clarity, non-retroactivity, publicity, universality, and consistency, the rule of law may very well enhance populist rule. The tension between populism and the rule of law arises when respecting these criteria frustrates the enactment of populist law. In the words of Lacey, 'if law is used merely as a means to an end, the distinctive mode of mutually respectful agency-recognizing association reflected in the ideal of the rule of law is not present'.[71] This is where the instrumentalism – and the ensuing arbitrariness – of populism vis-à-vis the most

68 Joseph Raz, *The Morality of Freedom* (Clarendon Press, 1979).

69 Lon L. Fuller, *The Morality of Law* (Yale University Press, 1969); Jeremy Waldron, 'The Rule of Law and the Importance of Procedure', *Nomos* 50 (2011): 3–31.

70 See Emre Turkut, 'The Venice Commission and Rule of Law Backsliding in Turkey, Poland and Hungary', *European Convention on Human Rights Law Review* 2 (2021): 209–40.

71 Nicola Lacey, 'Populism and the Rule of Law', *Annual Review of Law and Social Science* 15, vol. 15 (2019): 82.

basic requirements of the rule of law appears. Since the claim of this section is that populism corrupts the rule of law, I shall zoom in on the thin account of the rule of law: if populist rule fails to meet this account, while still claiming to genuinely employ the same concept, that concept is corrupt.

The literature emphasizes instrumentalism when scholars observe the salient traits of populist rule in practice. Krygier for example speaks of the judiciary as an 'instrument of legitimation'.[72] One of the clearest effects of populist rule concerns the independence of the judiciary and its subordination to the executive and/or the parliament – in particular, if the former enjoys a strong majority in the latter. As we shall see in later chapters, populist governments typically purge presidents of courts, pack judicial councils, interfere with judicial proceedings, investigate judges for the substance of their judgments, defame legal officials, refuse to publish or simply ignore legal decisions.[73] All these effects conflict with thin accounts of rule of law, but surely they do not necessarily result from populist rule – and, as such, these effects are not themselves distinctive of populism. It is therefore required, here again, to explain how the ideational account of populism can specifically make sense of these effects. To take just one example here, the Fundamental Law of Hungary (adopted in 2011) amended the old constitution with the effect of repealing the decisions taken by the Constitutional Court taken prior to the entry into force of that Law with a wide range of consequences[74] – and this counts as a blatant violation of the criterion of the non-retroactivity of the law. Certainly, the more one fuels the rule of law with thicker components, the more populism corrupts. If one understands the function of the rule of law as 'tempering power', as Krygier does, corruption appears when one notices an 'institutional logic systematically at odds with the tempering ambitions of the rule of law, even when allegiance is mouthed to it'.[75]

The upshot here is that populist rule of law corrupts even the thin account of the rule of law. As Lacey explains, 'any institutional structure that questions that political expression, tends to place constraints on its

[72] Martin Krygier, 'The Challenge of Institutionalisation: Post-Communist "Transitions", Populism, and the Rule of Law', *European Constitutional Law Review* 15, no. 3 (2019): 547.

[73] Ibid., 547.

[74] Gábor Attila Tóth, 'Illiberal Rule of Law? Changing Features of Hungarian Constitutionalism', in *Constitutionalism and the Rule of Law: Bridging Idealism and Realism*, ed. Maurice Adams, Anne Meuwese, and Ernst Hirsch Ballin (Cambridge University Press, 2017).

[75] Krygier, 'The Challenge of Institutionalisation', 568.

execution, or divides the people's power via checks and balances is liable to come into conflict with the populist leader'.[76] Why is that so? I suggest that the populist rule of law, when it corrupts the thinnest criteria, largely supervenes on the ontological antagonism examined earlier. That is the analytic link between the distortion of democracy and the rule of law – and its corruption. When the rule of law cannot operate its taming role, the spectre of arbitrariness appears. Toth neatly explains the Hobbesian dimension of such arbitrariness in the context of Hungary:

> from a Hobbesian perspective, in the Hungarian legal system the two-thirds parliamentary majority is led by a person in charge, that is, the party leader and prime minister is the highest legal power, i.e. the Sovereign. Since the majority of voters gave this entity the authority to enact laws, everybody should obey the imposed regulations, regardless of disrespected individual interests or moral rights.[77]

3.5 Moving Forward

The conceptual and normative analysis offered in this chapter helps carve out the space for articulating the nexus between the distortions of democracy – deliberation and representation – on the one hand and the corruption of the rule of law on the other hand. The aversion for deliberation and representation obliterates the requirement of addressing and representing the people's plural claims and, ultimately, appealing to justification as the currency of democratic deliberation. Further, populism does not only corrupt the rule of law in the name of its sacrosanct 'will of the people', but it also assumes that the rule of law may facilitate the domination of the 'elite' over the people. Since the thinnest criteria of the rule of law are distinctively formal, even these criteria form part of the domination by the 'elite'. In the words of Krygier, the formalism of the law 'invisibilizes the informal power of the networks, while at the same time it blocks effective action against them'.[78] However, that seems entirely opportunistic: populists use both the content and the form of the law supportively when it suits them and denounce their domination over the people when it does not.[79] The

[76] Lacey, 'Populism and the Rule of Law', 87.
[77] Tóth, 'Illiberal Rule of Law?', 405.
[78] Krygier, 'The Challenge of Institutionalisation', 112.
[79] Mudde, 'Are Populists Friends or Foes of Constitutionalism?'; Pablo Castillo-Ortiz, 'The Illiberal Abuse of Constitutional Courts in Europe', *European Constitutional Law Review* 15, no. 1 (2019): 48–72.

same applies to judicial interpretation – for instance, scholars have suggested that populists do not favour any particular or principled approach to interpretation[80] with the only simple and obvious exception that judges should obviate any openness to interpreting the law when the legislator has not allowed for it. In the context of Poland, for example, 'the populist government quite often appeared to be very principled about holding on to the literal meaning of the constitution, especially when the party launched its assault on the independence of the judiciary'.[81] But that is only one pattern, and as other scholars have pointed out, it remains difficult to find a type of relationship beyond instrumentalism.[82]

In other words, deliberation and representation on the one hand and the rule of law (thin or thick) on the other hand employ a similar set of values that populism equally undermines. They both call to reasonably accommodate contingency, uncertainty, opposability, and fallibility – in the words of Nässtrom, they ask us to 'start anew'. Sadurski puts the point in the context of judicial review in Poland: 'the element of contingency, instability and revocability of "reforms" inherent in any robust system of judicial review, uncontrollable by the executive and/or parliamentary majority, is something that an illiberal authority can hardly tolerate'.[83] This is due to the rigidity of the antagonism that permeates populism as an ideational construct. As I shall explain in later chapters, one could take proportionality as a more precise example of a rule of law principle whose normative role has precisely been conceived along the lines of democratic reason.[84] In employing justification and not authority as the paradigm of adjudication,[85] courts may tackle the ontological antagonism of populism. Cohen-Eliya and Porrat put the point of proportionality in combating populism as follows: 'rather than preferring one worldview or set of

[80] Anna Gamper, 'An "Instrument of Government" or "Instrument of Courts"? The Impact of Political Systems on Constitutional Interpretation and the Case of Populism', in *Populist Challenges to Constitutional Interpretation in Europe and Beyond*, ed. Fruzsina Gárdos-Orosz and Zoltán Szente (Routledge, 2021), 19.

[81] Wojciech Brzozowski, 'Whatever Works: Constitutional Interpretation in Poland in Times of Populism', in *Populist Challenges to Constitutional Interpretation in Europe and Beyond*, ed. Fruzsina Gárdos-Orosz and Zoltán Szente (Routledge, 2021), 184.

[82] Zoltán Szente, 'Populism and Populist Constitutionalism', in *Populist Challenges to Constitutional Interpretation in Europe and Beyond*, ed. Fruzsina Gárdos-Orosz and Zoltán Szente (London: Routledge, 2021).

[83] Sadurski, *Poland's Constitutional Breakdown*, 66.

[84] Mattias Kumm, 'The Idea of Socratic Contestation and the Right to Justification'; Kai Möller, *The Global Model of Constitutional Rights* (Oxford University Press, 2012).

[85] Moshe Cohen-Eliya and Iddo Porat, *Proportionality and Constitutional Culture* (Cambridge University Press, 2013).

values to the other, it views all worldviews as worthy of respect and attempts to resolve complex conflicts with important and hard considerations for each side, according to a reasoned and elaborate balance'.[86] The rule of law, like democratic deliberation and representation, requires operating and remaining within the realm of reason, justification, opposability, and openness. Populism undermines this value system through and through.

[86] Ibid., 25.

4

The Court's 'Democratic Society'

Preliminaries

To recall, Chapter 3 aimed to explain how the ideational core of populism distorts democracy and corrupts the rule of law. I started by granting the basic point that while populism as an ideational construct can speak to the basic constitutional and democratic understanding of the people as the locus of legitimate political authority – and, as such, can employ a superficially democratic register – it cannot account for the core values of democratic deliberation and representation. Populism obliterates the functions of deliberation and representation that I take to be central to the legitimacy of the democratic process.

Now, there is undoubtedly significant debate about the various claims made in that chapter among scholars of populist governments and parties. For example, Mansbridge and Macedo object that the reliance on a strong, embodied leader does not apply to some populist governments and parties. It may be valid, say, in the case of the Orbán government in Hungary, say, but not of the Podemos party in Spain; this reinforces its relevance to authoritarian populism as the variant utilized in this investigation. It is also important at this point to recast the findings of Chapter 3 in the overall context of the investigation. To recall, Chapter 3 started building the nexus between populism and the Court. The nexus is that the Court has been distinctively but minimally concerned with protecting democratic and rule of law values through rights and obligations. If populism amounts to a distortion of democracy and a corrupt rule of law, it becomes crucial to scrutinize the Court's practice of protecting these values via relevant rights and obligations. However, if the Court has defined its protective role against categorical and external threats to democracy, as Chapter 2 argued, then the question becomes: is it equipped to respond to an internal threat such as populism?

In this chapter, I articulate the other side of the nexus by setting out in more detail how the populist distortion and the corruption of the rule of law are specifically relevant to the Court's role and practice. As explained in earlier chapters, it is key that the Court's response to populism integrates the Court's legal and judicial parameters. The chapter therefore operates as a transition from the theoretical discussion to the specifically legal and judicial context of the Court. However, it is not yet an investigation of how the Court understands the democratic and rule of law rights of the Convention – these will be addressed in cluster-based chapters (Chapters 6, 7, and 8). Rather, I here suggest placing some basic legal and judicial parameters that generally shape the Court's role in interpreting these rights. These parameters reflect the specifically international and subsidiary jurisdiction of the Court. Chapter 2 has already explained how the Court's minimal account of democracy is historically linked to this jurisdiction. In so doing, this chapter enters legal considerations proper.

In what follows, I explore two parameters of the Court's international and subsidiary role, one procedural and one substantive, which need to be considered when evaluating what the Court can do in its particular position. In reference to recent developments in case law, I shall first emphasize what has been called 'procedural review' – a growing interpretive trend whereby the Court retreats into a review of the procedural (-democratic) pedigree of the right(s)-interfering norm of the respondent state, the so-called procedural-embedding phase picked up by former President Spanó, referred to in Chapter 1. This notably means that the Court does not independently balance rights (or proportionality *stricto sensu*) on its own terms. The procedural review of the Court in my view epitomizes the principle of subsidiarity as conferring authority to the lower(-state) level to adjudicate the content and limits of rights (if Convention standards have been duly considered). While it certainly only speaks to the interpretive dimension of subsidiarity – subsidiarity also matters at the admissibility and remedial levels, as we shall see – procedural review is particularly relevant to the international coordinates of the Court. It indicates the fundamental concern for the democratic and sovereign nature of the subjects of the Court and its epistemic and normative limitations as a supranational supervisory organ.

Importantly, procedural review is channelled to another subsidiarity-related concept specific to the Court's adjudication, namely the margin of appreciation. However, there is a contingent rather than necessary relation between the two: engaging in procedural review may or may not culminate in a margin of appreciation accorded to the respondent state party. Whether there is a European consensus may also inform the Court's findings, for example. The justifications for procedural review and the margin of appreciation overlap: while some are epistemic ('national authorities are better placed' in the Court's parlance), others are normative and democratic ('national authorities benefit from democratic legitimation' in the Court's parlance), as we shall see. As I explain later, the international and subsidiary position of the Court is not devoid of normative premises: it adjudicates over and above forty-seven states constructed as liberal democracies. This premise is of utmost importance to the Court's response to populism: whether the domestic democratic process, as defined by the standards of procedural review, is sufficient in the context of populism.

Second, I introduce a substantive concept that can shed further light precisely on the Court's account of democracy and its relation to populism, that of 'democratic society'. The concept is found in many locations in the Court's reasoning with reference to most Convention rights, which indicates how important an interpretive role it has played. I shall concentrate on its location in the Court's proportionality test – that is, when the Court turns to the justification(s) for why, and to what extent, the respondent state party may interfere and limit Convention rights. That is where the concept is the most incisive and where democratic considerations operate, often in an adversarial manner. Indeed, at the third and last step of the test, the Court determines if this or that interference was 'necessary in a democratic society'. In turn, this helps highlight the issue that our following chapters will explore with respect to various clusters of rights: when is procedure sufficient to justify deference, and when is it insufficient to respond to and counter populism?

Overall, therefore, the legal and judicial parameters of the Court matter as they help situate and discuss the adjudicatory role of the Court as opposed to apex courts domestically or to other international courts – both structurally (in its jurisdictional position vis-à-vis state parties) and substantively (with respect to the content and limits of rights). However, these situational points do not replace the case law analysis that I will conduct in the next, cluster-based chapters (Chapters 6, 7, and 8), which offer a deeper dive into the Court's case-based reasoning.

Finally, I explain in more theoretical terms why democracy and the rule of law play such an important role in the proportionality test, and therefore why it is highly relevant to look at them in the context of an adjudication-based response to populism. Based on proportionality theory, I show that the Court's proportionality test embodies the same set of values (participation, deliberation, justification, and openness) that I used to evaluate the populist distortions (of democracy) and corruption (of the rule of law) in earlier chapters. It is therefore not only that the content and scope of rights inform the Court's approach to democracy. The very function of proportionality, I shall explain, has a built-in democracy- and rule of law-tracking function that can be of assistance in crafting the response to populism – an argument I shall build in the Chapter 9.

4.1 Subsidiarity and the Procedural Turn

In this section, I explain how subsidiarity generally matters to the Convention system and then zoom in on the procedural review as an expression of the principle at the interpretive level. Again, the goal here is to have a better sense of the parameters – defined in legal and judicial terms – in which the Court operates, one that in turn also informs the Court's reasoning in crucial ways. Subsidiarity in human rights law generally concerns the implementation of a review mechanism that is external and secondary to that of the state party. In the words of Besson, it refers to 'the introduction of minimal internal institutional, and especially judicial, mechanisms of implementation of those rights and monitoring/review thereof that are complemented by some form, whether judicial or political, of international and hence external human rights monitoring'.[1] The Convention system reflects this complementarity in that the obligation to secure rights (Article 1 of the Convention) is not only the (primary) responsibility of the state party but also of the Court. In other words, there is a shared duty – or 'shared responsibility' as the 2015 Brighton Declaration emphasizes – between the state party and the Court in performing that rights-securing function. In the words of Çalı, 'the ECtHR's vision for international judicial review, therefore, is that it takes place in tandem with domestic judicial review, not at the expense of it'.[2] The basic point of subsidiarity is to allocate authority in the performance of that reviewing and monitoring function.

Importantly, this basic definition does not specify how to allocate authority between the domestic and the international levels – what Besson calls the 'sequencing of judicial monitoring or review competence'.[3] This is where delving into the theory of subsidiarity is

[1] Samantha Besson, 'Subsidiarity in International Human Rights Law: What Is Subsidiary about Human Rights?', *The American Journal of Jurisprudence* 61, no. 1 (2016): 77.

[2] Başak Çalı, 'International Judicial Review', in *Handbook on Global Constitutionalism*, ed. Anthony F. Lang and Antje Werner (Edward Elgar Publishing, 2017), 298.

[3] Besson, 'Subsidiarity in International Human Rights Law', 92.

required. On the one hand, subsidiarity requires that the smaller, lower, or more basic level should have priority in operating the review function (commonly called 'primarity'). As Carozza seminally pointed out, subsidiarity requires that the higher level should not 'arrogate to itself' a function that the lower level can perform.[4] More precisely, as Føllesdal puts it, 'principles of subsidiarity, theorems in normative political theory, urge a rebuttable presumption for the local'.[5] On the other hand, subsidiarity requires that the higher-level authority comes in when the smaller, lower, or more basic level does not operate this function satisfactorily (not sufficiently or not sufficiently well): 'generally, central bodies must offer comparable effectiveness or efficiency when they exercise authority over the constituent bodies'.[6] As a result, there is an evaluative step for allocating authority to the higher level that the theory of subsidiarity does not definitively answer – when and why should the Court step in? Answering that question requires distinguishing between various dimensions of subsidiarity and elucidating the criteria used by the Court for each.

Before addressing that question, note that this basic concept of subsidiarity is specific to human rights law on two levels. First, human rights subsidiarity concerns the allocation of authority for the purpose of reviewing and monitoring human rights violations. Therefore, it applies to the Convention rights of individuals against any state authority (legislative, executive, judicial). As Føllesdal puts it, 'the normative conception of subsidiarity used here is person-centered rather than state-centered'.[7] The 'rebuttable presumption for the local' concerns the reviewing and monitoring of the Convention rights. Second, human rights subsidiarity links two entities that are not the same – the state level and the Court level, which are called the 'subjects' of subsidiarity.[8] Unlike state authorities, the international level – in our case the Court – does not have any other function

[4] Paolo G. Carozza, 'Subsidiarity as a Structural Principle of International Human Rights Law', *American Journal of International Law* 97, no. 38 (2003): 38–79.

[5] Andreas Føllesdal, 'Subsidiarity and International Human-Rights Courts: Respecting Self-Governance and Protecting Human Rights – or Neither?', *Law and Contemporary Problems* 79, no. 2 (2016), 148; Andreas Føllesdal, 'The Principle of Subsidiarity as a Constitutional Principle in International Law', *Global Constitutionalism* 2, no. 1 (2013): 37–62; Andreas Føllesdal, 'Survey Article: Subsidiarity', *Journal of Political Philosophy* 6, no. 2 (1998): 190–218.

[6] Føllesdal, 'Subsidiarity and International Human-Rights Courts', 148.

[7] Ibid., 149.

[8] Besson, 'Subsidiarity in International Human Rights Law'; Gerald L. Neuman, 'Subsidiarity', in *The Oxford Handbook of International Human Rights Law*, ed. Dinah Shelton (Oxford University Press, 2015).

but to review and monitor the human rights records of states. Unlike other forms of subsidiarity (e.g., in federalism), human rights subsidiarity concerns that limited relationship between a public(-state) authority and an international court. Therefore, 'the object of subsidiarity is the (judicial or not) competence or power or to monitor or review'.[9] The domestic object of subsidiarity can apply to other functions (legislative, executive, or judicial) – what Besson calls a 'complete institutional competence'.[10] It is also worth recalling that the ECtHR only declares whether a respondent state has violated one or several articles of the ECHR in a particular case. The pilot procedure, which notably aims at reducing the backlog of cases, usually implies infrastructural considerations as to the reforms needed in the domestic legal order, but it is not the principled function of the Court as an international and subsidiary organ.

Now, subsidiarity takes several forms in the Convention system. For the sake of conciseness, I distinguish between the jurisdictional and the substantive dimensions of subsidiarity before zooming in on the latter. Jurisdictional subsidiarity comes chronologically prior to the substantive as it consists of an admissibility criterion for the Court to examine the merits of a case (Article 35(1) of the Convention). Further, the delegation from the state level to the international level operates in a particular way in that context. Indeed, unlike substantive subsidiarity that generally involves 'zones of discretionary decision-making',[11] Article 35(1) rather requires evidence that individuals have exhausted domestic avenues, which means having appealed to and lost at the highest judicial body of the given state party, usually the apex court. This is seen in the Court simply finding (or not finding) whether the domestic remedies have been exhausted or not and, more precisely, whether the remedy was 'available and effective'. The Court's Guide to Article 35 states that the obligation to exhaust domestic remedies forms part of customary international law and that the Court's interpretation of the exhaustion of the domestic remedies rule flows from general principles of international law and international human rights law. The Court constructs this rule as a basic principle[12] and an indispensable part of the functioning of

9 Besson, 'Subsidiarity in International Human Rights Law', 89.

10 Ibid., 90.

11 Andreas von Staden, 'Subsidiarity, Exhaustion of Domestic Remedies, and the Margin of Appreciation in the Human Rights Jurisprudence of African Sub-Regional Courts', *The International Journal of Human Rights* 20, no. 8 (2016): 1114.

12 *Demopoulos and Others* v. *Turkey* (GC), 26 January 2010, Application Nos. 46113/99, 3843/02, 13751/02, 13466/03, 10200/04, 14163/04, 19993/04, and 21819/04, paras. 69 and 97.

the protection system under the Convention.[13] It should be noted that the Court has made exceptions to the exhaustion of domestic remedies for admissibility at the Court, incrementally developing an account of when the remedy system within the state party fails to be 'available' and/or 'effective'.[14]

In contrast, substantive subsidiarity concerns the merits stage of the proceedings – that is, when the Court, having admitted the application, having reviewed the trajectory of the complaint in the domestic system, and having found a prima facie violation based on established interpretive canons, examines whether the respondent state party has struck a fair balance between competing rights and interests as part of the proportionality test. This is also where the Court may ultimately allocate a margin of appreciation to the respondent state, a margin that gives that state latitude in establishing whether there ultimately was a violation of the Convention in specific circumstances.[15] As the literature has shown, however, the allocation of the margin operates on various grounds and problematically so: either the Court reviews the state's proportionality analysis on its own terms and concludes that the state ought to benefit from a margin (implying that the Court has an independent metric for setting the margin) or the Court simply refrains from balancing in the first place.[16] In both cases, substantive subsidiarity has the same function as jurisdictional subsidiarity, namely allocating the reviewing and monitoring functions, albeit with application to the merits of an application. Yet there is something very different between the two, in that substantive subsidiarity is not governed by a rule (jurisdictional subsidiarity is governed by Article 35). It is the Court's own creation – without even a trace in the *travaux préparatoires* of the Convention – that helps modulate its scope of review on an ad hoc basis.

[13] *Vučković and Others* v. *Serbia* (preliminary objection) (GC), 25 March 2014, Application Nos. 17153/11, 17157/11, 17160/11, 17163/11, 17168/11, 17173/11, 17178/11, 17181/11, 17182/11, 17186/11, 17343/11, 17344/11, 17362/11, 17364/11, 17367/11, 17370/11, 17372/11, 17377/11, 17380/11, 17382/11, 17386/11, 17421/11, 17424/11, 17428/11, 17431/11, 17435/11, 17438/11, 17439/11, 17440/11, and 17443/11, para. 69.

[14] *Ringeisan* v. *Austria*, 16 July 1971, Application No. 2614/65, para. 89.

[15] Yukata Arai-Takahashi, 'The Margin of Appreciation Doctrine: A Theoretical Analysis of Strasbourg's Variable Geometry', in *Constituting Europe: The European Court of Human Rights in a National, European and Global Context*, ed. Andreas Føllesdal, Birgit Peters, and Geir Ulfstein (Cambridge University Press, 2013).

[16] George Letsas, 'Two Concepts of the Margin of Appreciation', *Oxford Journal of Legal Studies* 26, no. 4 (2006): 705–32.

Now, while the distinction between jurisdictional and substantive subsidiarity matters significantly in understanding the Court's role in systemic terms, only the latter will be explored in depth in this investigation in conformity with the project of evaluating the Court's interpretive equipment when a case reaches the merits stage of the process – that is, when the Court evaluates applications on an substantive, article-based level. This does not mean that jurisdictional subsidiarity does not matter to the project of reforming the system through the admissibility channel – indeed, it has been argued that the Court should better align the grounds of subsidiarity between the jurisdictional and the substantive.[17] As we shall see in the next section, the justifications for subsidiarity cut across the distinction, and therefore one could examine and potentially revise both in conjunction. In addition to the interpretive practice of the Court, state parties may also abuse the jurisdictional dimension of subsidiarity by delaying or complicating the application's journey until domestic remedies are exhausted.

4.2 Justifying Subsidiarity

There are two categorically distinct justifications for subsidiarity (both jurisdictional and substantive) in the context of the Court. First, one may view the 'rebuttal presumption for the local' context as a presumption in favour of the rule of law-abiding and democratic states – a family of which all state parties to the Convention are presumed to be members. Importantly, however, authority attribution in the Convention system is not a competition over which level (domestic or international) is the most democratic and rule of law-abiding – that is precisely because the relation is between a democratic community and an international judge. There is only one democratic community at play here – the community of the state (party). From this angle, subsidiarity incorporates not only a 'rebuttal in favour of the local' but, one may say, a 'rebuttal in favour of the rule of the law-abiding and the democratic'. This justification is important to this investigation: when is a state party sufficiently law-abiding and democratic to enjoy primacy and benefit from subsidiarity? This question again requires delving into the criteria of the Court when it does, and when it does not, accord a margin of appreciation on grounds of democratic credentials. As

[17] Alain Zysset and Başak Çalı, 'Exhausting Domestic Remedies or Exhausting the Rule of Law? Revisiting the Normative Basis of Procedural Subsidiarity in the European Human Rights System', *Transnational Legal Theory* 14, no. 2 (2023): 157–77.

I explain in the next section on procedural review: provided that the respondent state party demonstrates democratic and rule of law engagement in debating, enacting, and enforcing the right-interfering norm in various key institutional fora – especially the parliament and the judiciary – the Court will not substitute its own views for those of the domestic courts. In the famous case of *S.A.S.* v. *France*, in which the Court ruled that the French principle of 'living together' justifies the ban on clothing covering the face in public spaces, the Court held that:

> It is also important to emphasise the fundamentally subsidiary role of the Convention mechanism. The national authorities have direct democratic legitimation and are, as the Court has held on many occasions, in principle better placed than an international court to evaluate local needs and conditions. In matters of general policy, on which opinions within a democratic society may reasonably differ widely, the role of the domestic policymaker should be given special weight.[18]

Here, the perceived contestability of an issue, which is a normative matter, justifies attributing a margin of appreciation *ex ante*. The second justification, in contrast, dwells on epistemic grounds. This type is well known for the justification of allocating a margin of appreciation when the Court holds that 'domestic authorities are better than an international court to evaluate local needs and conditions'.[19] The wording here varies. At times, the Court speaks of domestic authorities as being 'in direct and continuous contact with the vital forces of their countries'. The empirical justification operates the same function as the substantive one, which is to defer the potential finding of a violation to national authorities engaging with the Convention on their own terms. Now, one should notice, as Besson does, the Court presumes, rather than demonstrates, that the state parties are 'better placed' – it remains at the discretion of the Court to determine which question(s) are epistemically contentious.[20] Furthermore, it is rather clear that the Court allocates a margin of appreciation on empirical grounds also when the issue is already normatively contentious politically in the respondent state party's jurisdiction. Because this other justification remains empirical and therefore independent from the normative nature of the subjects of subsidiarity (namely, a democratic(-state) community and an

[18] *S.A.S.* v. *France* (GC), 1 July 2014, Application No. 43835/11, para. 129.
[19] *S.A.S.* v. *France*, 129.
[20] Besson, 'Subsidiarity in International Human Rights Law', 93.

international judge, as mentioned earlier), the justifications of subsidiarity are not mutually exclusive – they can sit alongside and reinforce the purpose of subsidiarity.

4.3 Procedural Review

In this section, I explain how in recent years the Court has amplified its subsidiary role by adopting an increasingly procedural kind of review of applications lodged before it. In a nutshell, rather than reviewing how the respondent state party has performed proportionality – a requirement for most, but not all, provisions – the Court concentrates on the process under which the right(s)-interfering norm was adopted within the respondent state party to ultimately establish whether a violation of the Convention occurred. This leads to the Court dispensing itself from reviewing the proportionality analysis on its own terms. The literature documenting this evolution is now rich and comprises contributions from scholars in law and political science. In terms of the roles that procedural review is intended to play, Brems explains how both an *efficacy-based* approach and a *subsidiarity-based* approach can justify procedural review: the former assumes, under a consequentialist and empirical framework, that the quality of the process will lead to a better outcome in terms of Convention compliance.[21] The latter speaks to the idea advanced in the previous section that the epistemic and normative justification could go as a far as dispensing the Court from reviewing the substantive outcome of the domestic process if there is evidence that the 'impact of a proposed measure on Convention rights has been expressly and extensively discussed, whether the reasons invoked to justify interference with a Convention right are among those that the Court accepts, and whether and how the proportionality of such interference was assessed, that is to say that it should scrutinize domestic human rights scrutiny'.[22]

Clearly, the two approaches are not mutually exclusive. Political scientists aim to explain this rise of procedural review by a more general pressure on the Court to retreat from excessively intrusive

[21] Eva Brems, 'Procedural Protection: An Examination of Procedural Safeguards Read into Substantive Convention Rights', in *Shaping Rights in the ECHR: The Role of the European Court of Human Rights in Determining the Scope of Human Rights*, ed. Eva Brems and Janneke Gerards (Cambridge University Press, 2014), 19.

[22] Ibid., 25.

modes of review – via proportionality review and 'expansive' or 'dynamic' approaches to interpretation,[23] which are perceived as departing from the terms of the Convention to which state parties consented.[24] The amendment to the Preamble to the Convention in Protocol 15 allegedly crystallizes this retreat.[25]

The section first makes the claim that terming this review 'procedural' as opposed to 'substantive' is not optimal: a significant number of 'procedural' standards pertaining to the quality of the domestic process are continuous with the obligations attached to the substantive content of rights by the Court. They speak of the same values of a deliberative and representative democracy. The Court does not, in other words, derive the standards of its procedural review *stricto sensu* from any substantively distinct grounding other than its own, right-based ones, as we shall see in what follows. The former can be linked back to the latter conceptually. The term 'procedural' may have descriptive and analytical value but does not loom large normatively because both procedures and rights may speak to the same normative values. Still, in terms of the Court's scope of review, the processual values can be pursued at the expense of the substantive, explicitly right-based ones and questioned for that very reason – as in *Animal Defenders International* v. *United Kingdom*: drawing on the Court's extensive protection of political speech, which should grant a narrow margin of appreciation, judges Ziemele, Sajó, Kalaydjieva, Vučinić, and De Gaetano argue in their dissenting opinion that

[23] Miles Jackson, 'Judicial Avoidance at the European Court of Human Rights: Institutional Authority, the Procedural Turn, and Docket Control', *International Journal of Constitutional Law* 20, no. 1 (2022): 112–40; Mikael Rask Madsen, 'From Boom to Backlash? The European Court of Human Rights and the Transformation of Europe', in *The European Court of Human Rights*, ed. Helmut Aust, Esra Demir-Gürsel, and Georg Forster (Edward Elgar Publishing, 2021); Mikael Rask Madsen, 'The Narrowing of the European Court of Human Rights? Legal Diplomacy, Situational Self-Restraint, and the New Vision for the Court', *European Convention on Human Rights Law Review* 2, no. 2 (2021): 180–208. Pin, 'The Transnational Drivers of Populist Backlash in Europe'.

[24] Spanó, 'The Future of the European Court of Human Rights'.

[25] 'Affirming that the High Contracting Parties, in accordance with the principle of subsidiarity, have the primary responsibility to secure the rights and freedom defined in this Convention and the Protocols thereto, and that in doing so they enjoy a margin of appreciation, subject to the supervisory jurisdiction of the European Court of Human Rights established by this Convention.'

> it should follow, at least in our view, that nothing justifies a departure from the well-established methodology of proportionality analysis where one starts with the analysis of the nature of the right, which analysis is decisive for effective human rights protection.[26]

This passage suggests how, for these judges, the substantive value of public debate should take precedence over the procedural value of the quality of the domestic process. This significantly matters in studying the response of the Court in the populist context: whether the Court can privilege procedural review depends on how robust that review is, and therefore whether it is tailored to detect and counter the distortion and corruption relevant of populist forces – we shall explore this crucial point in cluster- and right-based Chapter 6, 7, and 8.

Let me first reconstruct what the literature understands by 'procedural' review before offering my own take and linking it back to the main concern of this investigation. On the one hand, the Court's review is procedural when it emphasizes the procedural obligations falling within certain Convention articles and makes it decisive to the case. Here, the Court's review is not more procedural than what the procedural obligations of this or that provision are. Articles 5 (right to freedom), 6 (right to a fair trial), and 13 (right to an effective remedy) have been prominent examples of procedural obligations derived from the rule of law.[27] Still, the Court has also read procedural obligations into Articles 2, 3, and 8 and Article 1 Protocol 1 of the Convention. To give just one example, on the issue of the right to abortion under Article 8 of the Convention and the case of *A., B. and C.* v. *Ireland*, the Court held: while emphasizing that 'the profound moral views of the Irish people as to the nature of life'[28] justify allocating a wide margin of appreciation to the Irish state, the Court nonetheless found that national authorities failed to comply with their positive obligation to secure to the third applicant effective respect for her private life by reason of the absence of any implementing legislative or regulatory regime providing an accessible and effective procedure by which the third applicant could have established whether she qualified for a lawful abortion in Ireland.[29] This clearly shows how a procedural obligation (positive or negative) is established. In Chapter 6, I show more

26 *Animal Defenders International* v. *United Kingdom,* (GC), 22 April 2013, Application No. 48876/08, Joint Dissenting Opinion of Judges Ziemele, Sajó, Kalaydjieva, Vučinić, and De Gaetano, para. 3.

27 Brems, 'Procedural Protection', 137.

28 *A., B. and C.* v. *Ireland* (GC), 16 December 2010, Application No. 25579/05, para. 241.

29 *A., B. and C.* v. *Ireland,* para. 267.

precisely how the Court has also established procedural obligations with respect to Articles 10–11, which are relevant to the infrastructural effects of populism. In Chapter 7, I turn to Article 6 and the Court extending the protection of access to the Court as another example. In these cases, the procedural obligations will form the basis for the Court to examine 'necessity in a democratic society'.

On the other hand, the Court's review is procedural when the Court emphasizes the conditions under which the right(s)-interfering norm was issued domestically, which, when deemed sufficient, comes at the expense of the Court's own assessment of proportionality of that same norm (proportionality *stricto sensu*). This implies primarily, but not only, looking at the parliamentary and judicial engagement with Convention norms – including proportionality. Parliamentary review performed by the Court, for example, consists of evidence that the national parliament, in plenary or in committees, has considered in good faith the impact on Convention rights of the legislation in question. As Saul explains, 'for committee work, the Court has been interested in consultations and reports; for plenary sessions, the Court has valued debates and votes'.[30] If that is the case, the Court tends to refrain from reviewing on its own terms the balancing performed by domestic authorities between the protected provision and the right(s)-interfering norm on its own terms. As Saul puts it:

> where the margin is widened on the basis of good process, the scope for rights violations to go unchecked is increased. This is because, although good process can improve the prospects that an outcome will be rights compliant (by, for instance, helping to ensure that a decision is taken with a fuller awareness of the different interests at stake), it does not entail the consistency of outcomes with rights.[31]

It is not necessarily the case that procedural review is performed at the expense of proportionality review, though. The Court may very well do both. When the two correlate – that is, when the emphasis on procedure is made at the expense of proportionality (especially balancing), the Court may allocate a margin of appreciation. As the Court puts it in *Animal Defenders International* v. *United Kingdom*,

> in order to determine the proportionality of a general measure, the Court must primarily assess the legislative choices underlying it. The quality of

[30] Matthew Saul, 'The European Court of Human Rights' Margin of Appreciation and the Processes of National Parliaments', *Human Rights Law Review* 15, no. 4 (2015): 762.
[31] Ibid., 760.

> parliamentary and judicial review of the necessity of the measure [under consideration] is of particular importance in this respect, including to the operation of the relevant margin of appreciation.[32]

There is still, in other words, a high degree of indeterminacy around what the procedural review consists of – for example, how much engagement, and whose engagement, is sufficient – but also around what its consequences are and could be. In cases like *Animal Defenders International* v. *United Kingdom*, the Court accorded a margin of appreciation based on the evidence of an extensive parliamentary debate even though the right-interfering norm was an extensive ban, whereas in *Hirst* v. *UK* the Court found that in the absence of such debate, a ban on prisoners' right to vote violated the Convention, highlighting in particular the absence of proportionality assessment.[33] It should be clarified that procedural review *stricto sensu* is typically applied when the Court faces an acute conflict between two protected rights with particular emphasis on Articles 8–11. To give just one example, in *Von Hannover* v. *Germany* (No. 2) the Court had to balance freedom of expression (Article 10) against the right to private life (Article 8):

> The Court observes that, in accordance with their case-law, the national courts carefully balanced the right of the publishing companies to freedom of expression against the right of the applicants to respect for their private life. In doing so, they attached fundamental importance to the question whether the photos, considered in the light of the accompanying articles, had contributed to a debate of general interest. They also examined the circumstances in which the photos had been taken.[34]

In this case, the Court paid particular attention to whether two photographs depicting a royal family on holiday contributed to a debate of public interest – a criterion that is central to the Court's 'democratic society' under Articles 10 and 11, as we shall see in more detail in Chapter 6.[35] In the words of Gerards, the Court 'generally has to accept the outcomes of such a (non-problematic) procedure, even if it reflects

[32] *Animal Defenders International* v. *United Kingdom*, para. 108.

[33] *Hirst* v. *United Kingdom* (No. 2) (GC), 6 October 2005, Application No. 74025/01. Peter Cumper and Tom Lewis, 'Blanket Bans, Subsidiarity, and the Procedural Turn of the European Court of Human Rights', *International & Comparative Law Quarterly* 68, no. 3 (2019): 611–38.

[34] *Von Hannover* v. *Germany* (No. 2) (GC), 7 February 2012, Application Nos. 40660/08 and 60641/08, para. 124.

[35] Zysset, 'Freedom of Expression, the Right to Vote, and Proportionality at the European Court of Human Rights'.

a different balance or a different choice than the Court's judges would have preferred'.[36] As we saw earlier, there are two kinds of justification for (substantive) subsidiarity: normative and empirical.

This also may reinforce the Court engaging in procedural view – but not necessarily. In *A., B. and C.* v. *Ireland*, the Court for instance offered a clear empirical justification for deferring substantive review to national authorities:

> by reason of their direct and continuous contact with the vital forces of their countries, the State authorities are, in principle, in a better position than the international judge to give an opinion, not only on the 'exact content of the requirements of morals' in their country, but also on the necessity of a restriction intended to meet them.[37]

The normative justification of subsidiarity is more salient in *S.A.S.* v. *France* where the Court faced the question of whether the wearing of the full-face veil in public fails within the scope of Article 8:

> in such circumstances, the Court has a duty to exercise a degree of restraint in its review of Convention compliance, since such review will lead it to assess a balance that has been struck by means of a democratic process within the society in question. The Court has, moreover, already had occasion to observe that in matters of general policy, on which opinions within a democratic society may reasonably differ widely, the role of the domestic policy-maker should be given special weight.[38]

The Court held that view after having emphasized the subsidiary role of the Court's system:

> The national authorities have direct democratic legitimation and are, as the Court has held on many occasions, in principle better placed than an international court to evaluate local needs and conditions. In matters of general policy, on which opinions within a democratic society may reasonably differ widely, the role of the domestic policymaker should be given special weight.[39]

As explained earlier, the same democratic and epistemic concerns that justify subsidiarity apply to procedural review. It should be repeated, however, that the margin of appreciation is only a contingent and not a necessary implication of the Court's procedural review. Similarly, the

[36] Janneke Gerards, 'The Prism of Fundamental Rights', *European Constitutional Law Review* 8, no. 2 (2012): 173.
[37] *A., B. and C.* v. *Ireland*, para. 232.
[38] *S.A.S. v. France*, para. 154.
[39] *S.A.S. v. France*, para. 129.

procedural and substantive review can co-exist and do not necessarily function as substitutes for one another. The Court may acknowledge that national authorities sufficiently considered Convention standards but still review the substantive (proportionality-based) merits and diverge from the domestic determination.[40]

Now, when the Court does defer substantive(-proportionality) review, which evaluative standards take prominence? As already explained, the Court insists on the deliberative process of norm-making and norm-adjudicating across constituted powers (legislative, administrative, and judicial). Gerards for example speaks of the 'quality of the process and deliberations underlying a certain piece of legislation'.[41] These conditions are all democracy- and rule of law-based and include participation, inclusiveness, pluralism, independence, transparency, and proportionality across all constituent powers. In *Animal Defenders International* v. *UK*, for example, the Court insisted on the quality of the procedure across parliamentary and judicial channels that underlined the general prohibition of political advertising in broadcasting:

> The Court, for its part, attaches considerable weight to these exacting and pertinent reviews, by both parliamentary and judicial bodies, of the complex regulatory regime governing political broadcasting in the United Kingdom and to their view that the general measure was necessary to prevent the distortion of crucial public interest debates and, thereby, the undermining of the democratic process'[42]

This example provides evidence that those procedural requirements – in this case, the necessity of the interference – form part of Convention rights and values. For example, when the Court assesses that the interfering norm was 'prescribed by law', it is using the first prong of the proportionality test that it usually applies for alleged violations of Articles 8–11 of the Convention. The standards of procedural review are part and parcel of the Convention's interpretive apparatus.

Positively, procedural review also consists of reviewing whether the domestic authority has considered Convention standards at the domestic level. This is salient for instance in *Axel Springer* v. *Germany* (No. 2), in which the Court held that 'where the balancing exercise between those

[40] See, in particular, *Lindheim and Others* v. *Norway*, 12 June 2012, Application Nos. 13221/08 and 2139/10.

[41] Janneke Gerards, 'Procedural Review by the ECtHR: A Typology', in *Procedural Review in European Fundamental Rights Cases*, ed. Eva Brems and Janneke Gerards (Cambridge University Press, 2017), 127.

[42] *Animal Defenders International* v. *United Kingdom*, para. 116.

two rights has been undertaken by the national authorities in conformity with the criteria laid down in the Court's case-law, the Court would require strong reasons to substitute its view for that of the domestic courts'.[43] This corresponds to the procedural review *stricto sensu.*

4.4 Procedural Only in the Name?

It appears that procedural review *stricto sensu* does not consist of standards that are substantively distinct from the obligations falling within the Convention's scope, which then blurs the distinction between procedural review and the 'standard' review of the Court.[44] A good example is the requirements of pluralism and contribution to public debate under Article 10, which were central to the Court's conclusion in *Von Hannover* v. *Germany* (No. 2) and are part of the core content and scope of the right to freedom of expression and the right to assembly and association, as we shall see in more detail in Chapter 6. In other words, while the literature dissociates the two kinds of review (procedural and substantive), the standards used in procedural review *stricto sensu* are not foreign to the Court's understanding of Convention rights, even if these standards are not referred to as right-based in the text of the judgment. As Arnardóttir explains, 'the focus is not on if and how procedural elements are made explicit as part of the protective scope of Convention rights, but on their significance among the balance of reasons when the Court pronounces on the substantive merits and assesses the proportionality or reasonableness of a measure'.[45] This again suggests that often the Court is not explicit about whether it is engaging in procedural review at the expense of proportionality.

This overview has aimed to place an important parameter that is distinctive of the Court's international and subsidiary position – yet one that can also inform our study on the response to populism. Legal scholars have discussed the normative significance of procedural review but have not (yet) linked it back to the populist threat specifically. There is a lively debate, however, on whether and for what procedural review is beneficial. As already mentioned, there is clear consensus in the recent

[43] *Axel Springer AG* v. *Germany (No. 2)*, 10 July 2014, Application No. 48311/10, para. 88.

[44] I develop this point further in Alain Zysset, 'A Culture of Justification or a Culture of Presumption?'.

[45] Oddný Mjöll Arnardóttir, 'The "Procedural Turn" under the European Convention on Human Rights and Presumptions of Convention Compliance', *International Journal of Constitutional Law* 15, no. 1 (2017): 9–35.

literature that the rise of procedural review responds to a 'political crisis'[46] of the Court, which the Brighton Conference in 2015, followed by the amendment to the Preamble of the Convention referring to subsidiarity and the margin of appreciation in Protocol 15, can be seen as attempting to mediate. While it is beyond the scope of this chapter to cover the whole range of factors driving the crisis, it suffices to distinguish between the still very relevant (practical) issue of the backlog of cases and a (descriptive) explanation targeting the legitimacy of the Court's approach to interpretation, which has gone quite far in scrutinizing state practices – in the words of Miles, 'this dynamism takes place in a legal structure with few concessions to shifting political interest, whether by carve-outs or exceptions for particular states or by amendment on substantive matters'.[47]

Moving from explanation to justification, the literature has highlighted the risk that procedural review poses to legal certainty.[48] What matters more for our purposes is the link between procedural review and democracy. On the one hand, Kleinlein for instance explains that 'the current reformulation or refinement of the principle of subsidiarity has the potential both to enhance the democratic legitimacy of the Court's rulings and to stimulate domestic democracy' that does not amount to 'a retreat or deterioration of international human rights as fundamental values or a decline of the rule of law'.[49] In the same vein, Spanó calls procedural review a 'qualitative, democracy enhancing approach' that essentially 'reformulates the principle of subsidiarity'.[50] In a more recent article, he develops the idea of an 'organic' evolution of the Convention's embeddedness in domestic legal orders: from a substantive embeddedness, the Court has moved to an 'effective procedural embedding phase' whose role is to increase the general level of Convention protections at domestic level, subsidiarity-based deference being premised on good-faith domestic engagement with Convention principles.[51] On the other

[46] Jackson, 'Judicial Avoidance at the European Court of Human Rights', 115.

[47] Ibid., 118.

[48] Patricia Popelier and Catherine Van De Heyning, 'Procedural Rationality: Giving Teeth to the Proportionality Analysis', *European Constitutional Law Review* 9, no. 2 (2013): 230–62.

[49] Thomas Kleinlein, 'The Procedural Approach of the European Court of Human Rights: Between Subsidiarity and Dynamic Evolution', *International & Comparative Law Quarterly* 68, no. 1 (2019), 110.

[50] Robert Spanó, 'Universality or Diversity of Human Rights? Strasbourg in the Age of Subsidiarity', *Human Rights Law Review* 14, no. 3 (2014), 499.

[51] Spanó, 'The Future of the European Court of Human Rights', 492.

hand, Nussberger writes that 'the very function of human rights review is to counter-balance majority decisions: This cannot be done by reviewing the procedure only'.[52] As we saw, the consequentialist approach underpinning procedural review is difficult, if not impossible, to reconcile with the deontological nature of rights, so that any enhancement on rights compliance is a contingent one.

Given the high degree of contingency and indeterminacy involved around when, how, and why procedural review is applied, one can wonder if an abstract discussion only on its general merits can shed light on the Court's relation to democracy and the rule of law. As we saw, procedural review embodies standards – sometimes explicitly, often implicitly – that form part of the obligations that correlate to Convention rights themselves. In my view, therefore, a joint discussion of the standards of procedural review viewed together with the Court's right-based approach to democracy and the rule of law is necessary. That is why, in Chapters 6, 7, and 8, I reconstruct both the substantive and procedural principles underpinning the Court's approach. In what follows, I offer a preliminary overview of the context in which this approach to democracy operates in the Court's review, namely proportionality, and then explain how the Court's notion of 'democratic society' encapsulates the Court's overall approach to democracy.

4.5 The Court's 'Democratic Society' and Proportionality

As already indicated, I will use the notion 'democratic society' as a heuristic device for reviewing the Court's case law in the following chapters. It is worth pondering why, methodologically, the Court's 'democratic society' can offer a vantage point for exploring the Court's actual and potential response to populism. I show how 'democratic society' plays a key role in proportionality testing – as a matter of description of what the Court does, but also as a matter of theory in showing how the very notion of proportionality can be tied to (promoting) democratic values.

As we shall see in Chapter 7, recent contributions have focused on the range of provisions that help the Court decipher abuses of the grounds for interfering with Convention rights. For example, Article 18 can be

[52] Angelika Nussberger, 'Procedural Review by the ECHR: View from the Court', in *Procedural Review in European Fundamental Rights Cases*, ed. Eva Brems and Janneke Gerards (Cambridge University Press, 2017), 167.

used to track 'illegitimate' or 'ulterior' purposes for interfering with rights. This approach has important merits. For example, as we shall see in Chapter 8, Article 18 notably enables the Court to consider the wider (infrastructural) context in which interferences occur, so that the Court can place an interference within a wider pattern and better grasp (or infer) which purpose(s) is taken to preside over the interference. The main issue with focusing on Article 18 is that it often fails to elaborate that this Article is in fact remedying deficiencies of the proportionality test routinely applied by the Court. That is, focusing on 'illegitimate' and 'ulterior' purposes overlaps with the more general question of the legitimate aim pursued by the state party for interfering that occurs under all derogable rights of the Convention (Articles 8–11).

In zooming in on the Court's 'democratic society', I aim to offer a more comprehensive approach. It assumes, as we saw in Chapter 2, that the Court's system itself was primarily designed to protect a 'democratic society' through specific rights and obligations. More precisely, it makes the case that the Court's 'democratic society' and its mobilization in the proportionality test offers a vantage point to grasp the Court's approach to democracy. In other words, I believe that this notion, taken in its specific jurisprudential environment, is the most appropriate to discuss and problematize the Court's equipment to respond to distortive forces such as populism.

This jurisprudential environment is that of the proportionality test, a test whose generic purpose is to evaluate reasons offered by the respondent state party and potentially allow it to interfere with protected rights in particular circumstances. Not all the rights examined in this study have this status under the Convention. In most cases before it, however, the Court conducts proportionality analysis as a separate exercise, as we shall see in the next chapters. It usually follows the application of 'established principles' of interpretation to the particular facts of the case at hand. Having considered its own canons for finding a violation, the Court turns to the reasons that the respondent state party offers for interfering with Convention rights. Importantly for our purposes, proportionality analysis displays a *substantive* and *adversarial* kind of reasoning. Indeed, having to consider a protected provision (duly interpreted) and to weigh it against competing reasons advanced by the respondent state generally requires the Court to reassert, and potentially revisit, the rights' foundations, content, and scope in the specific circumstances of a case. For example, the Court's higher level of protection of freedom of expression heavily depends on the Court's finding that the views expressed constituted a matter of public interest, as we shall see in greater detail in Chapter 6.[53]

More precisely, the proportionality test follows a four-step process: (1) determining whether there is interference with rights, (2) verifying whether this interference is 'prescribed by law', (3) assessing whether the interference pursues a 'legitimate aim', and finally (4) examining whether the interference is 'necessary in a democratic society'. The fourth stage is particularly significant, as it assesses if there is a 'pressing social need' justifying the interference. This stage includes an analysis of suitability, necessity, and balancing, where the Court weighs the state's reasons against the impact on the individual rights. While each stage is distinct, in practice, they often overlap, particularly during the final balancing stage, when the Court often reconsiders the right's foundations, content, and scope considering competing state interests.

Now, while proportionality is presented as a test, it has a normative significance that is of utmost importance in the context of crafting the Court's response to the populist distortion of democracy and rule of law corruption. While a fuller argument will be articulated later in the investigation (Chapter 9), I here outline the nexus between proportionality and democracy (distortion) informed by our discussion of deliberation and representation (in Chapter 3) to set the stage for upcoming chapters where the Court's case law will be reviewed. The core claim is that proportionality, via the various stages just outlined, constitutes a distinct exercise of democratic deliberation. It is relatively straightforward that when a state party fails to demonstrate the foreseeability of the law criterion (its violation) under the 'prescribed by law' requirement (second stage), it is violating the rule of law (thinly construed, as we saw in Chapter 3). But when does democracy enter the stage, more specifically?

On the one hand, in asking state parties to demonstrate that the inference was rationally connected to a legitimate aim, and that it took the least restricting measure to achieve such an aim, proportionality entails that public authorities must continuously compare, weigh, and measure the impact of a right-inference upon the exercise of Convention rights. This connects with our findings in Chapter 3 about the vacuum of democratic representation. As much as elections involve a vacuum as to the locus of political power, proportionality implies a vacuum as to the justifiability of

[53] *Refah Partisi and Others (The Welfare Party)* v. *Turkey*, para. 87. See also *Animal Defenders International* v. *United Kingdom*, para. 116. More recently, see *Szurovecz* v. *Hungary*, 8 October 2019, Application No. 15428/16, para 61.

interferences with rights. All the stages of proportionality assessment introduce elements of contingency, uncertainty, opposability, and fallibility that are all equally toxic to the logic of authoritarian populism. This is highly relevant to the interferences impacting individuals and groups that play a key role in sustaining a 'democratic society' normatively construed, as we shall see in the next chapter. For example, as far Article 10 (freedom of expression) is concerned, the Court in its routine practice closely examines interferences in the freedom of the press, which the Court conceives as the 'watchdog of a democratic society'.[54]

On the other hand, deliberation operates here through the state party's requirement that the right-interfering measure being 'necessary to democratic society' (in normative terms) refers to that measure being justifiable to all democratic subjects, in contradistinction to the populists' exclusionary understanding of the 'people' delimiting the realm of subjects to whom reasons are owed. In Chapter 9, the connection between proportionality and democratic deliberation is further explored through Rainer Forst's concept of the 'right to justification'[55] and Mattias Kumm's account of proportionality as a 'test of public reason'.[56] In a nutshell, Forst argues that human rights are based on the ability of individuals to demand justifiable reasons for any action or law that affects them. Human rights ensure equal standing in political and social life and require a political-legal authority to provide justification. For Forst, the moral basis for human rights is respect for the overarching moral rights to demand acceptable reasons for actions and laws that affect them. Kumm, in turn, builds on this basis and links up the right to justification to proportionality in human rights adjudication. He suggests that the proportionality test helps assess whether state actions can be justified in terms of 'public reason' in the Rawlsian tradition, meaning that the state

[54] *Jersild* v. *Denmark* (GC), 23 September 1994, Application No. 15890/89, para. 31. See also *Thorgeir Thorgeirson* v. *Iceland*, 25 June 1992, Application No. 13778/88, para. 63, and *Bladet Tromsø and Stensaas* v. *Norway* (GC), 20 May 1999, Application No. 21980/93, para. 62. More recently, see *Szurovecz* v. *Hungary*, para. 61.

[55] Forst, 'The Justification of Human Rights and the Basic Right to Justification'; Forst, *The Right to Justification*.

[56] Kumm, 'The Idea of Socratic Contestation and the Right to Justification'; Mattias Kumm, 'Is the Structure of Human Rights Practice Defensible? Three Puzzles and Their Resolution', in *Proportionality: New Frontiers, New Challenges*, ed. Mark Tushnet and Vicki C. Jackson (Cambridge University Press, 2017); Mattias Kumm and Alec D. Walen, 'Human Dignity and Proportionality: Deontic Pluralism in Balancing', in *Proportionality and the Rule of Law: Rights, Justification, Reasoning*, ed. Bradley W. Miller, Grant Huscroft, and Grégoire Webber (Cambridge University Press, 2014); Zysset, 'The Right to Justification in the Context of Proportionality'.

party must offer reasons that every citizen, being free and equal, could reasonably accept. Proportionality and in particular the stage of 'necessity in a democratic society' thus allows individuals, via the Court's review, to challenge the justifiability of rights-interfering measures, based on reasons, ensuring that those actions have democratic legitimacy normatively construed. In this sense, proportionality *stricto sensu* has a distinct equality- and democracy-enhancing function that can respond to the distortion of authoritarian populism.

Now, while this offers a normatively informed framework to explain where proportionality and authoritarian populism intersect, it does not follow that, in practice, the Court's record of proportionality testing aligns with this framework. Some aspects resemble it, other less so, but in all cases the framework can help normatively evaluate the Court's record critically. As Chapters 6, 7, and 8 will illustrate, the Court develops a form of *holistic* reasoning across the range of rights, which provides the basis for scrutinizing the justifications offered by respondent states to potentially outweigh the upholding of these rights in specific factual circumstances. As a matter of description, 'democratic society' operates as the non-derivative normative grounding for these relations – and can be used as the 'heuristic device' for identifying and evaluating the Court's response. To give just one example, when the Court discusses the freedom of expression of judges and prosecutors, it often ultimately relies on this notion in justificatory (and non-derivative) terms, stressing that 'issues relating to the separation of powers can involve very important matters in a democratic society, which the public has a legitimate interest in being informed about and which fall within the scope of political debate'.[57]

Now, it is important to repeat that democracy is not the only referential framework governing proportionality testing. The Court may find a violation only based on rule of law considerations pertaining to the law's 'foreseeability' (at the 'prescribed by law' stage of the test), for example. Similarly, it may be found that the extent of interference was not strictly necessary to achieve the aim pursued (at the 'legitimate aim' stage of the test) – an epistemic issue. Still, overall, the adversarial character of the proportionality test offers space for the tension between the rights of an individual exercising their autonomy (say, expressing one's view in a newspaper), on the one hand, and the prerogative of the

[57] *Kövesi* v. *Romania*, 5 May 2020, Application No. 3594/19, para. 201; see also *Baka* v. *Hungary*, para. 165.

state exercising its collective autonomy, on the other, to deploy 'necessity in a democratic society'.[58]

Therefore, I shall not exclude the two previous stages ('prescribed by law' and 'legitimate aim') from my reconstructive analysis of the Court's 'democratic society' in the next chapters. This is because, while the Court addresses these steps separately, there is no strict distinction between, say, the 'legitimate aim' of pursuing 'the protection of public morals' and the collective (and democratic) interest underlying it, which may be unpacked and discussed at the last step of 'necessity in a democratic society'. The list of acceptable legitimate aims found in the text of various provisions all aim to give due consideration to a collective interest, which irremediably speaks to democratic values understood in basic majoritarian fashion. In fact, the Court has predominantly operated the step of 'legitimate aim' as a mere exercise of descriptive classification (asking whether there is an apparent aim based on the Convention's predetermined list) while the more substantive, principled, and adversarial discussion is found at the step of 'necessity in a democratic society'.[59] At that final stage, the Court may very well return again to the claims made at the previous steps, since that question amounts to specifying, discussing, and ultimately balancing Convention rights against one or several of these legitimate aims previously identified. The absence of a clear demarcation between these steps, and their conceptual overlap as referring to collective and democratic interest described in opposition to rights, explains why I shall not circumscribe 'democratic society' to one portion of the test.

I hope this adds some flesh to the methodological claim that the Court's 'democratic society' is suitable for studying the Court's interpretive equipment to detect and counter populism. This focus primarily has to do with the central yet pivotal role that the notion plays in reasoning: on the one hand, it affirms and strengthens the rights' normative ground(s), content, and scope vis-à-vis countervailing considerations in a principled manner. On the other hand, the Court sometimes uses the same notion of 'democratic society' to defer interpretive authority to the respondent state party – by saying that the interference was 'necessary in a democratic

[58] Zysset, 'Searching for the Legitimacy of the European Court of Human Rights'; Zysset, 'Freedom of Expression, the Right to Vote, and Proportionality at the European Court of Human Rights'; Zysset, 'The Right to Justification in the Context of Proportionality'.

[59] The same pattern is observed across constitutional systems. See, for example, Dieter Grimm, 'Proportionality in Canadian and German Constitutional Jurisprudence', *The University of Toronto Law Journal* 57, no. 2 (2007): 383–97.

society', which then pivots its meaning as expressing a collective interest of the respondent state, which the respondent state will have the discretion to balance. Procedural review matters here too as a principled discretion to the respondent state constructed as a sovereign and democratic entity in shaping the content and limits of the Convention's rights. Moreover, as briefly mentioned in the last chapter, deference by the Court to the respondent state is particularly salient as far as electoral processes and institutions are concerned (with reference to P1-3, the right to free elections, specifically),[60] so that while procedural review can be described as conditional discretion afforded to the respondent state party, it still builds upon varying degrees of deference that have been constant, sometimes over decades, with regard to democratic rights of the Convention. The literature on this provision has been abundantly clear that the Court is at best 'pragmatic' when extending its scrutiny to these democratic credentials.[61]

To sum up, I believe that the relatively open space in and around the proportionality test is not only suited to reconstructing the Court's account of democracy as an exercise of scholarship, but it can also serve as a heuristic device to assess the Court's interpretive equipment to respond to populism. This is because, on the other side of the equation and very much like the Janus-faced character of the Court's 'democratic society', populism also operates within a conceptual space that is seemingly democratic. To reiterate its distinctive traits identified in Chapter 3, authoritarian populism is anchored in an ontological antagononism between the 'corrupt elite' and the 'real people'. In the name of the latter and against the former, populists in power pass legislation to take control of the media landscape and of the electoral process and plead for (and often achieve) much wider access to popular referenda and constitutional reform. Throughout these patterns, they disregard rule of law standards (at the stages of norm adoption, norm interpretation, or norm enforcement). All that apparatus is ornamented by a veneer of democracy.

As a result, one may wonder where, and how, populist governments will instil their distorted account of democracy in the context of the Court's case law previously outlined. From where could they opportunistically draw some form of support for their project through the

[60] Zysset, 'Freedom of Expression, the Right to Vote, and Proportionality at the European Court of Human Rights'.

[61] Dmitry Kurnosov, 'Pragmatic Adjudication of Election Cases in the European Court of Human Rights', *European Journal of International Law* 32, no. 1 (2021): 255–79.

same mode of operation, which consists not of circumventing the law, but of perverting it? One may hypothesize that populist governments may use the Court's malleable, ambiguous, and indeterminate 'democratic society' to that end. This is not only a hypothesis, but also an increasingly clear pattern at the Court when respondent state parties offer justifications for their interferences. As we shall see in more detail in the next chapters, populist governments may very well justify their capture of the judiciary – for example, dismissing or shortening the term of judges by relying – on one of the grounds for restricting rights as authorized by the ECHR (e.g., 'the authority and impartiality of the judiciary' – one of the 'legitimate aims' listed). In doing so, they are effectively exploiting the malleable space of the proportionality test, in particular the room left for their seemingly democratic argumentation to deploy, as we shall see in the next chapters. For example, in reforming its judicial system and modifying the mode of appointment of judges through controlling the National Council of the Judiciary (NCJ), Poland argued that '"democratization" of the NCJ election procedure constituted an important public interest which justified in turn the early termination of the term of office of the NCJ's judicial members'.[62]

Equally, the Court may very well use that same space to counter this erosion by strengthening its account of 'democratic society'. Yet, because of the deep tension built into it, I submit that the Court has not yet offered a comprehensive account of democracy tailored to respond to populism. As I explained in Chapter 2, the Court has not significantly moved on its account of democracy as primarily aiming to contain existential threats to democracy. As also mentioned in that chapter, some commentators have claimed that the Court has gradually come to fulfil a second function of 'protecting individuals and groups from the excesses of majoritarianism in healthy democracies'.[63] There is evidence of this in the Court's case law at the level of wording – in particular, its repeated assertion that 'democracy does not simply mean that the views of the majority must always prevail. A balance must be achieved which ensures the fair and proper treatment of minorities and avoids any abuse of

[62] *Grzęda v. Poland*, para. 187

[63] Paul Mahoney, 'The Changing Face of the European Court of Human Rights', in *Trends in the International Law of Human Rights: Studies in Honour of Professor Antônio Augusto Cançado Trindade*, ed. S. A. Fabris, Vol. 2 (2005), p. 258

a dominant position'[64] – a proposition that the Court has elevated to a mantra in its case law.

4.6 Moving Forward

The rise of procedural review and the margin of appreciation, and the persistent lack of a principled account of when, and why, it ought to be allocated, suggests that no clear paradigmatic shift in understanding democracy has in fact occurred. In my view, as it stands, the ambiguous and pivotal role of the Court's 'democratic society' does not supply enough substance, clarity, and consistency – and therefore insufficient resistance – across its democratic rights jurisprudence to effectively respond to authoritarian populism. This applies, it must be repeated, to the conjunction of historical, jurisdictional, and substantive considerations reinforcing each other. I believe that the Court's account of 'democratic society' is still severely influenced by the self-restrained mandate of minimal supervision of the domestic democratic process, which then explains the level of deference to domestic authorities via procedural review and the margin of appreciation at the level of adjudication.

While processual in nature, these devices are underpinned by the Court's 'democratic society' and its associated rights. In particular, the distortions of deliberation and pluralism is inherent to this form of institutional capture: why should commissions, councils, committees, or any supervisory organ engaging with democratic rights and rule of law standards stay immune to the requirements of deliberation and pluralism when, in some of the Court's case law, these values are effectively elevated to supremacy? For example, why does the Court celebrate the vital contribution that diverse political parties make to a 'democratic society' if these organs, which previously had to represent the party spectrum, are not composed of members securely selected by the executive?

Yet is the Court disposed and equipped to detect these insidious tactics? Despite the Court's mantra of 'pluralism, tolerance and open mindedness' in its record on freedom of expression and assembly, the Court refrains from scrutinizing this type of structure and their practice in any significant depth. Since these structures fall deep into the state's constitutional and administrative order, the Court is unlikely to examine

[64] *Young, James and Webster* v. *United Kingdom*, para. 63.

them and that is again due to its subsidiary function. They are the prototypical cases of allocating the margin of appreciation that may combine both empirical and democratic justifications. To give a more concrete example, an individual may apply to the ECtHR arguing that their right to free and fair elections was violated based on the biased and selective media coverage undertaken by public broadcasting.[65] To this, the Court could reply that there was an available procedural avenue for contesting the fairness of the elections via an electoral commission, for example. But it will neither scrutinize the composition of the commission nor its actual record. The mere existence of an avenue for contestation deemed sufficient illustrates the entrenched limits of the Court's scrutiny – and, by the same token, of the reach of the Court's 'democratic society'. Again, this is reminiscent of the Court's reluctance to intrude in the state's infrastructure.

It is worth finally mentioning that this oscillation also speaks to the initial, 'alarm-bell' function the Court was supposed to serve. As briefly showed in Chapter 2, from its beginnings the Court had to navigate this tension between protecting the basic conditions of the democratic process (via its catalogue of rights and duties of political participation), on the one hand, and not interfering with that nascent democratic process, on the other hand. In that sense, the Court's 'democratic society' is eminently multifaceted but also ambiguous, and this further justifies digging into the Court's case law and zooming in on specific (groups of) rights.

[65] *The Communist Party of Russia and Others* v. *Russia*, 19 June 2012, Application No. 29400/05.

5

The Effects of Populist Rule

An Overview

In the last chapter, I placed the second piece of the nexus between populism and the Court for the purpose of crafting a response, namely, the jurisdictional and adjudicatory parameters in which the Court operates. The subsidiary and international role of the Court remains of prime importance. It explains why designing the Court's response may differ from other apex or supranational courts. Indeed, subsidiarity shapes the Court's role when it comes to jurisdiction, interpretation, and remedies alike. We saw in Chapter 2 that, unlike the constitutional structure of state parties to the Convention, populist governments cannot easily bend the architecture of the Convention system to their advantage. In this supranational context, however, I highlighted the infrastructural risk that authoritarian populism, considered as an ideational construct, poses to the same (democratic) procedure when it operates formally but remains substantively distorted.

In Chapter 4, I also emphasized the rise of procedural review at the level of interpretation of the Court, which highlights how important the democratic process and its associated rights and values are to the Court's intensity and scope of review – namely, that a duly conducted democratic process domestically justifies granting a margin of appreciation to the respondent state party in conducting proportionality and balancing. The Court requires the state to provide evidence of compliance with established Convention standards, which are themselves central to the Court's 'democratic society' normatively construed. Procedural review in this sense also reflects the Court's historical role of protecting the necessary conditions of the democratic process argued for in Chapter 2. Procedural review is a byproduct of the subsidiary role of the Court at the level of interpretation.

In this context, I have hypothesized that populist governments at the Court can and will attempt to abuse the discretion that procedural review offers them. This is not only because democracy is one of the core justifications of subsidiarity, and because populism thrives on the celebrated 'will of the people'. It is also because a populist government with experience of the Court's process and standards may very well engage with these while ultimately justifying curbing them in the very name of (a distorted) democracy. In this hypothesis, the key issue is whether the Court's minimalist account of democracy can tackle the populist attack on the substance of democracy (defined as the triad of deliberation, representation, and the rule of law). A wide margin of appreciation derived from procedural review confers populist governments a window for potentially abusing the (democratic) values that preside to its allocation. In this sense, populism may constitute a threat to the jurisdictional foundations of the Convention system.

Another takeaway from Chapter 4 is that since procedural review is often conducted at the expense of proportionality analysis, the latter should retain our full attention when we scrutinize Strasbourg cases where the Court's failure to track the specific populist mode of subverting the Convention could enable populist forces. This is what Chapters 6, 7, and 8 are intended to provide. Equally, a thorough examination could pinpoint avenues for strengthening the proportionality test's capacity for detecting these attacks, as Chapter 9 will explore. As already indicated in Chapter 1, proportionality testing constitutes a tool that enhances democracy and the rule of law when it scrutinizes (both factually and normatively) the rationale offered by the respondent government for having interfered with Convention rights. In other words, exactly how populist forces subvert proportionality, and how the Court may respond, needs unpacking.

However, to conduct such an examination, one needs a better idea of which Convention rights are relevant, and of how to go about finding that methodologically. Therefore, in this chapter and the next, I turn to an intermediary juncture of the book: the analytical link between the distortion of democracy and the corruption of the rule of law surveyed in Chapter 3, on the one hand, and the Convention provisions, on the other hand. To bridge these two variables, I propose to first examine what populist governments prototypically do to their subjects (both institutions and individuals) when they reach elected office. I offer an overview of the effects that have been observed so far and delineate the extent to which Convention rights are relevant to these effects. Now, some effects of populist rule are also effects of (competitive) authoritarianism or even autocracy.[1] This is because the erosion of democratic and rule of law

[1] Levitsky and Ziblatt, *How Democracies Die*.

safeguards are observable effects independent of their ideational underpinnings. Yet not all the effects of authoritarian rule are found in the populist register, and certainly not all of these effects can be conferred a populist meaning. A nuanced account of these effects at the level of description and of their meaning at the level of normative assessment is needed. I shall therefore complete this chapter by offering a populist account of the archetypical effects of populist rule in light of the parameters set in Chapter 3, namely, the distortion of democracy and the corruption of the rule of law.

I also note that the hypothesis that the populist governments may attempt to profit from the Court's subsidiary position echoes patterns observed in the domestic constitutional context. For example, it recalls Landau and Dickson's concept of 'constitutional borrowing', which refers to 'the use of concepts, designs, principles from core aspects of liberal democratic constitutionalism, but which are turned into attack on the minimum of electoral democracy'.[2] It also echoes Martinico's point that 'populists rely on the ambiguity of the concepts belonging to the toolbox of constitutional theory',[3] which we surveyed in Chapter 2. I suggest that the same applies to the concepts and toolbox used by Court – in particular, to the pivotal notion of 'democratic society' and all the facets of subsidiarity. In other words, this investigation is also about detecting where, in the Court's adjudication, populists may (ab)use the Convention provisions and the subsidiarity framework that organizes the allocation of jurisdiction between the Court and domestic authorities. However, only a robust normative and analytical framework informed by the Court's coordinates, on the one hand, and a review of the prototypical effects of populist rule, on the other hand, can ultimately do the job of explaining how populists use and abuse the Convention at the Court.

5.1 Three Relevant Domains

The claims I defend here are situational: they aim to approximate the domains in which the effects of populist rule are Convention-relevant, and to explain why these effects can be viewed as populist in the first place. Chapters 6, 7, and 8 will then zoom in on the Court's practice with respect to specific provisions in the case law. Using constitutional and

[2] Dixon and Landau, *Abusive Constitutional Borrowing*, 36.

[3] Giuseppe Martinico, *Filtering Populist Claims to Fight Populism: The Italian Case in a Comparative Perspective* (Cambridge University Press, 2021), 154.

social scientific studies, I focus on three relevant domains that populist forces prototypically target after arriving in power. The first concerns the media and the informational and deliberative functions that democracy demands of it. What immediately appears when reviewing this domain is the infrastructural nature of the capture by the government (and its associates), for example, buying outlets and radio and television channels, and controlling the supervisory, regulatory, and oversight agencies involved. These attacks create an enormous asymmetry between the pro-government and opposition media in informing and discussing public affairs. They strengthen the distorted account of democracy by incapacitating voices and discourses challenging the official stance through informational and deliberative channels, creating a powerful chilling effect, yet without necessarily and directly affecting the individual exercise of democratic rights. In the words of Krygier, 'capturing media watchdogs, for example, can become a way for populists to amplify their own (often nearly universal) presence while dampening that of their opponents'.[4] This is highly Convention-relevant as a matter of principle: the Court has defined the overarching role of the media as the 'watchdog of a democratic society' under Articles 10 (freedom of expression) and 11 (freedom of assembly and association), as we shall see in the next chapter. Can these provisions track and respond to the specifically populist attacks on the media apparatus?

The third domain concerns the electoral system and the conditions in which the electoral competition is organized. Here, populist governments prototypically amend the (constitutional) rules pertaining to elections to facilitate their entrenchment in power if they can and, similarly to the media domain, deprive electoral bodies of deliberative and representative functions. While celebrating the electoral process that initially brought them to (share) power – proclaiming that the elections allowed the 'true people to finally speak' and claiming victory from within the established democratic procedures – they tend to quickly claim immunity from the need for renewed popular consent at regular intervals (defined as one canon of electoral integrity). How can one make populist sense of these effects? Recall that elections are not conceived of as 'starting anew' (in Nässtrom's sense) in the populist discourse, as we saw in Chapter 3. Rather, populist representation embodies the so-called

[4] Martin Krygier, 'Illiberalism and the Rule of Law', in *Routledge Handbook of Illiberalism*, ed. András Sajó, Renáta Uitz, and Stephen Holmes, 1st ed. (Routledge, 2021), 301.

true people pre-existing the electoral process – the 'pre-political people'[5] – in the figure of the leader. The electoral process becomes a plebiscitary exercise ornamented by considerations of efficacy and immediacy of governmental action – an 'instantaneous translation of the political will into binding, legally enforceable rules and policies'.[6] It is not just that populists have a distorted and opportunistic approach to democratic(-electoral) procedures.[7] In addition, the key function of democratic representation of enabling an additional space for discussing, contesting, and deliberating public matters (in Urbinati's sense surveyed in Chapter 3) becomes redundant. From the perspective of the Court's practice, the right to free and fair elections, namely Article 3 (Protocol 1) (free elections), as well as its interaction with Articles 10 (expression) and 11 (assembly and association), are key to study. As we shall see in the next chapters, the margin of appreciation accorded to this domain may be highly problematic in addressing these effects.

The second relevant domain concerns the administration of justice and the independence that the rule of law demands of its institutions. Populist governments almost systematically capture the prime counter-majoritarian agent, namely the judiciary (ordinary and/or apex). The judiciary is conveniently portrayed as the 'undemocratic' elite that frustrates the necessarily virtuous 'will of the people'. Rather, judges should facilitate and protect the expression and the implementation of that will defined in (ethno)nationalist terms. The prototypical populist effects here include altering the rules of appointment, transfer, promotion, and termination for judges, as well as the stripping of jurisdiction (e.g., by leaving some key matters outside of the scope of judicial review) at the level of judicial competence. However, it is short-sighted to only examine the judiciary – indeed, these effects potentially extend to any representative and adjudicative body where democratic deliberation and representation ought to operate, and here the question will be whether the Court's interpretive apparatus under Article 6 (the right to a fair trial) extends to matters that are better depicted by the concept of the separation of powers, a notably vexed issue in the Court's practice, as we shall see in more detail in Chapter 8. This second domain further indicates how quintessentially infrastructural these effects are – they are not necessarily about one or the other domain of law and policy, but about the

5 Blokker, 'Populism as a Constitutional Project', 542.

6 Sadurski, 'Institutional Populism, Courts, and the European Union', 511.

7 Rostbøll, 'Second-Order Political Thinking'. See also Rostbøll, *Democratic Respect*.

conditions under which law is enacted, adjudicated, and enforced. True, populists may decidedly target specific individuals – political opponents in particular – through libel indictment when the prosecution is also captured, hence raising the costs of dissent.[8]

It appears from studying these three core domains of ruling that populism in power does not dismantle the institutions established to protect democratic subjects from the abuses of arbitrary and potentially rights-violating rule. Sadurski is correct that 'populists work within the inherited institutional architecture and subvert it for their purposes'.[9] Unlike fascism, for example, the facade of institutions protecting democratic subjects from arbitrary rule is preserved – and in fact populists may even establish additional rights-protective bodies to operate a seemingly virtuous function and further create the impression that institutional protection of democracy and the rule of law is reinforced, as we shall see later (in the Chapter). More generally, the democratic process is preserved formally: political parties still compete; bills are still passed before parliament; administrative bodies still adjudicate disputes; and courts still review legislation and state action. In the words of Krekó and Enyedi describing Hungary, populists 'enjoy the secret ballot, face no threat of violence, live in a country belonging to that club of democracies called the European Union, and get news from journalists who need fear no jail time'.[10] What is therefore problematic with populist rule in terms of its effects on Convention rights, one may provocatively ask?

There is one important caveat to be added to the claims of this chapter. As already explained in Chapter 1, populists may very well attack other provisions of the Convention that are not specifically examined here. In the context of freedom of assembly and association (Article 11), for example, Poland in 2016 amended its Peaceful Assembly Statute to prohibit counter-demonstrations against periodic assemblies, which effectively prevented anti-governmental activists from registering their own assemblies prior to government-sponsored assemblies.[11] In the same vein, Poland in 2018 established an offence of publicly making Poland responsible for crimes against humanity during the Second World War.[12] While acknowledging these effects, this chapter

[8] Sadurski, *Poland's Constitutional Breakdown*.
[9] Wojciech Sadurski, *A Pandemic of Populists* (Cambridge University Press, 2022), 49.
[10] Péter Krekó and Zsolt Enyedi, 'Explaining Eastern Europe: Orbán's Laboratory of Illiberalism', *Journal of Democracy* 29, no. 3 (2018), 41.
[11] Sadurski, *A Pandemic of Populists*, 151.
[12] Ibid., 154–7.

deliberately concentrates on the right-based conditions of the democratic process and the rule of law infrastructurally, rather than more surgical and direct attacks carried out on specific groups and individuals.

5.1.1 Zooming In on Media Capture

There is vibrant social scientific literature on the relationship between populism and the media in a liberal democratic society. This literature aims to explain how populism relates to the media and which causal direction this relationship takes: does populist discourse attract more media interest and coverage, or does it simply respond to and/or accelerate a largely pre-existing and large-scale transformation in concert with a mutation of the political system as whole – one in which 'mainstream parties became less appealing to the electorate and reacted by becoming increasingly populist themselves'?[13]

Indeed, populist discourse is considered particularly 'newsworthy' against a wide set of media logics. As Moffit explains, the newsworthiness of populism includes, for example, 'sports-based dramatization and polarization', 'anti-establishment attitude', 'personalization', 'steretotypization', 'simplification', and 'emotionalization'.[14] Surely whether and to what extent these stylistic issues prevail in which specific populist context is an empirical issue.[15] Further, the empirical literature emphasizes the strongly strategic relationship of populism to the media located at the outskirts of the political and electoral system – that is, populist movements and leaders tend to heavily invest in media presence to make up for the absence of a party base with associated resources and recognition. As Kenny explains, populist movements are different from 'programmatic or bureaucratic parties', which 'are deeply institutionalized

[13] Luca Manucci and Edward Weber, 'Why the Big Picture Matters: Political and Media Populism in Western Europe since the 1970s', *Swiss Political Science Review* 24, no. 4 (2017), 316.

[14] Benjamin Moffitt, *The Global Rise of Populism: Performance, Political Style, and Representation*, 1st ed. (Stanford: Stanford University Press, 2016), 76.

[15] Luca Manucci, 'Populism and the Media', in *The Oxford Handbook of Populism*, ed. Cristóbal Rovira Kaltwasser, Paul Taggart, Paulin Ochoa Espejo, and Pierre Ostiguy (Oxford University Press, 2019), 467–88; Gianpietro Mazzoleni, 'Populism and the Media', in *Twenty-First Century Populism: The Spectre of Western European Democracy*, ed. Daniele Albertazzi and Duncan McDonnell (Palgrave Macmillan UK, 2008), 49–64.

and expect to outlive any particular leader or period of government'.[16] It should hardly be a surprise that populist parties and movements blame the (public) media when they encounter defeat – for example, when Orbán in Hungary lost the elections in 2022.[17]

However, there is less research on how populist forces, once in power, shape and reshape the media landscape, public and private.[18] In addition to the 'newsworthy' character of the populist discourse, the privilege of elected office – often combined with a strong parliamentary majority – confers populist forces the power to effectively (re)organize and orchestrate the media system from within official procedures and institutions, most often with the tactic of changing the rules governing the composition of existing bodies. This mode of operation has the unrivalled advantage of preserving a facade of democratic accountability. As a result, understanding the distortion of democracy and the corruption of the rule of law methodologically requires immersing oneself in an environment that is highly institutionalized and legalized – and which remains irremediably country-specific. While it is beyond the scope of this inquiry to comprehensively study specific legal landscapes where multiple relevant sources – constitutional, administrative, and competition law – matter and interact, I delve just enough into the law and politics of specific jurisdictions to illustrate the distortion of democracy and the corruption of the rule of law in context, insights that will permit evaluating the Court's interpretive equipment in responding to these phenomena.

A preliminary way to proceed is by eliminating the manoeuvres that populist rulers do not typically deploy. Despite enjoying a monopoly on the legitimate use of force, populist governments do not persecute, arrest, and indict journalists on spurious legal bases. Media headquarters and premises are not raided and/or seized by the security and judicial apparatus of the state; intellectuals, experts, academics, and dissidents are not exiled or even in hiding. True, Hungary in 2017 adopted a Russian-style 'foreign agents' law for non-governmental organizations (NGOs) that receive foreign grants, which reinforced a 'general climate of

[16] Paul D. Kenny, '"The Enemy of the People": Populists and Press Freedom', *Political Research Quarterly* 73, no. 2 (2020), 265.

[17] Sadurski, *A Pandemic of Populists*, 72.

[18] For emerging research in this area, see e.g., Václav Štětka and Sabina Mihelj, 'The Rise of the Illiberal Public Sphere', in *The Illiberal Public Sphere: Media in Polarized Societies*, ed. Václav Štětka and Sabina Mihelj (Springer, 2024): 25–59.

government-inflamed anti-foreign paranoia'.[19] Also true, populist governments may identify and intimidate opponents by launching libel or civil proceedings, for example.[20] But these coercive techniques remain only one – and one could say a minor – effect of populist rule. To that extent, populist rule does not necessarily resort to (all the) coercive measures to silence opposition even when the prosecution and/or the judiciary may already have been captured. Unlike the authoritarian governments of Russia or Turkey (the latter being still a member of the CoE as of 2025), populist rulers do not indict or detain journalists indefinitely without due process, mistreat, or even assassinate them. This is because populists remain tied, I believe, to the (distorted) commitment to respect democracy. If they resort to coercion, they risk losing the democratic facade that conferred on them legitimacy in the first place. Unlike authoritarians *simpliciter*, authoritarian populists need societal support,[21] and, as far as European countries are concerned, they are tightly constrained by European instruments, the Convention being the prime example in the human rights realm.

A subtler and more infrastructural approach may still prove effective as far as the distortion of deliberation and representation in wider society is concerned. In conformity with their wider attempt to play by the pre-existing rules, procedures, and institutions, the attack rather focuses on the background conditions in which journalists and outlets operate, with ramifications in both the public and the private domains of media regulation. On the one hand, the infrastructural approach includes the capture of key monitoring and oversight bodies with the power to regulate and/or oversee the activities of the press (in print or online), radio, and television alike. On this level, populist rule bends the rules for sitting on and for governing these institutions so that the power to regulate – to include, to sanction, and to exclude the voices that can take part in deliberation and representation – is held by and only by agents of the government and the majority. Key to this capture for our analytical framework is the incapacitation of democratic deliberation and representation in these institutional fora, which has devastating effects on the very possibility of a pluralistic debate on public affairs.

As far as deliberation is concerned, these captured bodies typically fail to give reasoned decisions when reviewing applications and adjudicating

19 Sadurski, *A Pandemic of Populists*, 74.
20 Sadurski, 'Poland's Constitutional Breakdown'.
21 Sadurski, 'Populism and Human Rights in Poland', 62.

disputes and are more generally prone to expedite processes altogether. This could concern the licensing of channels, the review of complaints pointing to government propaganda dressed as public information campaigns, or the practice of mergers and acquisitions in the field. As far as representation is concerned, captured bodies with seats occupied by ruling party members only and accountable to the government that appointed them blatantly fail to include political opposition and dissent in clear breach of established canons and principles of shared power. In these senses, the requirements of deliberation and representation that are central to democratic legitimacy are suppressed.

However, that is not all. On the other hand, the capture of the media market develops via the often-aggressive takeover of outlets critical of government by government-friendly media or, if they remain independent, via more surgical measures such as state advertisement or subsidies. For the sake of concision and illustration, I shall focus here on newspaper publishing and on the effects that disproportionately affect and imperil the very material and economic conditions of independent and opposition media outlets. On that level too, it is not that freedom of expression – and, more specifically, freedom of the press – is directly curtailed. Rather than the sword, it is via the purse that the capture is effectuated. This helps clarify how infrastructural effects differ from direct, coercive, and individualized effects on journalists and editors – yet the effects on a society's capacity to hold an informed and open debate are nonetheless extremely serious. It is in this light that the role and the equipment of the ECtHR shall subsequently be assessed – a reality that seems, at least on the face of it, to pose a serious challenge to the Court's minimalist approach to democracy.

Hungary and Poland in recent years have witnessed a significant deterioration precisely along these lines. As explained in Chapter 1, these two contexts are not highlighted only because of their mere membership in the CoE and therefore as parties to the ECHR. It is true that their trajectories as post-Soviet states whose transition to liberal democracy and the rule of law was accompanied, and often consolidated, by the standards of the ECHR make them particularly attractive to study. There are some longer-term and entrenched regional dynamics that are still impacting how media structures and institutions, both public and private, operate today – this aspect would undoubtedly deserve its own specific study as far as the explanation for their perdurance is concerned. Importantly, Poland and Hungary have experienced a distinctively authoritarian populist turn in the last couple of decades that very much reflects the traits of democratic distortion as far as the media domain is concerned. And given the perdurance of these governments since their arrival in power in the 2010s – still ongoing in Hungary, but recently brought to a halt in Poland in late 2023 – a significant number of issues relevant to democratic distortion (and rule of law corruption, as we shall see in the next chapters) have reached the Court, which then provides for an optimal point of observation for the purpose of evaluating the Court's response and equipment.

In both Hungary and Poland, it is via monitoring, regulatory, and oversight institutions that media capture has primarily taken place, although its relevant legal form (constitutional or standard legislation) varies. In Hungary, what has been described as 'structural revamping of the media system that will cement for the long haul the dominance of the current ruling parties in the public domain'[22] has taken a sharply constitutional form, whereas the Polish constitution has remained untouched throughout the entire period of populist rule, while there was massive legislative activity in the media domain. Now, for this deterioration to occur, one surely needs a significant majority in parliament to pass enabling legislation (primary and secondary). The specific way in which the capture occurs of course remains highly context-sensitive, and this concerns both the public and private aspects. This requires delving into the particulars of each country and then critically reconstructing these phenomena through the lens of democratic distortion and rule of law corruption.

In the Hungarian context, the most salient instance of the capture of a media oversight public body concerns the Media Council, which came into existence shortly after the Fidesz party won the elections in 2010. The appointment procedure to the Council has specifically been captured: its members are appointed by an ad hoc parliamentary committee composed of members with a power commensurate with their parliamentary representation,[23] which in a parliamentary supermajority implies total control over the composition of the body. The effect is that the government holds control not only of media legislation but also of content monitoring, distribution of frequency, and allocation of public media funding.

[22] Mertek Media Monitor, 'Centralised Media System – Soft Censorship 2018 (Mertek Booklets 18)', 13 December 2019, 125, https://mertek.eu/en/2019/12/13/centralised-media-system-soft-censorship-2018-mertek-booklets-18/.

[23] Ibid., 141.

This is paired with the merger and centralization of public media providers into the Media Service Support and Asset Management Fund (MTVA) headed by a chief executive officer appointed by the Media Council. As Mertek Monitor puts it, 'the MTVA is subject to the review of a single organization: the Media Council. Media Council members were delegated by the ruling party, so there is no independent control over the MTVA.'[24] Capture also transpires from actual decisions of the Council. For example, in 2010 the Media Council annulled a public service tender awarded for a frequency in Budapest, declared an unknown bidder the winner, and justified the annulment of the previous winner based only on the lack of signature on the blank backing sheets. In 2016, Mertek Monitor complained to the Council that the broadcast of the communication campaign 'Hungarian reforms work!' amounted to political advertising rather than serving the public interest. The Council refused to launch an administrative procedure, invoking the absence of any suspected infringement.[25] By 2017, Fidesz effectively controlled all regional newspapers, the second-largest commercial television company, and the second-most-popular news website, its sole national commercial radio network, its only sports daily, and its only news agency.[26] By 2019, it was estimated that 78 per cent of journalists in Hungary were pro-government.[27]

Furthermore, while the Council preceded the first Orbán government, a new supervisory body – the National Media and Telecommunications Authority – was created and empowered to impose fines on outlets that may (among other things) fail to offer balanced coverage of the news. In effect, the head of this new body can 'issue decrees that are binding on everyone, and to supervise and sanction the content of the broadcast media, print and Internet outlets'.[28] The parliament elected Fidesz members to all the seats of the new body. The constitutional court of Hungary did not find the sanctions imposed on the media by the authority

[24] Mertek Media Monitor, 'Media Landscape after a Long Storm: The Hungarian Media Politics since 2010 (Mertek Booklets 21)', 7 December 2021, 38, https://mertek.eu/en/2021/12/10/media-landscape-after-a-long-storm-the-hungarian-media-politics-since-2010-mertek-booklets-25-2/.

[25] Ibid., 32.

[26] Ibid., 46.

[27] 'Hungary: Almost 78% of the Media Are Pro-government', European Federation of Journalists, 9 May 2019, https://europeanjournalists.org/blog/2019/05/09/hungary-almost-78-of-the-media-are-pro-government/.

[28] Tóth, 'Illiberal Rule of Law? Changing Features of Hungarian Constitutionalism', 398.

inherently against the constitution.[29] All members of supervisory bodies are elected with nine-year mandates. The new authority also has the power to appoint the executive directors of the public media providers, which speaks to the infrastructural features of entry/exit or promotion/demotion found prominently in the capture of the judiciary.

The private media market has witnessed a similarly serious process of capture via the channel of mergers and acquisitions, reinforcing the process of centralization in the hands of the government and the ruling party. Following the election of a new two-thirds majority in 2018, the limits to market concentration in the radio market were effectively removed. Indeed, the creation in 2018 of the Central and Eastern European Media Foundation (KESMA in Hungarian) illustrates the process of capture in terms of ownership concentration of private outlets. The concentration amounted to a total of 476 government-friendly media brands merged into a single stock corporation owned exclusively Gabor Liszkay, a figure very close to the prime minister Victor Orbán. Importantly, this merger was made possible by a 2013 amendment to the Competition Act, giving the government the discretion to exempt certain mergers from the obligation to scrutinize them if they are deemed of 'strategic national importance' – and that was the case with KESMA. And this concerns both the risk of dominant market position and the risk to media pluralism. In the words of the Mertek Media Monitor:

> as in any situation involving the merger of such value, the Hungarian competition authority would have been obliged to examine whether the merger substantially reduced competition in the relevant market, especially in terms of creating or reinforcing a dominant market position. At the same time, the Hungarian media act provides that the media authority needs to review how the merger affects media pluralism.[30]

Concurrently, the capture of the media domain also occurred via the nationalization of media distribution, as in the case of Antenna Hungaria, which operates the terrestrial digital platform for broadcasting: 'this also means that the composition of the digital terrestrial television packages depends on the unregulated and uncontrolled decisions of a state-owned company'.[31] It is important to note that the media outlets outside the KESMA umbrella that can be qualified as independent still exist and can operate. But their capacity to do so may still be hampered by

[29] Ibid., 'Centralised Media System – Soft Censorship 2018', 131–2.
[30] Mertek Media Monitor, 'Media Landscape after a Long Storm', 10.
[31] Ibid., 23.

other factors, which again points to the infrastructural character of the attack on the media domain. For example, the sub-domain of state advertising spending is illustrative of media outlets close to the government being favourably treated, as well as the further centralization of communication with, for instance, the creation in 2014 of the National Communications Office with decision-making subordinated to the prime minister's Cabinet Office. In the words of Dragomir, state advertising is a very effective tool for media capture – 'as the economic crisis ravaged media industries all over the world for nearly a decade now, state advertising has become an even more powerful tool to keep critical media outlets in check'.[32]

Now, one may expect the judiciary to step in and strike down laws that effectively violate the canons of media pluralism. Yet, as we shall see in the next chapter with respect to the capture of the judiciary, the concomitant captures of the media and of the judiciary ensure alignment. For example, the constitutional court of Hungary found that 'the establishment of the one-sided supervisory body of public service broadcasting poses a "less serious constitutional threat" against the freedom of expression than the non-functional public service media advisory boards in the absence of the presidency'.[33] The notions of 'media colonization',[34] 'soft censorship',[35] and 'stealth'[36] have been used in the literature to emphasize the subtle, insidious, and infrastructural character of the capture: 'it may target all the media – public and private alike – but its primary targets are the regulatory authorities and public broadcasters that parties may oversee more easily than private outlets, since the appointment mechanisms of their supervisory boards are designed in ways that enable parties to delegate supporters to these institutions'.[37] In the words of Varol, stealth 'serves as a way to protect and entrench power when direct repression is not a viable option'.[38]

In contrast to Hungary, the PiS government in Poland attacked the media domain without a constitutional overhaul but with the full force of statutory amendments, and the capture and its effects are similarly

[32] Marius Dragomir, 'Control the Money, Control the Media: How Government Uses Funding to Keep Media in Line', *Journalism* 19, no. 8 (2018), 1137.

[33] Mertek Media Monitor, 'Centralised Media System – Soft Censorship 2018', 141.

[34] Bajomi-Lázár, 'The Party Colonisation of the Media'.

[35] Mertek Media Monitor, 'Centralised Media System – Soft Censorship 2018'.

[36] Varol, 'Stealth Authoritarianism'; Ozan O. Varol, 'Structural Rights', *The Georgetown Law Journal* 105, no. 1001 (2017): 1001–53.

[37] Bajomi-Lázár, 'The Party Colonisation of the Media', 23.

[38] Varol, 'Stealth Authoritarianism', 1678.

infrastructural. One prime example concerns the Media Broadcasting Council (KRITT) being stripped of its authority over the appointment of members of management boards and supervisory committees of public media, which the 2015 Broadcasting Act Amendment permitted (the 'Small Media Act'). As Fomina and Kucharczyk explain, 'the new law gave each broadcaster a new board temporarily controlled by the Treasury Ministry, and sidelined the constitutional body that is charged with guarding media independence'.[39] The government appointed a PiS spin doctor as president of public television and 'promptly conducted a purge of journalists and media workers suspected of lacking enthusiasm for the government's political agenda'.[40]

As already mentioned, populist government do not only pack existing monitoring and oversight bodies, but they also create new ones and apply the veneer of virtuous institution – exemplifying the point made in Chapter 3 that captured institutions perform a function that is antithetical to their initial purpose. This can be illustrated with the National Media Council (NMC) of 2016, in charge of appointing the management and supervisory boards of public media. In the words of Sadurski, 'this was a largely bureaucratic body with cumbersome procedures that leaders of the party feared (without good grounds, as events have shown) would not be easily controllable. So, PiS established, by a statute enacted by parliament they controlled, a five-person malleable council',[41] while officially aiming at establishing an independent body. Guzek and Grzesiok-Horosz note that the act establishing the NMC did not return to the system of employment competition for the positions of members of the supervisory boards or management boards in public radio and television broadcasting units. Nor did it provide for the participation of other entities in the process of selecting or recalling members of management boards or supervisory boards of public media.[42]

In the same vein as its Hungarian counterpart, the PiS government also accelerated a trend towards renationalization of the media. Very much in line with the populist tenet that foreign ownership amounts to a capture by the 'elite', the government engaged in the purchase of individual

39 Anna Wójcik, 'Restoring Poland's Media Freedom', *Verfassungsblog*, 2023, https://verfassungsblog.de/restoring-polands-media-freedom/.
40 Joanna Fomina and Jacek Kucharczyk, 'Populism and Protest in Poland', *Journal of Democracy* 27, no. 4 (2016), 63.
41 Sadurski, *A Pandemic of Populists*, 52.
42 Damian Guzek and Agnieszka Grzesiok-Horosz, 'Political Will and Media Law: A Poland Case Analysis', *East European Politics and Societies* 36, no. 4 (2022), 1250.

media. For example, in 2020 the state-owned company PKN Orlen S. A. signed an agreement to buy all the shares of the German Verlagsgruppe Passau Capital Group in Polska Press Sp. Z o o, which effectively gave that company a monopoly on regional dailies. As Sadurski mentions, 'one scenario apparently envisaged is to create rich investment vehicles based on state-owned companies, which would then offer foreign publishers and broadcasters "proposals they cannot refuse"'.[43] This naturally raises the issue of excessive media concentration. With respect to the press market, the share of the four leading press groups in the overall circulation of the press market reached around 70 per cent in 2013 and 77.5 per cent in 2014.[44] As Klimkiewicz explains, 'current media and competition laws do not contain specific rules that could promote more competition and at the same time, prevent a high degree of cross-ownership between the different media'.[45]

Another commonality with Hungary is the tool of state advertising.[46] It has been shown in the Polish context that state-owned companies spend much higher amounts on print and audio-visual media that support government policy. In 2021, the advertising budget of the Polska Press group increased significantly – in one instance by as much as 177 per cent, as Polish independent journalists have reported.[47] Central to their analysis is the project of building 'the personal brand of executives and politicians including the prime minister, justice minister and president of the National Bank'.[48] On the populist view, state advertising can help tremendously with strengthening the 'twist' of representation and the direct link between the ruler and the people, as discussed in Chapter 3. Certainly, state advertising is not a trend exclusive to Hungary or Poland, but its concomitance with the use of other tools of capture (not only in the media, but with respect to other key institutions, as we shall see in the next two chapters) illustrates the populist trait of attacking the

[43] Sadurski, *Poland's Constitutional Breakdown*, 140.

[44] Beata Klimkiewicz, 'State, Media and Pluralism: Tracing Roots and Consequences of Media Policy Change in Poland', *Publizistik* 62, no. 2 (2017): 197–213.

[45] Ibid.

[46] Aron Kerpel, 'Pole and Hungarian Cousins Be? A Comparison of State Media Capture, Ideological Narratives and Political Truth Monopolization in Hungary and Poland', *Slovo* 29 (2017): 68–93.

[47] Ben Koschalka, 'Polish State Firms Direct Advertising Cash to Government-Friendly Media, Data Show', *Notes from Poland* (blog), 1 April 2022, https://notesfrompoland.com/2022/04/01/polish-state-firms-direct-advertising-cash-to-government-friendly-media-data-show/.

[48] Ibid.

opposition in the informational and deliberative sphere. As Dragomir explains, 'in reality, they use this money to basically buy favours from media and journalists. In many countries, decisions not to buy advertisements in specific media outlets, particularly smaller, independent ones, condemn them to extinction.'[49]

Why does populist rule operate in such an infrastructural fashion? As outlined earlier, the same distortion of maintaining a democratic facade while paying lip service to the values of democracy becomes apparent. While infrastructure explains *how* the capture takes place, the values of deliberation and representation can help explain *what* is eroded about democracy in this instance. Importantly for our purposes, while the effects are infrastructural rather than individual, they still have 'chilling' consequences as far as individuals embedded in infrastructure are concerned – in the first place, self-censorship. The effect sought was 'rather that editorial offices might adapt and make compromises to avoid conflicts relating to the regulation or the authority, and that the media policy might aim to manipulate the less politically active and less politically conscious media consumers of the public with one-sided information'.[50] In the literature on media freedom, scholars have indeed referred to the chilling effect in both coercive and infrastructural terms to 'describe overt censorship such as a government banning publication of a book, as well as subtler controls such as ambiguous legislation and high legal costs that provoke uncertainty and fear among writers and journalists'.[51]

However, as far as individuals (readers and consumers) at large are concerned, infrastructural capture does not directly erode freedom of expression (Article 10 of the Convention) or the right to assembly and association (Article 11 of the Convention). That is where the analytical gap lies: since the capture is infrastructural, one should examine which infrastructural features are significant to the exercise of these rights, their purpose, content, and limits. As I explain in Chapter 6, the case law on the 'procedural arm' of Articles 10–11 may be the most appropriate portion of the Court's practice of deriving obligations that are infrastructural. For now, one may approximate media capture by reference to the evaluative lens articulated in Chapter 3. Unlike (competitive)

[49] Dragomir, 'Control the Money, Control the Media', 1133.

[50] Mertek Media Monitor, 'Centralised Media System – Soft Censorship 2018', 132–3.

[51] Judith Townend, 'Freedom of Expression and the Chilling Effect', in *The Routledge Companion to Media and Human Rights*, ed. Howard Tumber and Silvio Waisbord (Routledge, 2017), 73.

authoritarianism, which does not necessarily require a clear guiding ideology and where ill-defined norms abound, the ideational basis of populism surveyed in Chapter 3 and these aforementioned patterns suggest the following normative link: since the pre-existing media is systematically portrayed as (a part of) the 'corrupt elite' in the populist discourse, taking effective control of it supposedly restores the standing of the 'people' and further vilifies the 'elite' in the public sphere. On this view, the media does not have the role of mediating the language that should inform, contest, and revise the terms of public debate.

In sum, therefore, it is not just the selective and favourable coverage of media content and the slow path towards self-censorship that are slowly induced here. It is not just the participation of democratic subjects through information gathering and deliberation that is affected either. As a result of hollowing out regulatory, supervisory, and oversight institutions specifically, the value of democratic representation – typically, in preserving a pluralistic composition of an oversight body that reflects the political spectrum, and the deliberative mode of decision-making associated with it – is also gravely attainted. In the words of Urbinati, 'direct representation does not call the indirect structure of decision-making into question; it questions the management of that decision-making and the actors that perform it'.[52] In this sense, the effect of populist rule in restoring the 'will of the people', claiming to ameliorate democracy, in fact generates the opposite effect. According to Enyedi and Whitefield, populists 'undermine liberal democracy, but, simultaneously, provide large groups of citizens with the feeling of regaining ownership over the state and a genuine representation of their preferences'.[53] So it is one thing to recall the elective affinity between populism and the media through their mutually reinforcing logics. It is yet another thing to measure democratic loss when the government authoritatively impoverishes a democratic society through its core infrastructure. It is, in the succinct words of Urbinati, *the substitution of the whole by one of its parts*[54] in theory, but also, I would add, *the substitution of the whole by one or a few within that part* in practice.

[52] Urbinati, *Me the People*, 178.

[53] Zsolt Enyedi and Stephen Whitefield, 'Populists in Power: Populism and Representation in Illiberal Democracies', in *The Oxford Handbook of Political Representation in Liberal Democracies*, ed. Robert Rohrschneider and Jacques Thomassen (Oxford University Press, 2020), 22.

[54] Urbinati, *Me the People*, 151.

It is important to reiterate the normative framework against which this assessment develops. It is only when we assign democratic values a constructive function – more precisely, the egalitarian function of openly deliberating and justifying the terms of living together as explained in Chapter 3 – that the populist distortion of democracy through media capture can be accurately identified. This is relevant to the populist model of representation as embodiment – and it extends to other domains, as we shall see, whether media-focused, judiciary-focused, or elections-focused; one witnesses the strength of 'hierarchical, state-dependent structures and the reduction of the participation of lower strata'.[55] A democratic society does not only require recognizing the rights that enable individual political participation. It also requires the infrastructural and institutional conditions for democratic subjects, and their representatives, to collectively define and justify the terms that apply to them – and one needs to situate and justify the role of (Convention) rights in preserving, supporting, and enhancing these conditions.

The democratic loss is accurately measured – in normative terms – if and only if the egalitarian horizon is grounded in substantively democratic procedures, rather than in aggregation or derived from a 'pre-political' will of the people. The values of participation, deliberation, justification, and openness inform the procedure, the fulfilment of which legitimately establishes the terms of the democratic settlement. These procedures are inherently and purposefully collective and relational. Chambers characterizes that loss succinctly, namely 'dismantling the procedural conditions that give force to the claim to be exercising popular sovereignty'.[56] From that normative perspective, the infrastructural effect of media capture under populist rule is to prevent the exercise of that sovereignty.

5.1.2 Zooming In on the Rule of Law and the Independence of Justice

The capture of the judiciary, ordinary and/or apex, has become almost definitional of populist authoritarian rule. It is highly illustrative of a key overarching institution whose formal function remains intact but is

55 Enyedi and Whitefield, 'Populists in Power: Populism and Representation in Illiberal Democracies', 21.

56 Simone Chambers, 'Proceduralising the People: Deliberative Democracy, Majority Rule and the Rule of Law', in *Rule of Law vs Majoritarian Democracy*, ed. Giuliano Amato, Benedetta Barbisan, and Cesare Pinelli (Hart, 2021), 103.

substantively hollowed. In general, constitutional and statutory procedures are followed, decisions are rendered, and the courts' authority is respected. One may distinguish between two ways in which the capture of the judiciary remains harmful to democracy. On the one hand, packing courts with government or party affiliates undoubtedly violates the rule of law by disrespecting the independence of the judiciary. On the other hand, the effect of capturing the judiciary is to disable the counter-majoritarian role of the judiciary – and this applies to the democratic function, rather than only the constitution, of the body. As we shall see in the following chapters, the democratic function is for example manifest in the proportionality assessment (the lack thereof) that the domestic judiciary must operate under the Convention.

Across the board, the archetypical effect is the altering of the appointment procedure of judges of apex and/or ordinary courts – enabled by a concerted effort between government and parliament – when it previously was conducted by a peer-based, multi-party, deliberative, and consensual process. In Hungary, for example, the members of the Supreme Court, the 'Curia', used to be elected by parliament upon nomination by a committee in which every parliamentary group had one representative. As a result of lowering the retirement age of judges from seventy to sixty-two (as of January 2012), more than a hundred judges had to leave judicial office.[57] As we shall see in Chapter 7, this manoeuvre has been subject to a number of applications that reached the ECtHR, and it will be crucial to grasp the extent to which the Court addresses the systemic problem diagnosed here. One issue concerns the competence(s) assigned to the apex court of the state governed by the populist Fidesz. Hungary provides a case where constitutional alterations to competences – and the stripping of reviewing competence, for example – directly responded to a pre-existing limitation to governmental power adduced by the former constitutional court itself. It is widely established that the then-constitutional court had acquired a prominent status and a taste of an 'eclectic interpretive practice'.[58] In the words of Szente, 'the Court reached a pre-eminent position in the Hungarian constitutional system and has had much success in elaborating and standardizing the living constitutional law'.[59]

57 Tóth, 'Illiberal Rule of Law? Changing Features of Hungarian Constitutionalism'.

58 Zoltán Szente, 'The Interpretive Practice of the Hungarian Constitutional Court: A Critical View', *German Law Journal* 14, no. 8 (2013), 1597.

59 Ibid., 1595.

Moving from the judiciary's composition to its proper powers, the Hungarian Fundamental Law enacted in 2012 only allows the constitutional court to review procedural aspects of these challenges and not the substantive ones. As Bodnar explains, 'in doing so, the constitution-making power excluded the possibility of letting the Constitutional Court interpret its competence extensively'.[60] In a similarly restrictive vein, the Fundamental Law removed the very possibility of *actio popularis* allowing every individual or organization to initiate proceedings before the constitutional court about the constitutionality of legislation. Like the Italian example of parliamentary seats being reduced, considerations of efficiency were presented: 'we can presume that although the official goal was to reduce the burden on the Court, limiting its power in politically sensitive questions was also one of the real aims'.[61] Now, as for the media and the elections, populists in Hungary have strengthened their grip by changing the internal rules of the committee that appoints Supreme Court judges. Here again, the manoeuvre was to exclude opposition members from the body altogether. The hearings of the committee can be closed at the discretion of the committee.[62] If that was not enough, the parliament elects the president of the Constitutional Court for a period that can extend to twelve years, when the pre-populist constitution limited that period to three years.

The case of Poland shows that comparable infrastructural changes – in particular, concerning the composition of the Constitutional Tribunal and the Supreme Court – without including the constitutional overhaul distinctive of Hungary. As a result of ordinary parliamentary statutes and governmental acts, in Poland fourteen of the fifteen judges of the Constitutional Tribunal were replaced, half of the judges of the Supreme Court were exchanged, and the oversight body of judges – the National Council of the Judiciary – was captured.[63] Now, as outlined previously, the link to (Convention) rights may not be direct – the Polish constitution and its body of rights remain intact – yet, undoubtedly, it is expected that capture will affect how rights are interpreted by the judicial branch

[60] Eszter Bodnár, 'Disarming the Guardians: The Transformation of the Hungarian Constitutional Court after 2010', in *Anti-constitutional Populism*, ed. Martin Krygier, Adam Czarnota, and Wojciech Sadurski (Cambridge University Press, 2022), 265.

[61] Ibid., 267.

[62] Ibid., 278.

[63] Mirosław Wyrzykowski and Michał Ziółkowski, 'Illiberal Constitutionalism and the Judiciary', in *Routledge Handbook of Illiberalism*, ed. András Sajó, Renáta Uitz, and Stephen Holmes (Routledge, 2021); Sadurski, *Poland's Constitutional Breakdown*.

across the country. In the words of Sadurski, 'with the effective paralysis of the Constitutional Tribunal (CT) and the conversion of this rights-protective body into a branch of the legislature invariably taking the side of the dominant party, the interpretation of the legitimacy of statutory restrictions on constitutional rights has become the prerogative of the political leadership'.[64] The emphasis on restriction of rights in the Polish context mirrors the issue that animates our overall investigation, namely the (ab)use of the content and scope of rights. And here again, personal rule seems to predominate the initiation of the change. Indeed, the president elected in 2015, Andrzej Duda, simply refused to appoint the judges who were nominated in accordance with the constitutional rules in place then. Wyrzykowski and Ziółkowski explain that judges elected lawfully before the 2015 parliamentary elections 'became systematically excluded from almost all panels in cases concerning the constitutionality of laws adopted after 2015'.[65] After the landslide parliamentary victory later in 2015, Sjem, the Polish parliament, passed a resolution that declared the previous election invalid and selected candidates for judges of the Court itself.[66]

In some respects, however, the Polish populists went further than their Hungarian counterparts in capturing the body in charge of controlling the ordinary function of judges, the National Council of the Judiciary, as we shall see in more detail in Chapter 7. This helped introduce, for example, a disciplinary chamber for sanctioning the conduct of judges directly and, one can safely say, arbitrarily so. Indeed, the president of the chamber can designate the competent court for addressing disciplinary cases at hand. As we shall see in Chapter 7, the very conditions in which disciplinary cases are heard – in particular, the obligations derived from due process – pose questions that are directly relevant to Article 6 of the Convention, and these questions have already reached the Court in recent years. Other notorious effects on the judiciary include the merge of the position of the justice minister with the position of public prosecutor – and, unsurprisingly, changing the rules of membership in the National Electoral Commission whereby the members are elected by parliament.

64 Sadurski, 'Populism and Human Rights in Poland', 61.
65 Wyrzykowski and Ziółkowski, 'Illiberal Constitutionalism and the Judiciary', 520.
66 Michał Stambulski, 'Constitutional Populism and the Rule of Law in Poland', in *Anti-constitutional Populism*, ed. Martin Krygier, Adam Czarnota, and Wojciech Sadurski (Cambridge University Press, 2023), 339–40.

5.1.3 Zooming In on the Electoral System

The third domain that populists have shown great interest in once in power is the electoral system. Now, it would be naive to assume that only populists aim to bend the electoral rules in their favour. What makes elections interesting in the populist context is the infrastructural manoeuvre of bending the electoral law(s) that brought populist parties to power in the first place. This reflects the point made in Chapter 3 that populists cannot account for the independent role of democratic procedures – they do support elections when they win the bid but claim that they are rigged when they do not. This explains that once in power the pattern of 'executive aggrandizement' reinforces itself – namely, to again 'hamper the power of opposition forces to challenge executive preferences'.[67] Now, while these effects overlap with (competitive) authoritarianism, the means do not necessarily align.

True, upon close examination of its effects on elections, populist rule exemplifies the authoritarian potential surveyed in Chapter 3, since altering electoral law – under an embodied model of representation – entails the risk of turning executive aggrandizement into personal rule. While the sliding from electoral legitimacy to self-entrenchment fits our theoretical model in which democratic deliberation and representation are repressed in the name of the 'people', in practice it often facilitates embodied arbitrary rule. There is a fine line between an acclaimed governmental leader whose legitimacy is to rule in the name of the 'will of the people' at the level of discourse and rhetoric, on the one hand, and the same leader that rules unilaterally, on the other hand. This does not imply, again, actively and coercively silencing dissent and opposition, but by surgically making it a lot more difficult to challenge the incumbents – for example, by handing hefty fines to opposition parties in the electoral domain, as is the case in Hungary.[68] To exercise that kind of authority, the 'referees', as Ziblatt and Levitsky call them, must be captured, which makes the capture infrastructural in the first place.

Yet again, while some effects overlap, the authoritarian populist approach is limitedly infrastructural. There are two angles to infrastructural change in the electoral domain. One is the general system of elections – in particular, the choice between majoritarian and proportional variants, whose effects on enabling the rise of populism is noticeable. The other is the specific institutions in charge of running and

[67] Nancy Bermeo, 'On Democratic Backsliding', *Journal of Democracy* 27, no. 1 (2016), 10.
[68] Krekó and Enyedi, 'Explaining Eastern Europe', 41.

overseeing the electoral process. In Hungary, for example, the electoral system was bent towards a majoritarian model, by, for instance, redrawing the boundaries of single-member constituencies and by increasing the percentage of single-member seats – both in the Fidesz party's favour – which helps explain the electoral landslides of 2014, 2018, and 2022, when Fidesz received 44, 49, and 54 per cent of the vote, respectively. As a matter of fact, a proportional system rarely enables the formation of a strong parliamentary majority – rather, it tends to favour the formation of coalitions – whereas a majoritarian system, whether 'first-past-the-post' and 'ranked choice' or 'preferential' voting system – has favoured the emergence of the populist party as a majority party. This is because, when they are seeking power, populists have notorious difficulty in forming alliances and coalitions with the 'established' parties given their anti-system credentials. Indeed, 'populist leaders depict themselves as insurgents willing to ride roughshod over long-standing conventions, disrupting mainstream politics-as-usual'.[69]

Conversely, the proportional system often enables large 'established' parties to form coalitions with populist parties to marginalize the populists – but that shielding from within can operate only when the majority of parties in government resist populism. In Germany, for example, these parties have established a 'Brandmauer'[70] to exclude populist representatives from joining coalition governments. These findings, however, remain only indicative. The rise of PiS in Poland in 2012, for example, was enabled by a coalition of right-wing parties. In Italy, the rise of League and Five Star parties in 2017 suggests that populists may be able to coalesce with mainstream parties in order to secure participation in government.[71] This echoes Ziblatt and Levitsky's broader account of how the gatekeeping of democracy is located at the party level: 'although mass responses to extremist appeals matter, what matters more is whether political elites, and especially parties, serve as filters. Put simply, political parties are democracy's "gatekeepers".'[72] This calls for examining how the Court understands the role of political parties and the scope of its review of parties' rights within the electoral system.

[69] Pippa Norris, 'The Populist Challenge to Liberal Democracies', in *The Oxford Handbook of Political Representation in Liberal Democracies*, ed. Robert Rohrschneider and Jacques Thomassen (Oxford University Press, 2020), 547. See also Pippa Norris, *Why Electoral Integrity Matters* (Cambridge University Press, 2014).

[70] Norris, 'The Populist Challenge to Liberal Democracies', 554.

[71] Martinico, *Filtering Populist Claims to Fight Populism.*

[72] Levitsky and Ziblatt, *How Democracies Die*, 20.

The Italian context highlights another effect relevant to the domain of elections: the reduction of parliamentary seats in the national parliament. The 2020 constitutional reform, initiated by the coalition government inclusive of the Five Star movement and the League, had the laudable goal of saving public expenditure and making the parliamentary process more 'efficient'. While scholars suggest that the effects of the reform are yet to be seen, they are also wary about their nefarious effects on democracy. For example, the reform could affect the work of parliamentary committees and the representation of minorities within them, which raises the spectre of majoritarianism entrenching itself.[73] The reduction of parliamentary seats is also a salient trait in Poland, where parliament amended the constitution to reduce the number of seats by almost half, while non-appointed judicial staff were allowed to rule on minor offences.[74] In Hungary, the Orbán government and its parliamentary majority reduced the size of the unicameral parliament by half and replaced two rounds of elections – both measures to the advantage of the leading party.[75] This was accompanied by more surgical measures such as the classic of gerrymandering – blending traditionally left-wing districts with traditionally right-wing ones, so that candidates of the former have less of a chance to win seats.[76] Allowing ethnic Hungarians living in neighbouring countries for decades to vote remotely was also deliberately orchestrated with the knowledge that these populations were strongly pro-Orbán.[77]

The Italian case offers another example where populists quite explicitly aimed for a more direct form of democracy that is distinctively critical of party politics, especially with the advent of new technologies and social media. That is an effect that reflects the *party-cratic* aspect of populism surveyed in Chapter 3.[78] The leader of the Five Star movement explicitly refused to qualify its movement as a party in the first place.[79] In a recent book, Martinico highlights that the Five Star movement's ideology clearly aims at restoring the older notion of 'imperative mandate' – a model in which 'representatives must respond immediately to the demands of the people with almost no autonomy in performing their public function, as

73 Martinico, *Filtering Populist Claims to Fight Populism*.
74 Tóth, 'Illiberal Rule of Law? Changing Features of Hungarian Constitutionalism', 397.
75 Sadurski, *A Pandemic of Populists*, 64.
76 Ibid., 61.
77 Ibid., 64.
78 Urbinati, *Me the People*.
79 Danielle Albertazzi and Duncan McDonnell, *Populist in Power* (Routledge, 2015).

though bound by a specific contract'.[80] Unsurprisingly, Martinico also suggests that the prohibition of the 'imperative mandate' is premised upon the autonomy of the parliamentarian – 'an autonomy which is crucial to facilitate decision-making on complex matters in a highly pluralistic society'.[81] In the United Kingdom – in particular, in the context of the Brexit referendum – it has been argued there is 'evidence of a shift in political debate, with parliamentarians focusing not on promoting the sovereignty of Parliament, but the sovereignty of the people and the political inevitability of Parliament needing to adhere to the outcome of the referendum'.[82] This aspect again echoes the theoretical argument articulated in Chapter 3 that democratic representation offers a surplus of democracy. The populist model of representation as embodiment calls for draining that surplus.

Now, as in the media domain, populists do not only change the primary rules of the electoral process. They also capture and control bodies in charge of regulating and overseeing the system. This is done by altering the rules by which the members of an electoral commission are appointed, for example. In Poland, the PiS significantly altered the electoral machinery by changing the composition of the National Electoral Commission (NEC) from judges to a combination of two members nominated by presidents of the two courts and seven members elected by the lower member of parliament (under the control of PiS).[83] In the same vein, electoral complaints are decided by a new chamber of the Supreme Court composed of judges appointed by the National Council of the Judiciary (NCJ), itself controlled by the parliamentary majority, as we shall see later (Chapter 7) – 'in this way, the party composed of a chamber that decides about its own victory or otherwise'.[84]

In capturing the infrastructural conditions of the electoral process, populist electoral reforms provide perhaps the best evidence that, while celebrating electoral victory, a determined logic of self-entrenchment best explains what populist government do when they reach elected office – one that evidently distorts democracy. In the words of

[80] Martinico, *Filtering Populist Claims to Fight Populism*, 150.
[81] Ibid., 160.
[82] Alison Young, 'Populism and the UK Constitution', *Current Legal Problems* 71, no. 1 (2018): 17–52; see also Alison Young, *Unchecked Power: How Recent Constitutional Reforms Are Threatening UK Democracy*, abridged edition (Bristol University Press, 2023).
[83] Sadurski, *A Pandemic of Populists*, 61.
[84] Ibid., 61.

Scheppele, 'populists may appear to valorize elections, but underneath they have no intention of leaving office. Instead of giving the people what populist ideology promises (all power to the people!), populists are crashing their constitutional democracies instead'.[85] The alteration of the electoral domain specifically also exemplifies the claim made in Chapter 3 that democracy more than constitutionalism serves the diagnosing of populism. Indeed, if the electoral system cannot be bent because of constitutional constraints, in populist eyes surely a landslide electoral victory is sufficient to modify constitutional arrangements in the first place.

Capturing the electoral system, in other words, entails a very serious derailment of the democratic process. The capture of electoral commissions, within or independently of parliament, deserves mention. It may be taken as a landmark example of a body whose alignment with democratic values quintessentially requires multi-party representation and, often, demands a mode of decision-making based on consensus and deliberation. In other words, democratic values are built into both the form (e.g., body members represent the political spectrum) and the substance of the body (e.g., the mode of decision-making). However, the populist rationale is to break the mediating position of the body for the sake of direct, embodied representation, to 'typically try to build bridges to the "real" people above the heads of intermediary institutions that in a constitutional democracy mediate between people and the exercise of power'.[86] From our normative standpoint, the effect is that the additional room for participation, deliberation, justification, and openness that these representative institutions ought to offer shrinks: 'the representation is entirely constituted by and through the relationship with her constituency'.[87]

5.2 Moving Forward

What is the intermediate conclusion one may draw from reviewing the effects of populist rule for the purpose of envisioning the Court's response? Zooming in on the effects of populist rule reveals how it deprives democratic subjects – including the 'people' that the populists claim to represent – of the conditions under which they may effectively

[85] Kim Lane Scheppele, 'The Opportunism of Populists and the Defense of Constitutional Liberalism', *German Law Journal* 20, no. 3 (2019), 330.
[86] Sadurski, 'Populism and Human Rights in Poland', 64.
[87] Urbinati, 'Continuity and Rupture', 212.

and equally participate and be represented in the democratic process, and of the rule of law protections against arbitrariness. Scholars of populism have employed several metaphors to describe the infrastructural and insidious characters of these effects. As we have already seen, 'stealth'[88] but also the 'Frankenstein state'[89] metaphorically express the idea that these effects are surgically and slowly, but deliberately, sought by populist forces. They operate within the formal settings of democratic and rule of law – and rights-abiding – institutions.

The core hypothesis that this chapter leads to is that if the effects of populist rule are primarily infrastructural, the Court's established practice requires a robust recalibration. Populist regimes, I submit, do not tend to place their attack on a coercive, individualistic, and therefore clearly identifiable plane. Packing an apex court, a media monitoring body, or an electoral commission does not necessarily result in affecting the exercise of Convention rights by individuals. This is neither because populist regimes target the domestic recognition of Convention rights specifically nor because once the institutional capture has occurred, these bodies may still operate in a Convention-compliant manner. More importantly, as we shall see in the next chapters, it is because the Convention's primary purpose is not to empower the Court to examine the infrastructural features of the state parties. Its international mandate implies it can only examine whether one or several Convention right(s) were violated in given, individual circumstances, and the appeal to infrastructural considerations underpinnings extends the Court's scope of review. Second, the subsidiary function of the Court makes it less inclined to extend its scrutiny over the infrastructural underpinnings of Convention violations. As argued in Chapters 2 and 3, the Court has been focused on existential threats to democracy.

[88] Varol, 'Stealth Authoritarianism'.

[89] Kim Lane Scheppele, 'The Rule of Law and the Frankenstate: Why Governance Checklists Do Not Work', *Governance* 26, no. 4 (2013): 559–62; Scheppele, 'The Opportunism of Populists and the Defense of Constitutional Liberalism'; Kim Lane Scheppele, 'How Viktor Orbán Wins', *Journal of Democracy* 33, no. 3 (2022): 45–61.

6

Deliberative Pluralism and the Media

In the last chapter, I offered an overview of the effects that one frequently finds in domestic jurisdictions under populist rule. Informed by social scientific as well as constitutional perspectives, I aimed to approximate how these effects reflect the ideational basis of populism in three key domains, and more specifically how these effects reflect the distortion of democracy and the corruption of the rule of law that I take to be normatively significant (based on the claims of Chapter 3). Methodologically, it is important to recall that Chapter 5 was a reconstruction of these effects through the populist lens, not an attribution of causation – in other words, that these the effects, which are factual, are conferred a populist meaning and justification, which is normative. As explained in the introductory chapter, it is not plausible to expect that one can identify clear, distinct, and explicit manifestations of populism (ideationally construed) either in the effects documented in Chapter 5 or, as we shall see now, in the Court's case law. Populism remains an analytical construct for the purpose of this book. Social and legal facts are reconstructed and evaluated through this conceptual lens.

However, the effects of populist rule can still inform and problematize the response of the Court. I concluded that these effects are best described as infrastructural. As a result, in addition to the core functions of the parliament and the judiciary, there is a clear tendency to target the regulatory, oversight, supervisory, and disciplinary bodies of public authorities. I suggested how this targeting may be viewed as continuous with the distortion of democracy and the corruption of the rule of law articulated in Chapter 3. It is not just that the infrastructural erosion reflects how authoritarian populism concentrates its efforts on the fundamentally 'democratic' domains of law-making (election and parliamentary law, media law, or the law of the judiciary, respectively). More importantly, the functioning of public authority is rendered void of deliberative and representative constraints in a democratic sense – and that makes these authorities distinctively populist according to our normative framework. In accordance with the ideational basis of populism, these authorities are not defined as (contributing to) constructing and mediating the democratic will – rather, their only role is to enable and/or enforce the sacrosanct and pre-political 'will of the people'. And if it is necessary to corrupt the rule of law to achieve this, then so be it.

Furthermore, the infrastructural effects of populist rule explain why the link to (Convention) rights is not necessary but contingent. Consequently, whether a (Convention) right is implicated – and possibly eroded – depends on how authorities, once altered by populist rule, interpret, rule, decide, adjudicate, sanction, or review. Otherwise put, the friction with, and the possible erosion of, (Convention) rights arises from *how* populist authorities perform their function in each case, which is a far more contingent and localized issue. This applies straightforwardly to the judicial function, but also to the range of adjudicators, arbiters, and referees in monitoring, supervisory, and oversight bodies covered in Chapter 5. Equally, I suggested in Chapter 4 that the tool of proportionality could operate as a detector of populism. On the one hand, populist governments are neither institution nor rights abolitionists. As suggested in Chapter 5, these governments are likely to recognize and accommodate Convention rights in domestic proceedings, but their authorities – when captured – are equally likely to ultimately exploit the room that the Court's proportionality assessment leaves to them, in particular the margin of appreciation. On the other hand, I argued in Chapter 3 that the steps of the proportionality test are democracy- and rule of law-enhancing. Proportionality embodies the cardinal values of participation, deliberation, justification, and openness – and therefore the Court may develop the analytical framework built into proportionality to detect and respond the infrastructural erosion distinctive of populism.

The overarching question I raised at the end of the last chapter, however, is whether the Court is apt to grasp the infrastructural character of these effects given the irremediably individual, limitedly right-centred, scope of its international and subsidiary mandate highlighted in Chapter 4. This is not just because the Court is an international court, the judgments of which only bind the parties to the case. It also remains that in principle the Court is not primarily required to do more than establish whether a violation of the Convention occurred in the individual and factual circumstances of a given application. As opposed to judicial economy, infrastructural erosion requires examining a wider context domestically, and then explaining how it enables and justifies a particular violation of a particular right in particular circumstances.

Furthermore, I also wonder if the Court's minimalist understanding of democracy and the rule of law surveyed in Chapter 2 will significantly limit its ability to identify and counter these enabling conditions. Answering that question, however, requires delving more deeply into the Court's case law, and showing how this minimalism shapes the Court's understanding of these rights and how it conducts proportionality considering these limitations. This issue should not be conflated with the repetition of the same individual violation, to which the 'pilot judgment procedure' (under Rule 61 of the Rules of Court) responded. Here, the issue concerns the Court's adjudicative reach based on its own interpretive apparatus and the limited facts to which it is applied, not the likelihood that the same violation is likely to occur.

In this chapter, I turn to the practice of the Court pertaining to the cluster of rights that are potentially implicated by populist rule in the three domains covered in Chapter 5. I start by examining how the Court has generally understood and protected the media domain under Articles 10–11 (freedom of expression and freedom of assembly and association) before moving to the administration of justice (Chapter 7) and the electoral system (Chapter 8). If populist governments are neither institution nor rights abolitionists, I expect these governments to incorporate these rights in domestic proceedings and claim compliance, since the Convention system makes them the primary interpreters and the only enforcers of them. Equally, they are likely to exploit the space – terminological and conceptual – that the Convention and the Court's practice allows for (ab)using the Court's minimalist account of democracy and the rights that underpin it. This is where returning to Court's legal and judicial parameters is key. In Chapter 4, I showed that procedural review – the renewed mode of emphasizing subsidiarity in the Court's case law – can amount both to deriving procedural obligations falling within the scope of a particular right and to evaluating the domestic process (legislative, administrative, judicial) of the right-interfering norm, which dispenses the Court from performing its own proportionality analysis. In this chapter, I reconstruct cases in which the Court has done both and evaluate the risk that such an approach poses to the Court's equipment in the populist context.

6.1 Can the Court Address Infrastructural Effects?

What are the core interpretive principles that the Court applies to the media domain under Article 10, and are these calibrated to address the infrastructural character of the populist attack observed in that domain?

The claim I defend in this chapter is that, on the one hand, the Court has undoubtedly built a strong interpretive apparatus for detecting when governments restrict Article 10 on distinctively non- or anti-democratic grounds. It does so by thoroughly examining whether views held, in particular those of journalists, contribute to a pluralistic public debate. In the populist context specifically, this applies for example to the critical view expressed by dismissed judges regarding infrastructural changes to the judiciary, which the Court has addressed in recent cases, as we shall see later (Chapter 7). While a populist stance will bend in favour of the government's aim of reforming the judiciary, the Court is keen to find a violation by explaining how a critical view of judicial reform falls within the realm of public interest.

On the other hand, the closest one finds in the case law to the infrastructural dimension of the populist distortion amounts to the procedural obligations attached to Articles 10–11. The Court's mode of inquiry appears far less inquisitive when it comes, for example, to oversight bodies or parliamentary committees imposing fines on journalists, where procedural obligations are irremediably basic. Furthermore, the broader infrastructural attack coming from media concentration and the capture of media – marginalizing dissenting media through the purse rather than the sword – does not feature in the Court's analysis. It becomes difficult for the Court to celebrate the media as 'the watchdog of a democratic society' when that function is infrastructurally impeded through concerted governmental distortion. A closer look reveals that the closer the Court's reasoning touches upon the infrastructural parameters underlying and enabling the violation in question, the more deferential its reasoning becomes, and the more salient the Court's subsidiary role becomes. This infrastructural aspect is distinctively vulnerable to populist erosion, I submit.

6.2 The Substantive Principles of Article 10

Let us first identify the broad principles that the Court employs for interpreting Articles 10 and 11 before assessing how these apply to the media domain in the context of the proportionality test. The value of deliberation is reflected specifically in how freedom of expression contributes to pluralism as a constitutive requirement of a 'democratic society'. Indeed, the Court's has relentlessly insisted that there is no 'democratic society' and, in particular, no democratic debate without 'pluralism, tolerance and broadmindedness'.[1] 'Deliberative pluralism', as we may call it, is the normative foundation that justifies the wide scope accorded to Article 10. Since the seminal *Handyside* case, freedom of expression applies 'not only to "information" or "ideas" that are favorably received or regarded as inoffensive or as a matter of indifference, but also to those that offend, shock or disturb the State or any sector of the population'.[2] In the Court's view, this applies first and foremost to what the Court terms 'free political debate':

> the promotion of free political debate is a fundamental feature of a democratic society. The Court attaches the highest importance to freedom of expression in the context of political debate and considers that very strong reasons are required to justify restrictions on political speech. Allowing broad restrictions on political speech in individual cases would undoubtedly affect respect for freedom of expression in general in the State concerned.[3]

This core definition has become the Court's mantra not only of Article 10 but also of Article 11 – in particular, on the question of the conditions under which a political party can be banned.[4]

To explore the link to populism in the next section, I highlight two implications that the Court draws from this emphasis on deliberative pluralism. First, when the Court finds that the view(s) interfered with by the government can qualify as pertaining to an issue of public interest, this view is protected – and this applies again equally to Article 10 and Article 11. This means that the Court actively and explicitly examines the facts presented to it through this lens. It is crucial to note that whether a public interest is indeed found is a matter of normative and not empirical analysis – that is, the Court usually relies on the facts and arguments brought by the applicant to establish whether there is indeed a public interest at stake, but the criteria for finding it are normative. Again, its subsidiary role generally prevents the Court from revisiting, or requesting, new factual information. Whether something counts as public interest heavily depends on that thing being debated in the public arena at the time where the views were expressed.

Correlatively, if such a public interest could be found, governments are required to thoroughly explain why these views ought to be nonetheless

[1] *Handyside* v. *United Kingdom*, para. 50.
[2] *Handyside*, para. 50.
[3] *Dupuis and Others* v. *France*, 7 June 2007, Application No. 1914/02, para. 40.
[4] *Refah Partisi* v. *Turkey*.

interfered with, which requires expanding on the restriction grounds listed in Article 10(2) and Article 11(2). That is where the link to the proportionality test appears: the burden of justification placed upon the respondent government substantially increases if such interest is to be found. As a result, if governments do not address the question of the existence of a public interest in the first place, it is highly unlikely that they will justify their interference accordingly. One may use the example of Islamism (in the context of Articles 10 and 11) and the numerous cases against Turkey to illustrate this reasoning. In *Gündüz* v. *Turkey*, for example, which concerned the leader of an Islamic sect defending sharia law on an independent Turkish television channel, the Court famously asserted that while sharia law is incompatible with a 'democratic society', the fact of defending the implementation of sharia law cannot be subject to restriction:

> [T]he applicant's extremist views were already known and had been discussed in the public arena and, in particular, were counterbalanced by the intervention of the other participants in the programme; and lastly, they were expressed in the course of a pluralistic debate in which the applicant was actively taking part. Accordingly, the Court considers that in the instant case the need for the restriction in issue has not been established convincingly.[5]

Since deliberative pluralism is inherently relational and contextual, it applies to both the speaker(s) and the listener(s) in the debate. For example, the Court insists on the 'right to reply', which engages Article 8 (the right to private and family life). Indeed, when does the freedom to contribute to public debate ('the speaker') encroach on the rights of others ('the listener(s)'), of which the right to privacy is an example? In another seminal case, *Melchynuk* v. *Ukraine*, which concerned the critique of the books of a recognized Ukrainian author, the then-Commission held that:

> the Court considers that the right of reply, as an important element of freedom of expression, falls within the scope of Article 10 of the Convention. This flows from the need not only to be able to contest untruthful information, but also to ensure a plurality of opinions, especially in matters of general interest such as literary and political debate.[6]

The importance accorded to deliberative pluralism, which mainly protects the right to 'offend, shock and disturb', does not extend to the

[5] *Gündüz* v. *Turkey*, 4 December 2003, Application No. 35071/97, para. 51.
[6] *Melchynuk* v. *Ukraine*, 5 July 2005, Application No. 28743/03, para. 2.

freedom to distort facts, however. This is because, in the framework of the Convention, freedom of expression – even in a political context – may ultimately violate 'the rights of others', including Article 8 of the Convention (the right to private and family life). The Court that journalists specifically act with 'an obligation to provide a sufficient factual basis for their assertions'[7] and 'provide accurate and reliable information'.[8] The distinction was seminally made in *Lingens* where the Court held that:

> in the Court's view, a careful distinction needs to be made between facts and value-judgments on this issue. The existence of facts can be demonstrated, whereas the truth of value-judgments is not susceptible of proof. The Court notes in this connection that the facts on which Mr. Lingens founded his value-judgment were undisputed, as was also his good faith.[9]

Now, again, the Court may relax these requirements of factual journalism if the views were expressed during a pluralistic debate where a public interest prevails, which reaffirms the tenets of deliberative pluralism. In *Dyuldin* v. *Russia*, the weaker requirement of factual support was decisive to the finding of a violation of Article 10:

> the Court would in any event observe that the distinction between statements of fact and value judgments is of less significance in a case such as the present one, where the impugned statement was made in the course of a lively political debate at local level and where elected officials and journalists should enjoy a wide freedom to criticise the actions of a local authority, even where the statements made may lack a clear basis in fact.[10]

This suggests that deliberative pluralism not only grounds but also extends to the content and the limits (via the proportionality test) of Article 10 (and Article 11). This is not necessarily the case for other democratic rights of the Convention, such as the right to free and fair elections (Article 3 Protocol 1), as we shall see in Chapter 8. The Court may assign equally strong deliberative foundations to that Article – in fact, the Court makes a strikingly strong connection between expression and vote in that respect, as we shall see – and yet may very well retreat into deference – via the margin of appreciation – when addressing the proportionality of the interference. The margin of appreciation as an

[7] *Cumpănă and Mazăre* v. *Romania*, (GC), 17 December 2004, Application No. 33348/96, para. 101.
[8] *Bladet Tromsø and Stensaas* v. *Norway*, para. 65.
[9] *Lingens* v. *Austria*, 8 July 1986, Application No. 9815/82, para. 42.
[10] *Dyuldin* v. *Russia*, 31 July 2007, Application No. 25968/02, para. 49.

expression of subsidiarity gains prominence at that specific location in the Court's review process.

6.3 Deliberative Pluralism as Populist Detector: Preliminaries

Deliberative pluralism offers a vantage point from which to envision how populist governments may attempt to either abuse or simply circumvent the Court's interpretive reach. Indeed, if one follows the logic of democracy being distorted (explained in Chapter 3), in which deliberation is superfluous to the formation and mediation of the democratic will, populists are likely to deny, diminish, or distort the 'public' or 'political' significance of exercising freedom of expression. One way to achieve this is to generally frame the issue at stake as *apolitical* and hence put more weight on the opposable right, in this case Article 8.

In the recent case of *Szurovecz* v. *Hungary*, in which a journalist was prevented from filming within the premises of a centre hosting asylum seekers, the Hungarian government, after insisting – without much justification – on the margin of appreciation that applies generally to Article 10, turned proportionality on its head by placing the burden of necessity and justification onto the applicant, thereby asserting that there were alternative means of achieving the end in question, namely the filming of the centre:

> The Government highlighted the margin of appreciation enjoyed by the State in the present case and in granting access to the requested information [. . .]. Any positive obligation under Article 10 ought to be construed in the light of the authorities' obligation to respect and ensure the enjoyment of other rights enshrined in the Convention and to strike a fair balance not only between private and public interests, but also between competing private interests – in the present case the applicant's right to receive information under Article 10 and asylum-seekers' right to respect for private life under Article 8, right to life and physical integrity under Articles 2 and 3, and right to personal liberty under Article 5 of the Convention.[11]

In its review of the Hungarian government's justification for interfering with Article 10, the Court deployed its account of deliberative pluralism with the search for public interest and pluralistic debate as guiding principles:

[11] *Szurovecz* v. *Hungary*, para. 36.

> At the material time there were a large number of asylum-seekers entering the territory of Hungary, a situation commonly characterised as a 'refugee crisis' and widely reported in the media [...]. In the face of these considerations, the Court finds that the domestic authorities should have paid particular attention to the public interest attached to the applicant's request, which consisted primarily in providing a first-hand report on the conditions prevailing at the facility. However, the Court cannot but note that the conclusion of the OIN [Office of Immigration and Nationality] in refusing the applicant access to the Reception Centre [...] was reached without any sensible consideration of his interest as a journalist in conducting his research or of the interest of the public in receiving information on a matter of public interest.[12]

In other words, the Court's reliance on deliberative pluralism prevents the government from arbitrarily selecting which aspect or interest counts as 'public'. This tension in turn entails two accounts of proportionality – and particularly two accounts of 'necessity'. For the government, the burden of justification falls upon the applicant to explain why it was necessary to film the premises of the asylum seekers' centre – what added value the filming of the centre's premises actually brings – whereas for the Court the burden of justification lies upon the government to justify its restriction on the reporting in the first place. The key difference is whether the living conditions were, at the time of the interference, the subject of a pluralistic public debate. This reconstruction also helps to see how one may view the government's adduced restriction as populist, namely the ex-ante delineation of the 'public' or the 'political'.

For the sake of the next steps of our analysis, I want to reiterate – as explained in more detail in Chapter 4 – that proportionality analysis is key to violation finding in the context of Articles 10 and 11. It is certainly not the case that any interference of a similar kind – any filming of any asylum centre – will trigger the Court's ethos of deliberative pluralism and justify the higher level of protection that the Court then affords to freedom of expression and assembly. What matters is whether the facts presented to the Court display the features of deliberative pluralism, in which case the government's burden of justification is heavier:

> domestic authorities have failed to demonstrate convincingly that the refusal of permission to enter and conduct research in the Reception Centre, which was an absolute refusal, was proportionate to the aims pursued and thus met a 'pressing social need'.[13]

[12] *Szurovecz*, para. 60.
[13] *Szurovecz*, para. 76.

In more philosophical terms, this is where the values of deliberation, participation, justification, and openness matter as an analytical evaluative framework. In Chapter 4, I explained how the balancing step of proportionality specifically plays a built-in democracy- and equality-enhancing function fit for further scrutinizing domestic records. In drawing on proportionality theory, I argued that balancing amounts to requiring public authority to justify disregarding the interest(s) of a minority – in the context of this case, the asylum seekers and their precarious conditions – in the public arena, constructed, again, as a deliberative and pluralistic one. It appears that the Court is responsive to this further level of justification when it identifies asylum seekers at risk of marginalization in public debate:

> The public interest in reporting from certain locations is especially relevant where the authorities' handling of vulnerable groups is at stake [. . .]. The matter of how residents were accommodated in State-run reception centres, whether the State fulfilled its international obligations towards asylum-seekers and whether this vulnerable group had the ability to fully enjoy their human rights was therefore undisputedly newsworthy and of great public significance.[14]

6.4 The Procedural Principles of Article 10

It appears that the Court's account of deliberative pluralism, in particular the guiding and normatively demanding function it plays in the proportionality test, seems particularly well geared towards detecting and diagnosing what I defined in Chapter 3 as the populist attempt to evade the requirement of democratic deliberation. But note that the requirement of deliberative pluralism here operates as a substantive principle: the requirement applies to the context of the right being exercised – namely, whether expression took place within an existing plural and adversarial debate – and to the content of the view held – namely, whether a public interest could be found. Often, the former will establish the existence of the latter.

However, as students of the Convention will know, Article 10 also has a procedural limb, which exemplifies the first kind of procedural review surveyed in Chapter 4, namely, when procedural obligations are attached to a Convention provision, and how these obligations outweigh the argument advanced by the government in the proportionality test

[14] *Szurovecz*, para. 61.

('necessary in a democratic society'). In what follows, I show that the Court's requirement of 'basic procedural guarantees' – highlighted in various notable cases against Hungary and Poland – is ultimately immune to the requirement of deliberative pluralism, and as a result it is vulnerable to the populist erosion of a infrastructural kind that we identified in Chapter 5. Indeed, the Court only examines whether procedural guarantees offered by domestic legislation meet some basic effectiveness and fairness criteria, but deliberative pluralism is not one of them – that is, the Court does not scrutinize how the appeal procedure is operated: how is the judicial or administrative body composed? Is it plural and adversarial? While the Court is principally correct that basic appeal procedures against decisions that interfere with Article 10 are meant to 'protect against abuse', the distinctively populist erosion does not concern the mere existence, availability, and basic fairness of these procedures, but *how* these procedures are fulfilled.

I first suggest exploring this issue by first closely examining the case of *Karácsony and Others* v. *Hungary*. The case pertains to the fines – what the Court terms 'ex post facto disciplinary sanctions' – imposed on opposition members in the Hungarian parliament who had used a placard, banners, and megaphone on the floor of the parliament to express their fierce objection to the government's policies on tobacco trading. As suggested in Chapter 4, one should look at the proportionality test to accurately examine the Court's interpretive equipment against populism. This case is no exception, and the decisive portion of the judgment is found under the last step of 'necessary in a democratic society', where the Court engages in balancing.

Further, and in principle, the parliamentary context is a particularly fertile terrain for examining the Court's ambivalent engagement with (the limits of) its 'democratic society' and populism. On the one hand, it is of prime importance that deliberative pluralism applies to this terrain, in particular the core proposition that Article 10 applies also to ideas and forms of expression that 'shock and offend', as we saw earlier in the chapter. On the other hand, the Court's potential interference with parliamentary affairs – a supranational and judicial interference – engages the issue of respecting, and not protecting, what the Court defines as a 'democratic society'. Parliamentary autonomy – and the parliament's overarching right to define the limits of MPs' immunity to sanctions and fine – is therefore located at another end of the Court's democratic universe, one where deference to domestic authorities is the norm from which the Court can only carefully and exceptionally depart.

The burden of justification falls on the Court, and this may partially explain why the case ultimately reached the Grand Chamber of the Court. Correlatively, the parliamentary context of this case also matters to our diagnosis of populism: parliament combines the democratic functions of deliberation and representation. As we saw in Chapter 5, controlling the parliament via a two-thirds majority was the first and enabling step of Hungary transitioning towards populism. Parliament, if anywhere, is the forum where deliberation and representation should be championed – and, as a result, a ruling and majoritarian populist party can equally distort these functions via the repression of deliberation and representation.

From a close reading of the 'necessary in a democratic society' portion of the case, the Court focuses on the general and specific conditions for imposing sanctions on MPs during their parliamentary exercise in the house, starting with the gross form of abuse of Article 10, namely the use of disciplinary sanctions to silence the opposition:

> Parliamentary autonomy should not be abused for the purpose of suppressing the freedom of expression of MPs, which lies at the heart of political debate in a democracy. It would be incompatible with the purpose and object of the Convention if the Contracting States, by adopting a particular system of parliamentary autonomy, were thereby absolved from their responsibility under the Convention in relation to the exercise of free speech in Parliament.[15]

Yet in *Karácsony* the Court does not concentrate on identifying whether indeed the aim of the interference was to suppress political opposition and democratic debate. Indeed, the Court in this case accepted that the government pursued a Convention-authorized 'legitimate aim' for restricting Article 10 (the second step of the proportionality test), namely the protection of the rights of others, which includes the rights of other MPs running a parliamentary session, as well as the prevention of disorder. Equally, the Court is 'satisfied that that the applicants did not receive sanctions for expressing their views on issues debated in Parliament, but rather for the time, place and manner in which they had done so',[16] which concerns the substance of Article 10. Rather, it is the ulterior imposition of sanctions on MPs that is at stake here – and the conditions under which these sanctions were imposed and contested. In this case, the process consisted of a proposal written by the speaker of the

[15] *Karácsony and Others* v. *Hungary*, para. 147.
[16] *Karácsony*, para. 150.

house to impose fines and its subsequent adoption by the plenary without any debate. And that is the core issue of the case defined as engaging with the procedural limb of Article 10. With the support of past similar cases, the Court established that the threshold for the procedure to count as Convention-compliant ought to be the 'right to be heard' for the sanctioned or fined MP:

> With regard to *ex post facto* disciplinary sanctions, the Court considers that the procedural safeguards available to this effect should include, as a minimum, the right for the MP concerned to be heard in a parliamentary procedure before a sanction is imposed. It notes that the right to be heard would indeed increasingly appear as a basic procedural rule in democratic States, above and beyond judicial procedures.[17]

Now, this threshold of procedures – or the absence thereof – is sufficient to establish a violation of Article 10. Indeed, in the present case the Court found that the procedural guarantees of Hungarian parliamentary law were insufficient: 'they were limited to a general possibility of making a statement in Parliament or petitioning certain parliamentary bodies without any guarantee that the applicants' arguments would be considered in the relevant disciplinary procedure'. In other words, the main concern of the Court is one of including fined or sanctioned individual(s) in the procedure via 'the right to be heard'. The Court insists that 'any *ex post facto* decision imposing a disciplinary sanction should state basic reasons, thus not only enabling the MP concerned to understand the justification for the measure but also permitting some form of public scrutiny of it'.[18]

Yet, from a populist standpoint, one may wonder if the Court is missing the characteristically infrastructural underpinnings of the violation. This suggests that an inclusive procedure, one that would render Hungarian parliamentary law Convention-compliant under the procedural limb of Article 10, is unlikely to effectively tackle the populist capture – whether it is the plenary or specific parliamentary committees. The requirement of including the sanctioned or fined individual falls short of extending deliberative pluralism to representative structures, in particular parliament. The Court's deference to 'parliamentary autonomy' and 'parliamentary law' is the flip side of the Court's relation to 'democratic society':

[17] *Karácsony*, para. 156.
[18] *Karácsony*, para. 158.

> where the underlying purpose of the relevant disciplinary rules is exclusively to ensure the effectiveness of Parliament, and hence that of the democratic process, the margin of appreciation to be afforded in this area should be a wide one. The Court observes that it has already acknowledged that member States have a wide margin of appreciation in the context of the regulation of parliamentary immunity, which belongs to the realm of parliamentary law.[19]

Now, as far the procedural limb of Article 10 is concerned, the Court applies the same line of reasoning in another recent landmark Article 10 case against Hungary, *Mándli and Others* v. *Hungary*.[20] This case adds a layer to our inquiry since it combines both the parliamentary conundrum just discussed and the cherished role that the Court assigns to journalists as 'watchdogs of a democratic society' – a notion that very much builds upon the foundation of deliberative pluralism. As I explain in the next section, in the Court's eyes, the 'watchdog role' is performed not only by the written press, but also by the wider audio-visual media system, as well as virtually every agent whose role is to contribute to a debate of public interest, from academics to NGOs and public intellectuals. In *Mándli*, the applicants were journalists who interviewed MPs on a controversial topic – alleged illicit payments in relation to the Hungarian National Bank – in an area of the parliament not designated for recording purposes. Further, the applicants asked their questions without prior notification either to the MPs themselves or to the speaker of the house. The disciplinary sanction in this case amounted to suspending the accreditation of the journalists in question – a suspension that lasted several months.

It should be noted from the onset that state parties by default enjoy a margin of appreciation in regulating parliamentary affairs, which the Court also includes in its 'democratic society': the Court considers that there is an overriding public interest in ensuring that parliament, while respecting the demands of a free debate, can function effectively and pursue its mission in a democratic society. Therefore, where the purpose of the relevant disciplinary rules is exclusively to ensure the effectiveness of parliament, and hence that of the democratic process, the margin of appreciation to be afforded in this area should be a wide one. Note, as explained in Chapter 4, that the Court does not specify the width of the margin but suggests that the normative and epistemic grounds matter and that is the case here too.

19 *Karácsony*, para. 146.

20 *Mándli and Others* v. *Hungary*, 26 May 2020, Application No. 63164/16.

In resolving *Mándli*, the Court focused on the 'necessary in a democratic society' step of the proportionality test, echoing again the centrality of that step explained in Chapter 4. In reaching that step, however, it is striking again that the Court did not engage in purposive analysis – that is, it did not dwell on the actual aim pursued and its legitimacy – very much as in *Karácsony*. Rather, the Court satisfies itself with establishing the rationality of the link between the sanction imposed and the Convention-listed aim claimed by the government:

> The Court therefore finds no reason to call into question that the impugned sanction imposed on the applicants for breaching the rules of conduct in Parliament was supported by reasons that were relevant for the legitimate aims pursued, namely the prevention of disorder and the protection of the rights of MPs'. [...] As regards the question whether those reasons as such were also sufficient to show that the disputed interference was 'necessary', the Court does not find it necessary to rule on the issue, but considers it more appropriate to focus its review on whether the restriction on the applicants' right to freedom of expression was accompanied by effective and adequate safeguards against abuse.[21]

While the Court rebutted that argument – 'the Court thus accepts that the subject matter of the applicants' recordings was journalistic coverage of an issue of public interest', as in *Karácsony* the Court's approach is not to examine the necessity of the interference itself by elucidating its purpose but to concentrate on the procedural limb of Article 10:

> The Court observes that, at the material time, domestic law, namely the Speaker's Order No. 9/2013 (see paragraph 13 above), contained a restriction on entry in the event of a breach of the relevant provisions, without requiring any assessment of the potential impact of the sanction or the relevance of the journalistic activity giving reason for the restriction. Furthermore, it did not provide for the possibility for persons sanctioned to be involved in the relevant decision-making procedure. The procedure in the applicants' case consisted of a letter addressed to the relevant editors-in-chief informing them of the suspension of the applicants' accreditation.[22]

It is the absence of 'procedural guarantees', in particular the absence of a right for the individual to be included and heard in that procedure, that justifies finding a violation of Article 10 in both *Mándli* and *Karácsony*. It is worth pondering why the Court exclusively opts for this procedural avenue – and why, as the Court puts it, it 'finds it more appropriate to

[21] *Mándli and Others* v. *Hungary*, paras. 70–1.
[22] *Mándli*, para. 73.

concentrate its review on whether the restriction on the applicants' right to freedom of expression was accompanied by effective and adequate safeguards against abuse'.[23]

6.5 Evaluating the Court's Equipment

On the one hand, one could view the emphasis on procedural guarantees as adding an infrastructural layer to the protection against the abuse of interferences with freedom of expression. One could further think that this reinforces the deliberative function of the domestic process – by asking domestic authorities to provide reasons for imposing a fine, for example. As the Court says, 'the Court considers that any *ex post facto* decision imposing a disciplinary sanction should state basic reasons, thus not only enabling the MP concerned to understand the justification for the measure but also permitting some form of public scrutiny of it'.[24] While requiring an infrastructural layer as a procedural obligation for that kind of interference, the Court does not attach requirements as to *how* that procedural obligation should be executed. The Court could have expanded on the requirements of such a process, rather than just requiring its existence. For example, it could have used its tenet of deliberative pluralism to extend requirements beyond the mere requirement of including the individual in the procedure. This is because it is not the very existence of institutions, channels, and procedures that is attacked by populist forces, but *how* these structures are operated. That is characteristic of populist rule: to maintain the facade of an institutional safeguard while running against its very purpose.

On the other hand, proceeding in this basic procedural way at the expense of purposive analysis is to turn a complete blind eye to the wider and infrastructural attack on the media that we documented in Chapter 5. Based on the findings of previous chapters, the reasons for this diagnosis are multilayered. Of course, the Court clearly assigns a great weight to the 'autonomy of Parliament' and the default, yet unspecified, margin of appreciation that goes with it, speaking to the normative justification of subsidiarity. Yet, as we saw in Chapter 4, the theory of subsidiarity does not by itself define the threshold beyond which the Court, as higher-level authority, should step in. As a result, by only relying on principles – 'autonomy of parliament' – rather than

23 *Karácsony and Others* v. *Hungary*, para. 151.

24 *Karácsony*, para. 158.

rules, it remains obscure *when*, and *why*, the principle is sufficiently strong in a particular case, and *against what* it should be balanced. Certainly, it is proportionality that could operate as the specifier, but in both *Karácsony* and *Mándli* the Court explicitly falls short of assessing the weight of principle in the 'necessity in a democratic society' step – rather, it is just blindly grants it to the respondent state. In my view, this amount to analytical failure: it is one thing to grant, say, parliamentary autonomy a significant normative weight *ex ante*, it is yet another to render it *conclusively* weightier *ex post facto*. Proportionality is supposed to mediate at this specific point and establish if indeed it was necessary at all.

More importantly, the Court blatantly fails to scrutinize the (legitimacy of the) aim pursued by the interference. Of course, it is logically deficient to conclude that an interference was rationally connected and necessary to reach an aim if that aim is not defined *a priori*. Yet my concern has more to do with placing an individual interference back in the infrastructural realm that we surveyed in Chapter 6. That is, I worry that the Court not engaging with purposive analysis disables the very possibility of considering the infrastructural breadth of populist capture of the media. Considering the media system currently in place in Hungary, which, as we saw in Chapter 5, is infrastructurally captured by both the purse (media ownership and concentration in the private sector) and the sword (media monitoring, supervision, and oversight in the public sector), it is particularly difficult, for a Court that makes deliberation the cornerstone of its 'democratic society', to seriously conclude that it is effectively responding to the populist attack by only requiring that procedural(-deliberative) obligations exist. As the Court has in many cases ascertained, governments often enact legislation and take decisions with the consequence (often intentionally, sometimes unintentionally) of creating a 'chilling effect' on the media. The Hungarian context provides perhaps an example of this without the coercive element of authoritarianism. Yet, without engaging in purposive analysis, the Court is unlikely to grasp this underlying yet critical aspect. This offers a clear example of where procedural review reviewed in Chapter 4 and understood as the Court focusing on procedural obligations comes at the expense of a thorough proportionality test. Note that a poor purposive analysis is also a legacy of the Court's case law, which has almost always treated the 'legitimate step' as an exercise of descriptive classification rather than analysis proper.

One could imagine the Court engaging in a wider analysis of the media system whose infrastructural variables are *a priori* relevant to the individual circumstances examined in a case. More precisely, this analysis could inform the Court's examination of not just the aim of the specific interference of a specific individual, but also to reason inferentially based on a combination between the individual and the infrastructural. Of course, it is a necessary requirement that the interference with a Convention right is manifest prior to the interpretation of the case – that is why this question comes prior to proportionality analysis in the Court's case law. But recognizing that does not absolve the Court from evaluating the parameters that are infrastructurally relevant to the interference. Typically, the Court could require the body in charge of determining the lawfulness of the interference initially, and the domestic courts reviewing its Convention compatibility subsequently, to address the wider infrastructural capture of the media system as background to the particulars of the case. As I explain in the next section, the Court has shown familiarity with media infrastructure, albeit with some severe limitations. In concrete terms, this approach could amount to a heightened burden of proof placed on these authorities at the step of 'legitimate aim' because that step engages purposive analysis specifically.

Furthermore, 'legitimate aim' is not just concerned with purpose – it is also concerned with 'legitimacy' proper. As I shall explain at more length in Chapter 9, I argue that the account of legitimacy should redefined by a renewed notion of 'democratic society' that includes the infrastructural dimension. Rather than engaging with 'democratic society' at the last, balancing stage, where the deontological ('has the view contributed to an issue of public interest?') and the instrumental ('was it necessary to do x?') are often unhelpfully intertwined, an enhanced 'democratic society' should operate as the normative framework against which the purpose of the interference should be evaluated at this step of the Court's review. It is for the states to demonstrate that they provide guarantees not only that journalists can express dissent individually, but that the infrastructure that sustains and has authority over this exercise does not hamper it – and it could rely not just on its tenet of deliberative pluralism but also on finding in a much more infrastructural fashion whether the government's capture of the media generates a chilling effect on the exercise of Articles 10–11. This shift does not represent a departure from the Court's widely established and principled account of 'democratic society' – rather, it is an 'updated' account of how its tenets are at risk of being violated in the populist context. Another way of specifying this is to bring the Court to break the distinction between the substantive content of Articles 10–11 and its procedural guarantees. It is undoubtedly clear that having a procedural guarantee only does not suffice in the populist context.

This is also where I want to return to the claims made in Chapter 2 about the Court's minimalist approach to democracy. By requiring the respondent state to address the wider infrastructural capture of the media, the Court would effectively recalibrate and enhance its 'democratic society' from the existential approach that its original mandate has been based on. That is, as argued for in Chapter 5, the infrastructural capture distinctive of populism is not coercive and cannot easily fall within the realm of threats that exist categorically outside the democratic realm. The Court ought to align its interpretive equipment with that evolution. While 'procedural safeguards' seem appealing, a closer look indicates that 'procedural guarantees' in fact constitute the weak link of the Court's interpretive apparatus.

The point also applies to the broader infrastructure being largely absent from the Court's reasoning applied to individual cases. In the case of *Matuz* v. *Hungary*, a journalist aimed to alarm public opinion by writing and publishing a book about alleged practices of censorship in the public broadcasting agency of Hungary. This case directly speaks to the effect of media capture reviewed in Chapter 5 – the appointment of a new director of the television company allegedly led to modifying the content of a cultural magazine programme. The Court did not link these allegations to broader concerns about the independence of the media in Hungary. Rather, it only examined how domestic courts used the established interpretive principles of Article 10:

> As a result, they [national courts] did not examine whether and how the subject matter of the applicant's book and the context of its publication could have affected the permissible scope of restriction on his freedom of expression, although it is such an approach that, in principle, would have been compatible with the Convention standards.[25]

It therefore appears that the Court swiftly applies the tenets of its 'democratic society' to cases involving the potential capture of public service media. If freedom of the media is one of the vehicles through which pluralism and deliberation are ensured, then the margin of appreciation left to states parties should be thin even if that impacts the other party significantly (such as in the conflict with the right to reputation

[25] *Matuz* v. *Hungary*, 21 October 2014, Application No. 73571/10, para. 49.

under Article 8). In the same *Matuz* v. *Hungary*, the Court held that 'if the national court demonstrates a lack of sufficient engagement with the general principles of the Court under Article 10 of the Convention, the degree of margin of appreciation afforded to the authorities will necessarily be narrower'.[26] This illustrates the limits procedural review applied to the media domain explained in Chapter 4 in that the Court's scrutiny does not extend beyond the Court's own standards of review which, as I argued throughout this investigation, were tied to an account of democracy that does not incorporate the features of authoritarian pluralism.

The erosion of freedom of expression may result from a broader and enabling ecosystem under indirect governmental control, as we saw in Chapter 5, which extends to dynamics of the public and private media market intersecting with various bodies of domestic law (e.g., competition law), as well as to the role of oversight, supervisory, and regulatory agencies, whether those agencies are specific to the media or to other domains, such as the judicial system. One example is *Baka* v. *Hungary*, where the Court found that the termination of the office of the former president of the Hungarian Supreme Court amounted, among other things, to a violation of Articles 10.[27] The Hungarian government argued that the termination of his office was justified on the basis of ongoing infrastructural reform aimed at 'de-politicising the selection process and enhancing the independence of the judiciary,[28] relying on the restriction clause of 'maintaining the authority and impartiality of the judiciary' within the meaning of Article 10. In response, while the Court did find a violation at the third stage of the proportionality test, namely necessity (whether the changes to the judicial apparatus required the termination of Mr Baka's office) and legitimacy (whether the government had a legitimate aim in the first place), it does not link up the erosion of judicial independence to the erosion of media infrastructure, remaining within the strict domain of the freedom of expression of members of the judiciary and civil servants.[29] In this connection, Kosař and Šipulová have well explained how focusing on Article 10 to tackle authoritarian populism is short-sighted in that it cannot reach the infrastructural

[26] *Matuz* v. *Hungary*, para. 35.

[27] For a similar case involving Article 8 ECHR, see *Erményi* v. *Hungary*, 22 November 2016, Application No. 22254/14.

[28] *Matuz* v. *Hungary*, para. 132.

[29] In this limited sense, see e.g., *Wille* v. *Liechtenstein* (GC), 28 October 1999, Application No. 28396/95, and *Harabin* v. *Slovakia*, 20 November 2012, Application No. 58688/11.

conditions that underpin, for instance, the system of judicial office nomination, as we shall also see in the next chapter.[30] Does the Court have a template for examining the infrastructure of the media domain, and how does it connect to its broader interpretive equipment under Article 10? As I shall exemplify in the next section, infrastructural consideration may enter the Court's reasoning where the state party in question is at risk of turning totalitarian, triggering intervention when the very core of its 'democratic society' is undermined.

6.6 Deliberative Pluralism and Media Infrastructure(s)

I mentioned previously that the Court is not unfamiliar with media infrastructure in its case law. In this section, I dig deeper into these limited cases where the Court has considered the infrastructural implications of its approach to Articles 10–11. As explained at the start of the chapter, the Court's democratic society is structured in a web of rights and correlative obligations, both negative and positive, assigned to both speakers and listeners. This web is particularly relevant to the Court's understanding not just of journalists doing their daily work, but also and more largely of the media system in a supportive and enabling fashion. In the Court's view, the media is chiefly understood as a 'public watchdog' of its 'democratic society' and as such the privileged enabler of deliberative pluralism – although this role can be equally performed by NGOs, scientists, intellectuals, bloggers, and so on. What matters is the function of contributing to existing pluralistic debate of public interest, not the nature of the individual or group exercising expression. Still, since the early days, the Court has principally identified the press and the media as the key enablers and guardians of deliberative pluralism. In another seminal case, *Jersild* v. *Denmark*, the Court clearly derived the role of the press from the right of the individual to be informed on issues of public interest:

> It is nevertheless incumbent on it to impart information and ideas of public interest. Not only does the press have the task of imparting such information and ideas: the *public also has a right to receive them*. Were it otherwise, the press would be unable to play its vital role of 'public watchdog'. Although formulated primarily with regard to the print media, these principles doubtless apply also to the audio-visual media.[31]

[30] Kosař and Šipulová, 'The Strasbourg Court Meets Abusive Constitutionalism'.

[31] *Jersild* v. *Denmark*, para. 31. See also *Thorgeir Thorgeirson* v. *Iceland*, 63, and *Bladet Tromsø and Stensaas* v. *Norway*, para. 62.

This rationale is the same for other persons or entities that perform the same role in society, such as audio-visual companies[32] and NGOs.[33] Now, deliberative pluralism is reinforced in the journalistic context by attaching duties to the deliberative role of journalists and the media. This aspect is particularly relevant to the link between populism and the sensationalist dimension of populism mentioned in Chapter 5. Here, the fine line between exaggeration or provocation as value judgments, on the one hand, and the distortion of facts, on the other hand, is relevant to the Court's assessment. As the Court held as in *Kania and Kittel* v. *Poland*:

> It is true that, when taking part in a public debate on a matter of general concern – like the applicants in the present case – an individual is allowed to have recourse to a degree of exaggeration or even provocation, or in other words to make somewhat immoderate statements [. . .]. However, the Court considers that there is a difference between acceptable exaggeration or provocation, or somewhat immoderate statements, and the distortion of facts known to the journalists at the time of publication.[34]

The Court has continually held that there a distinction between *information* and *value-judgment* on the grounds that the latter cannot be subject to the same factual assessment:

> in the Court's view, a careful distinction needs to be made between facts and value-judgments on this issue. The existence of facts can be demonstrated, whereas the truth of value-judgments is not susceptible of proof. The Court notes in this connection that the facts on which Mr. Lingens founded his value-judgment were undisputed, as was also his good faith.[35]

On the positive side, Strasbourg's 'democratic society' (driven by deliberative pluralism) culminates in a 'right of the public to be informed' on any issue of public interest. In other words, the Court's democratic society is not just a negative freedom to contribute, but a positive framework state parties ought to implement. In *Erdoğdu and İnce* v. *Turkey*, which concerned the interview of a sociologist on the conflict in Kurdistan, the Court asserted that 'domestic authorities in the instant case failed to have sufficient regard to the public's right to be informed of a different perspective on the situation in south-east Turkey, irrespective of how unpalatable that perspective may be for them'.[36]

32 *Radio Twist, A.S.* v. *Slovakia*, 19 December 2006, Application No. 62202/00, paras. 57–8.
33 *Vides Aizsardzības Klubs* v. *Latvia*, 27 May 2004, Application No. 57829/00, para. 42.
34 *Kania and Kittel* v. *Poland*, 21 June 2010, Application No. 35105/04, para. 47.
35 *Lingens* v. *Austria*, para. 42.
36 *Erdoğdu and İnce* v. *Turkey* (GC), 8 July 1999, Application No. 25067/94, para. 51.

While I cannot expand specifically on the limits of Articles 10–11 in this chapter, it is well established that for a particular view or opinion (of public relevance) to be restricted, an incitement to violence and hatred – or, in the context of Article 11 specifically, the risk that an anti-democratic political party is likely to seize power and endanger the democratic process itself once in office (notably by not respecting pluralism)[37] – must be engaged. In *United Communist Party of Turkey and Others* v. *Turkey*, in which the Turkish Communist Party was dissolved by Turkey's constitutional court, the Court held that 'there can be no justification for hindering a political group solely because it seeks to debate in public the situation of part of the State's population and to take part in the nation's political life in order to find, according to democratic rules, solutions capable of satisfying everyone concerned'.[38]

Yet again, the Court finds itself in its comfort zone when it comes to reasserting its classical account of 'democratic society' in the face of a existential threat – that is, where the means used by the domestic authorities and actors are (likely to be) non-democratic. Yet, considering that populist threats are endogenous rather than existential to the democratic realm, the Court may face more acute issues. As shown in Chapter 5, the attack on deliberative pluralism is primarily orchestrated through infrastructural means. To address this dimension, one must turn to the handful of cases pertaining to the public service media system and examine how the principle of deliberative pluralism plays out in the design of infrastructures and the positive obligations attached to it. An illustrative example in that respect is *Centro Europa 7 S.R.L. and Di Stefano* v. *Italy*, in which the applicant alleged that the Italian state unlawfully deprived the applicant's media company of the necessary frequencies for television broadcasting for more than ten years. The Court did find a violation of Article 10, suggesting that the principle of deliberative pluralism extends to an infrastructural level. Indeed, relevant here is the reference to the broader infrastructure of the media system in Italy at the time, and to the RAI-Mediaset duopoly over the available frequencies controlled by the government (under the then-prime minister Silvio Berlusconi). The Court observed that:

> In such a sensitive sector as the audio-visual media, in addition to its negative duty of non-interference the State has a positive obligation to put

[37] *Refah Partisi* v. *Turkey*, para. 87.

[38] *United Communist Party of Turkey and Others* v. *Turkey* (GC), 19 June 2012, Application No. 29400/05, para. 57.

> in place an appropriate legislative and administrative framework to guarantee effective pluralism [. . .]. This is especially desirable when, as in the present case, the national audio-visual system is characterised by a duopoly.[39]

But it is one thing to observe that infrastructural considerations are found in the text of the case, and yet another whether they matter to the Court's reasoning, and whether they are more broadly part and parcel of the Court's interpretive equipment. It is clear that the Court is presented with evidence pointing to the concomitance of media concentration and infrastructural reform, highlighting the risk of democratic distortion. For example, in reviewing the respondent state party's argument for the alleged violation, the Court touches upon the critical role of infrastructural reform ('the general reorganisation of national and local analogue frequencies in a context of limited availability').[40] Furthermore, when turning to its own assessment driven by general principles, the Court contemplates

> a situation whereby a powerful economic or political group in society is permitted to obtain a position of dominance over the audio-visual media and thereby exercise pressure on broadcasters and eventually curtail their editorial freedom undermines the fundamental role of freedom of expression in a democratic society.[41]

Yet, while making a clear link between infrastructure and deliberative pluralism, the decisive portion of the case does not dwell on it. Rather, the violation is found on the sole second step of proportionality, namely 'prescribed by law' (more precisely, 'foreseeability').[42] The Court established that during the transitional period of infrastructural reform between the broadcasting licence being awarded and the allocation of frequencies (explaining the lengthy period during which the applicant's company could not operate), the applicant was not provided with sufficient foreseeability as to when this allocation would take place:

[39] *Centro Europa 7 S.R.L. and Di Stefano* v. *Italy* (GC), 7 June 2012, Application No. 38433/09, para. 134. See also *Informationsverein Lentia and Others* v. *Austria* (GC), 24 November 1993, Application Nos. 13914/88, 15041/89, 15717/89, 15779/89, and 17207/90, para. 38, and *NIT S.R.L.* v. *the Republic of Moldova* (GC), 5 April 2022, Application No. 28470/12, para. 184.

[40] *Centro Europa 7 S.R.L. and Di Stefano* v. *Italy*, para. 117.

[41] *Centro Europa*, para. 133.

[42] For a more recent case illustrating this, see *Objective Television and Radio Broadcasting Company and Others* v. *Azerbaijan*, 18 February 2025, Application No. 257/12.

> [T]he Court considers that the domestic legislative framework lacked clarity and precision and did not enable the applicant company to foresee, with sufficient certainty, the point at which it might be allocated the frequencies and be able to start performing the activity for which it had been granted a licence.[43]

As a result, the Court's decisive reasoning did not address (the distortion) of infrastructure in principled terms, which the stages of 'legitimate aim' (third stage) and 'necessary in a democratic society' (fourth stage) would have potentially allowed. The distinct role that infrastructural erosion plays is overshadowed by the Court's narrow review of legality. While this narrow review certainly speaks to the corruption of the rule of law, it does uncover potential infrastructural distortion. The Court's 'democratic society' is infrastructural in principle, but not in action.

It is important to view these findings in light of the broader equipment of the Court in relation to the overarching principle deliberative pluralism and its applicability to media infrastructure. First, it is worth noting that while having a public service media generally matters to the pursuit of deliberative pluralism in the Court's eyes, in fact there is no (positive) obligation to set one up – rather, the requirement of pluralism applies once the service has been set up. Moreover, it does not follow from this that the Court derives a positive obligation to establish a framework against media concentration, the failure of which underpins the erosion of media infrastructure. While in the case just reviewed the Court does refer to the CoE's legislative activity in this domain – for example, resolutions of the Parliamentary Assembly or the opinion of the CoE's advisory body, the Venice Commission – the Court's decisive portion of the case does not depend on it; rather, the Court retreats into its proportionality considerations limited to 'prescribed by law'. As we saw in the preceding sections of this chapter concerning the procedural arm of Article 10, the Court is decidedly not inclined to enter purposive analysis in the infrastructural context either. This limitation, we shall see, also concerns other aspects of the democratic process, such as the right to free and fair elections in Chapter 8.

Second, this poses the question of when the Court *actually* and distinctively relies on (the failure to uphold) deliberative pluralism in the infrastructural domain to inform the decisive portion of its reasoning in the proportionality test. This is where I return to the broader argument held throughout the investigation, which is that the Court steps in when

[43] *Centro Europa 7 S.R.L. and Di Stefano* v. *Italy*, para. 154.

the necessary conditions of its 'democratic society' are at stake, pointing to a existential threat. Indeed, the obligation of deliberative pluralism in the infrastructural domain applies the most clearly when there is a concentration of ownership within the (public service) system characterized by a monopoly or a duopoly – and when there is virtually no guarantee for including (deliberative and representative) pluralism in the infrastructure of the media system. To see this more clearly, one can refer to the case of *Manole* v. *Moldova*, in which a journalist and presenter complained that her employer, Teleradio-Moldova (TRM), was under total control of the government after the 2001 elections, which saw the Communist Party win a large majority in the parliamentary elections – in particular, a number of senior managers at TRM were removed and replaced by persons loyal to the government – entailing systematic practice of censorship and government propaganda at the administrative level.

In this case, the Court is contemplating a situation where there is only one Moldovan broadcasting organization (TRM) producing television programmes available throughout the country. That is where the Court distinctively relies on pluralism to establish a violation of Article 10 on two counts: first, on the individual level, 'journalists, editors and producers at TRM's television station, must have been affected by these policies',[44] and second, on the infrastructural level, 'the legislative framework throughout the period in question was flawed, in that it did not provide sufficient safeguards against the control of TRM's senior management, and thus its editorial policy, by the political organ of the Government'.[45] To find the latter, the Court scrutinized the operation of the media oversight bodies in place, the 'Audiovisual Coordination Council' and the 'Council of Observers', and found that in the latter case, for example, only one seat was occupied by a representative of the political opposition. Generally, the Court concluded that since the parliament was controlled by one party, safeguards were insufficient, violating the positive obligation of pluralism:

> [D]omestic law did not provide any guarantee of political balance in the composition of TRM's senior management and supervisory body, for example by the inclusion of members appointed by the political opposition, nor any safeguard against interference from the ruling political party in these bodies' decision-making and functioning.[46]

[44] *Manole and Others* v. *Moldova*, 17 September 2009, Application No. 13936/02, para. 106.
[45] *Manole and Others* v. *Moldova*, para. 110.
[46] *Manole*, para. 110.

Here again, the Court finds itself in its comfort zone when it comes to reasserting its classical account of 'democratic society' in the face of a existential threat – that is, when it finds that only one broadcasting organization is under the total control of the majority government – in particular, the Communist Party benefiting from a large majority in parliament. In the authoritarian populist context, the facade is more complex and multifaceted and requires that the Court calibrate its interpretive equipment accordingly. This shows that the Court's review can extend to the infrastructural domain, but only superficially. In fact, in the more recent case of *NIT S.R.L.* v. *the Republic of Moldova*, one can observe how the Court has supervised Moldova's efforts in upholding the positive duty of pluralism in that manner. In that case, the television channel NIT's licence was revoked by the Audiovisual Coordination Council (ACC) in 2012 for failing to provide balanced political coverage, in particular because of accusations of biased support of the communist opposition party in Moldova at the time. While the case centres on the reasons for revocation and its basis in Convention standards, it also highlights, as pointed out the joint dissenting opinion,[47] that NIT was the only provider offering some national coverage of the main opposition party and that procedural safeguards were sufficient, considering the intrusive dimension of the interference, namely revocation. The dissenting judges precisely point to the lack of infrastructural reasoning in how the decision-making of the ACC suffered from methodological shortcomings. For example, the ACC based its findings (regarding the failure to comply with pluralism) on a period of just five days.[48]

6.7 Moving Forward

Pluralism also operates as a threshold for the Court to determine the (wide) limits of its interpretive authority, whether that is in the democratic arena or in the context of media infrastructure. One may draw the intermediary conclusion from this incursion that the Court is well equipped to ensure deliberation (as far as democratic participation and debate are concerned), namely, the protection of minor and dissenting views and entities that may be marginalized both by an authoritarian populist government or by a perceived 'corrupt elite' on the same terms, as well as its robust protection of its 'democratic watchdogs', in particular

[47] Joint Dissenting Opinion of Judges Lemmens, Jelić, and Pavli.
[48] Joint Dissenting Opinion of Judges Lemmens, Jelić, and Pavli.

the press and the media. The ECtHR has made this point most clearly in, for example, *Piermont* v. *France*: '[A] person opposed to official ideas and positions must be able to find a place in the political arena.'[49] In *Young, James, and Webster* v. *United Kingdom*, the Court specifically pointed to minority incorporation and protection in the democratic process: 'democracy does not simply mean that the views of the majority must always prevail. A balance must be achieved which ensures the fair and proper treatment of minorities and avoids any abuse of a dominant position.'[50]

However, in scrutinizing the Court's review of limitations adduced to Articles 10–11, one identifies the limits of its equipment to address the distinctive features of authoritarian populism. Most importantly, the Court is often reluctant to trigger purposive or necessity analysis, which closes the horizon for considering the infrastructural breadth of populist capture of the media system, public and private. The largely formal procedural safeguards afforded to opposition politicians to exercise dissent, we have seen, seem to limit the opportunities of the Court to broaden the horizon of scrutiny, in particularly when the 'procedural arm' effectively replaces the 'substantive arm' of the Court's review of Articles 10–11. The same limitations apply to the scrutiny of its positive equipment, namely the requirement of a pluralistic media system, where the Court seems to extend its examination to representative processes – for example, to the oversight bodies – only when there is apparent risk of total control over the body in question – the total absence of pluralism. This illustrates the ramifications in the Court's reasoning of its minimal account of democracy.

[49] *Piermont* v. *France*, 27 April 1995, Application Nos. 15773/89 and 15774/89, para. 76.
[50] *Young, James, and Webster* v. *United Kingdom*, para. 63.

7

The Rule of Law and the Independence of Justice

The last two chapters have attempted to shed light on how the populist distortion of democracy may be relevant to practices of deliberation and representation under Articles 10–11. This exercise involved viewing the government's submissions and the Court's review process in tandem to evaluate the Court's interpretive equipment in a holistic manner. In accordance with the claims of Chapter 5, I adopted an infrastructural lens to my reconstruction of the government's and the Court's reasoning. This infrastructural lens amounted to examining the extent to which the Court scrutinizes the deliberative and representative records of public authorities, given that deliberation and representation are two core values that populist governments tend to erode. In accordance with the methodological claims of Chapter 4, I focused on the Court's proportionality test and, in particular, on the last step of 'necessity in a democratic society' where the Court's account of democracy (and its limits) is put to test. Proportionality testing can detect the ideal-typical attacks of populism, I argued in that chapter, because of its democracy-, in particular, equality-, enhancing gear.

Yet whether the test as practised by the Court can detect these attacks depends on how democracy is conceived in the first place, which predetermines the scope of the Court's scrutiny. Central to this concern is the premise defended in Chapter 2 that the Court's role is historically associated with preventing the return of existential threats rather than detecting endogenous attacks on democracy. 'Deliberative pluralism', as the thick normative requirement of the Court's 'democratic society' under Articles 10–11, can help examine whether, and to what extent, the Court identifies and counters an interference constructed as populist under the terms selected for this investigation in Chapter 3.

The claim I defended in this chapter is that while the Court's reliance on 'deliberative pluralism' suggests that its interpretive apparatus is apt, in principle, to detect when governments restrict Article 10 on distinctively non- or anti-democratic grounds, the Court's scope of review still proves insufficient when it comes to detecting the infrastructural underpinnings of the violation. As an example, I used the obligation of 'procedural guarantee' for restricting freedom of expression (Article 10) and contesting sanctions imposed on journalists or MPs, which seemed insufficient to prevent the populist erosion of deliberation and representation specifically. It seems inadequate to simply require a public body – such as a parliamentary committee – to include the complainant in the procedure if that committee can expedite the process without much deliberative and representative constraints. Deliberative and representative pluralism qua normative tenets call for a more robust scrutiny of these procedures in the first place. What remains is the detecting function of the proportionality test, whose evaluative power could be augmented and adjusted; I expand on this in the conclusive Chapter 10.

The assumption that governments are applying the Convention in good faith still runs deep. As the Court itself holds, 'the whole structure of the Convention rests on the general assumption that public authorities in the member States act in good faith'.[1] The rise of authoritarian populism questions precisely that assumption and calls for the Court to adjust its scope of scrutiny to the infrastructural and insidious instances where deliberation and representation are repressed. Clearly, as evidenced in the government's argumentation, the references to the margin of appreciation and subsidiarity in that case, as well as the attempt to use and abuse the grounds for restricting the Convention, abound.

7.1 The Rule of Law in the Court's Practice

In this chapter, I turn to the second core trait of populist rule identified in Chapter 5, namely the corruption of the rule of law. The rule of law is a quintessentially infrastructural notion in that its requirements, whether thinly or thickly defined, applies to all realms in which legal and judicial authority is exercised upon individuals, as well as between public authorities (the separation of powers). In its case law, the Court often holds that the rule of law is 'inherent' to all the Convention provisions.[2] Some articles of the Convention are clearly constitutive of the rule law thinly construed, such as Article 6 (the right to a fair trial) or Article 13 (the right to a domestic remedy), but whether the other Convention rights are constitutive of the rule of law or only subject to its requirement is

[1] *Tymoshenko* v. *Ukraine*, 30 April 2013, Application No. 49872/11, para. 294.

[2] *Golder* v. *United Kingdom*, 21 February 1975, Application No. 4451/70.

a normative question. This chapter takes a reconstructive approach – it takes stock of the Court's self-defined attributes of the rule of law and examines them considering populist rule to test the adequacy of the Court's equipment. Former Court president Spanó describes the rule of law as 'a methodological point of departure in the examination of any arguable Convention complaint whilst at the same time creating a frame of reference when the Court interprets and applies the rights and freedoms'.[3] The question that guides this chapter is which aspect(s) of the Convention's rule of law, if any, is specifically relevant to how populist authoritarian rule operates in practice, and how equipped the Court is to address it.

In Chapter 4, I argued that the populist corruption of the rule of law does not take a principled shape in the way that democracy is distorted. Rather, the populist relation to the rule of law is instrumental and contingent all the way down and remains subordinated to the distortion of democracy itself ('the end justifies the means'), which may explain why the manifestations of rule of law corruption in populist regimes vary widely. This corruption can concern thin and rather formal criteria such as the generality and foreseeability of law, but it can also reach the thicker and more substantive requirement of proportionality *stricto sensu* (or 'balancing') and extend to the very existence of key infrastructure upholding the rule of law, such as an independent judiciary. In the latter case, the preconditions for upholding the Convention rights and therefore the primary role accorded to domestic authorities (in accordance with subsidiarity) are at stake. The purpose of the Convention system is at risk if the rule of law-derived requirements of judicial independence, for example, are void of any effectiveness. As we shall see, the Court makes this clear, but whether the protections added to its rule of law apparatus are sufficient is another question.

For the sake of clarity and concision, in this chapter I distinguish between two vantage points for reconstructing and evaluating the Court's response to the populist erosion of the rule of law. On the one hand, the Court generally applies basic and allegedly 'thin' rule of law criteria when it examines alleged violations of most, if not all, Convention rights. For example, the right-interfering norm may be vague, its violations unforeseeable, the ground(s) for restricting rights advanced by the government may be unsubstantiated or invalid, and so on – and these

[3] Spanó, 'The Rule of Law as the Lodestar of the European Convention on Human Rights', 215.

thin criteria importantly cut across all rights protected in the Convention, as the Court makes abundantly clear. It is in that context that Article 18 – as accessory to the Convention rights – deserves special mention and analysis. On the other hand, Article 6 of the Convention (the right to a fair trial) provides a key vantage point for understanding how the Court defines the rule of law, in particular the Court's understanding of the separation of powers and judicial independence via its accounts of 'access to a court' and 'tribunal established by law'.

My argument in this chapter is twofold. With respect to the core perimeter of Article 6, I reconstruct the Court's account of judicial independence that has occupied the Court in recent years. This development speaks directly to the attacks on the judiciary highlighted in a wave of cases against Hungary (through both constitutional overhaul and ordinary acts since 2011) and Poland (through the so-called Amending Act 2017) with references to various bodies and procedures for appointing, regulating, and disciplining judges. In what sense are these attacks populist, and how has the Court responded? Well, a close reading of recent cases shows that indeed governments prominently refer to democracy and subsidiarity to justify their reform of the judiciary. The margin of appreciation is recurrently if not systematically invoked. In the Court's response, what is striking is the novel posture of the Court resisting the idea, loudly defended by these governments, and previously articulated by the Court, that there is no 'universal system' for regulating the office of the judge. Recent cases show that the Court is ready to broaden the scope of the right of access to a court to members of an oversight body (e.g., national judicial councils) and making exceptions to this access more difficult to justify, for example. This shows that the Court can, considering the pernicious attempt to (ab)use the Convention, refine its lens to identify instances of rule of law corruption of a predominantly infrastructural kind.

In doing so, the Court seems to envision that countering the erosion of its 'democratic society' requires going beyond an interpretive approach largely dominated by test devices – in particular, the 'Ástráðsson' test[4] for defining 'tribunal established by law', and the 'Eskelinen' test[5] for the criteria justifying exclusion from access to a court – and examining the enabling and infrastructural factors, both legal and political, that

[4] *Guðmundur Andri Ástráðsson* v. *Iceland* (GC), 1 December 2020, Application No. 26374/18.

[5] *Vilho Eskelinen and Others* v. *Finland* (GC), 19 April 2007, Application No. 63235/00.

ultimately corrupt the rule of law in the domestic arena. In the Polish context, for example, it is quite striking that the Court engages in an all-encompassing analysis not just of the individual circumstances of the alleged violation, but also of the vast overhaul of the judicial system, taking a distinctly infrastructural perspective. But the implications of that interpretive stretch remain unclear: with respect to judicial independence, for example, I suggest that broadening the scope of the bodies and roles that ought to be independent and impartial in the (supra)judicial arena in fact could apply to a much wider set of oversight, supervisory, and regulatory functions beyond the judicial arena. The examples of disciplinary chambers[6] and national judicial councils,[7] we shall see, indicate that the issue has less to do with the judicial office per se and a lot more with the very values of independence and impartiality. When judicial independence is corrupt, 'fourth branch' or 'guarantor institutions' are at high risk of erosion too.[8] Moreover, as we shall see in the context of electoral rights in Chapter 8, the Court has enhanced its protection of the same values of independence and impartiality, pointing to a value-based convergence across Convention articles.

With respect to the thin rule of law criteria, I suggest another step of the proportionality test (in addition to the step of 'necessary in a democratic society' reviewed in Chapter 4) is vulnerable to populist corruption, namely the step of 'legitimate aim'. At this step, the respondent state party needs to specify if the interference pursued a legitimate aim listed in the Convention. The idea that restrictions adduced to Convention rights need to pursue a Convention-authorized aim is central to the Court's proportionality test, which, as a matter of theory, is one core component of the rule of law thinly construed. However, the demarcation between thin and thick criteria becomes far less clear when the Court has recourse to Article 18 to assess whether there was an ulterior purpose – a predominant one – and, effectively, to specify what a 'legitimate aim' can be. This article, we shall see, is supposed to filter the purposes of a right's interference, to ensure that these purposes are Convention-compliant, in particular the protection of democracy and the rule of law. It is not just that the triggering of Article 18 should be seen as an attempt to have recourse to broader factual, and allegedly

6 *Reczkowicz* v. *Poland.*

7 *Grzęda* v. *Poland.*

8 Tarunabh Khaitan, 'Guarantor Institutions', *Asian Journal of Comparative Law* 16, no. 1 (2021): 40–59. Mark Tushnet, *The New Fourth Branch: Institutions for Protecting Constitutional Democracy* (Cambridge University Press, 2021).

infrastructural, considerations to discern the actual and predominant aim pursued by the interference. In addition, the criterion of a 'hidden' but predominant purpose brings back the Court's conception and approach to democracy through the back door: before empirically finding whether there was indeed an ulterior purpose and therefore a government acting in bad faith, what makes a purpose legitimate, and how does one go about establishing that?

7.1.1 Article 6 and a 'Tribunal Established by Law'

In this first section, I examine how the Court has come to elaborate on the rule of law within the scope of Article 6 with particular emphasis on judicial independence. As previously indicated, the threat to judicial independence epitomizes the infrastructural kind of attack in the populist toolbox. Yet one cannot grasp the meaning of judicial independence in the Convention system without the notion from which it derives in the Court's practice, namely the rule of law – and that is also, but not only, because there is no self-standing (subjective) right to judicial independence in the Convention or in the case law. Now, one only need read the Preamble to the Convention to measure how foundational and all-encompassing the rule of law is to the Convention system as a whole in the minds of the Convention drafters: 'being resolved, as the governments of European countries which are like-minded and have a common heritage of political traditions, ideals, freedom and the rule of law'.[9] Now, this celebration should not hide the particularly elusive character of the rule of law when it comes to specifying its constitutive and peripheral requirements, and the Convention's relation to it is no exception. Furthermore, state parties often attempt to justify violations of the rule of law by relying on . . . the rule of law and democracy. As we have already seen in the last chapter, state parties may employ 'the independence and impartiality of the judiciary' to undermine the rule of law, such as the disciplining of judges. This explains why one must proceed carefully by zooming in on specific provisions and reconstruct how the Court scrutinizes state records in practice.

As one of the uncontested and constitutive requirements of the rule of law, Article 6 protects the right to a fair trial and can provide a point of departure for reconstructing the Court's definition in this domain. In the abstract, the right to a fair trial resonates with guarantees of due process

[9] Preamble to the Convention.

and equality of arms, and these encompass both criminal and civil proceedings. Yet examining the Court's record of obligations under Article 6 suggests an incremental development of its content through seminal cases brought before it. Most importantly, as scholars and students of the Convention will know, the perimeter of Article 6 has been primarily structured around the obligation to secure access to a court since the seminal case of *Golder* v. *United Kingdom*. From then on, the Court has been keen to make an intrinsic and direct link between Article 6 and access to a court and established that this link derives from the rule of law itself. In the words of Lautenbach, 'the rule of law should be seen as the main reason the ECtHR has broadened the scope of Article 6 to include access to court, both with regard to cases that concern civil rights and obligations and those that concern a criminal charge'.[10]

The second important step here is the Court's extension of the key notion of access to a court as potentially applying to civil servants, not only individuals in the general sense. In the case of *Pellegrin* v. *France*, the Court held that some public servants, despite holding a position in the exercise of 'protecting the general interests of the state',[11] may fall within the protections afforded by Article 6. In *Vilho Eskelinen* v. *Finland*, the Court specified its findings and held that state parties could exclude access to a court when domestic law expressly does so, or when such exclusion is justified on objective grounds in the state's interest. Why do these conditions matter, one may ask? Well, unsurprisingly, these conditions have subsidiarity at their core, as the Court holds:

> it is primarily for the Contracting States, in particular the competent national legislature, not the Court, to identify expressly those areas of public service involving the exercise of the discretionary powers intrinsic to State sovereignty where the interests of the individual must give way. The Court exerts its supervisory role subject to the principle of subsidiarity [. . .].[12]

As we shall see, these conditions – summarized as the *Eskelinen test* – have been at the centre of attention in recent cases pertaining to the dismissal of judges and membership of judicial councils. It is in that specific context of Article 6 and the conditions for excluding particular individuals and groups from access to a court that the issue of judicial

[10] Geranne Lautenbach, *The Concept of the Rule of Law and the European Court of Human Rights* (Oxford University Press, 2013), 130.
[11] *Pellegrin* v. *France* (GC), 8 December 1999, Application No. 28541/95, para. 63.
[12] *Vilho Eskelinen and Others* v. *Finland*, paras. 61–2.

independence in the Court's practice prominently arises. Yet this rather complex web of rights and obligations also matters because of the absence of an overarching (subjective) right to judicial independence in the Convention. As a result, judges have had to rely not only on Article 6 and its content, but also Article 10 and Article 8 to have their case assessed by the Court, as we also saw in Chapter 6 with respect to freedom of expression.

Still, Article 6 includes requirements that are prima facie specific to the office of the judge. A third step of the Court's incremental case law on the rule of law pertains to 'independence' and 'impartiality', which the Court defines vis-à-vis the other branches of government. Access to a court would be meaningless without having the conditions of its independence and impartiality secured – and as we saw in the last chapters, populist rule often preserves the facade of such rights and a rule of law-protective institution or body while corrupting and perverting its internal functioning. Taking a relatively recent case as an example, the general principles developed by the Court are that independence

> characterises both (i) a state of mind, which denotes a judge's imperviousness to external pressure as a matter of moral integrity, and (ii) a set of institutional and operational arrangements – involving both a procedure by which judges can be appointed in a manner that ensures their independence and selection criteria based on merit, which must provide safeguards against undue influence and/or unfettered discretion of the other state powers, both at the initial stage of the appointment of a judge and during the exercise of his or her duties.[13]

With respect to impartiality, the general principle under Article 6 is to operate

> (i) a subjective test, where regard must be had to the personal conviction and behaviour of a particular judge, that is, whether the judge held any personal prejudice or bias in a given case; and (ii) an objective test, that is to say by ascertaining whether the tribunal itself and, among other aspects, its composition, offered sufficient guarantees to exclude any legitimate doubt in respect of its impartiality.[14]

Now, the Court has established these principles with reference to the judicial office, but the question that populism raises is whether these

[13] *Xhoxhaj* v. *Albania*, 9 February 2021, Application No. 15227/19, para. 289.

[14] See also *Lavents* v. *Latvia*, 28 November 2002, Application No. 58442/00, para. 118; *Kyprianou* v. *Cyprus* (GC), 15 December 2005, Application No. 73797/01, para. 118; *Micallef* v. *Malta* (GC), 15 October 2009, Application No. 17056/06, para. 93.

principles, which the Court derives from a more encompassing account of the rule of law, should have their application confined to the judicial office given the infrastructural mode of attack characteristic of the authoritarian populist textbook, or whether they could inform the scrutiny of a wider family of supervisory, oversight, and regulatory bodies.

With this basic interpretive equipment in mind, one can turn to the wave of cases that the Court recently delivered with specific emphasis on judicial independence. One series of cases concerns the Disciplinary Chamber of the Supreme Court that the Polish government installed as a result of the now well-known Amending Act (2017), which granted the Polish parliament (Sjem) the competence to elect members of the new National Council of the Judiciary (NCJ). In the case of *Reczkowicz* v. *Poland*, for example, the applicant complained that her case was not examined by a 'tribunal established by law' under Article 6 and the guarantees of independence and impartiality precisely because the NCJ effectively controlled the functioning of the Disciplinary Chamber of the Supreme Court (since the NCJ recommends applicants to that chamber to the President).[15] This case is not only highly illustrative of how the infrastructural mode of attack pervades the Court's reasoning with respect to Article 6. It also provides insights on the instrumental use of the Convention by the Polish authorities and the (ab)use of the discretion attached to subsidiarity built into the Court's adjudication.

I shall emphasize two main points in this respect. First, the Polish government indeed defended its compliance with Article 6 by exploiting the space left to state parties by subsidiarity at the level of interpretation. It argued that the Convention does not prescribe a specific system of elections for judges and invoked the margin of appreciation in that regard:

> The Convention did not imply an obligation to apply a specific mode of appointment of judges to the highest courts of the Contracting States. The Convention did not require the appointment of judicial councils or their participation in the procedure for appointment of judges. Moreover, the Convention did not require the States to comply with any theoretical constitutional concepts regarding the permissible limits of the powers' interactions.[16]

[15] Subsequent similar cases include *Tuleya* v. *Poland*, 6 July 2023, Application Nos. 21181/19 and 51751/20; *Dolińska-Ficek and Ozimek* v. *Poland*, 8 November 2021, Application Nos. 49868/19 and 57511/19; and *Advance Pharma SP. Z O.O* v. *Poland*, 3 February 2022, Application No. 1469/20.

[16] *Reczkowicz* v. *Poland*, para. 196.

The government also reminded the Courts of its subsidiary role as a supranational adjudicatory body – in particular, the remedial form of subsidiarity analysed in Chapter 4: 'the Court was limited by the principle of subsidiarity, which allowed the High Contracting States to decide which measures to take to ensure the rights and freedoms of individuals and to implement the Convention guarantees'.[17] The reference to democracy is also visible in the government defending the mode of nominating new members of the NCJ – 'the new system allowing the candidates to be presented by a group of citizens or other judges ensured greater representativeness of the NCJ'.[18] As for Articles 10–11, examined in Chapter 6, this is evidence of the (ab) use of the Convention and the space preserved by subsidiarity, not of its denunciation as an international instrument.

Second, with respect to the specific requirement under Article 6 that a tribunal be 'established by law', the government made the formal claim that 'the constitution did not determine, however, who would elect these judges or how they would be elected'.[19] This is directly relevant to the Ástráðsson test according to which a tribunal fails to be established by law when there is a manifest breach of domestic law (first step). In response to these arguments, the Court had to go beyond the test device and appeal to both teleological and substantive considerations by examining whether the 2017 Amending Act, which regulates both the NCJ and the Disciplinary Chamber, includes sufficient guarantees of independence and impartiality. Indeed, taking a teleological approach, 'the Court has been unable to detect any attempt on the part of the Constitutional Court to explain its judgment why and how the new election model would better serve the interest of the judiciary and equal opportunities or whether, and if so how, it would impact upon the NCJ's primary constitutional obligation of safeguarding the independence of courts and judges'.[20] Taking a substantive angle, the Court asserted that the 2017 Amending Act 'practically removed not only the previous representative system but also the safeguards of the judiciary in that regard.' This, in effect, enabled the executive and the legislature to interfere directly or indirectly in the judicial appointment procedure [. . .]'.[21] It is therefore this

[17] *Reczkowicz*, para. 199
[18] *Reczkowicz*, para. 200.
[19] *Reczkowicz*, para. 199
[20] *Reczkowicz*, para. 239.
[21] *Reczkowicz*, para. 274.

detour through the substantive principles of independence and impartiality, which the Polish Supreme Court upheld against its counterpart, the Constitutional Court,[22] that allowed the Court to conclude that there was a manifest breach of domestic law as part of the Ástráðsson test, and to find a violation of Article 6. As we shall see later, this illustrates the Court's attempt to confine its reasoning within the tests established by its own practice while expanding the content and the substantive principles located herein.

7.1.2 Article 6 and the Broadening of 'Access to a Court'

As we have just seen, the Court in *Reczkowicz* examined the 2017 Amending Act and the compliance of the NCJ with Article 6 to address the question of whether the Disciplinary Chamber of the Supreme Court, which is controlled by the NCJ as a result of the Act, is a 'tribunal established by law'. I showed that the Court heavily mobilized its principles of independence and impartiality to ultimately assess the rule of law compliance of the Amending Act. As I further explain in what follows, this reasoning indicates the Court's disposition to move beyond thin criteria of the rule of law in favour of a more substantive approach. In other words, it indicates that domestic authorities cannot assume that Convention compliance is guaranteed by adhering to a formal law-making process – and, as such, may be viewed as an apt response to the hollowing out of that process by populist rulers. The larger question that emerges from this, however, is why these substantive principles ought to be confined to the judicial sphere if indeed they are constitutive of the rule of law in the Court's eyes. There are indications but no firm or clear strand of reasoning that the same principles of impartiality and independence could apply, for example, to a media oversight body.[23]

In *Grzęda* v. *Poland*, the Court had to examine the judges sitting on the NCJ having had their terms of office prematurely terminated by the same Act, which provides another angle on the Convention-based account of the rule of law compliance of the Polish judicial reform.[24] In that context, the Court had to grapple with the *Eskelinen* test, which allows state parties to exclude certain civil servants from access to a court as required by Article 6. Here again, the government did not only contend that sitting

[22] *Reczkowicz*, paras. 94–5.

[23] As analysed in Chapter 6, the Joint Dissenting Opinion of Judges Lemmens, Jelić, and Pavli in *NIT S.R.L.* v. *The Republic of Moldova*.

[24] See also *Żurek* v. *Poland*, 16 June 2022, Application No. 39650/18.

on the NCJ did not constitute employment and therefore could not benefit from access to a court under the first stage of the test – 'the fact of being a member of the NCJ could not be regarded as a right either under domestic law or under the Convention'[25] – but also argued at the same time that 'the subject-matter of the applicant's complaint related exclusively to the exercise of State power'.[26] More importantly for our investigation, the government appealed directly to democracy to justify the early termination:

> [T]he 'democratisation' of the NCJ election procedure constituted an important public interest which justified in turn the early termination of the term of office of the NCJ's judicial members. In this context, the Government submitted that under the 2017 Amending Act judicial members of the NCJ were to be elected by the *Sejm* from among the judges who obtained an adequate support from other judges or from citizens.[27]

This argument reflects the ideational basis of populism reviewed in Chapter 4 in that democracy is distorted by being deprived of its deliberative and representative requirements.

Turning to the Court's analysis of these arguments, one can discern an effort by the Court to strengthen the foundations of the rule of law in the absence of self-standing provision in the Convention protecting the rule of law. As explained earlier, Article 6 provides a pathway to the Court's account of the rule of law by its established criteria of access to a court. Yet, rather than focusing on the *Eskelinen* test directly, the Court first aimed at gathering evidence, in legal-positive terms, of the close nexus between its account of the rule of law and the requirement of judicial independence by citing, *inter alia*, the Preamble and the Venice Commission.[28] In the Court's view, 'it followed from the above that the independence of the judiciary was an underpinning element of the rule of law and thus of the protection of human rights'.[29] Still, the Court had to grapple with its *Eskelinen* criteria simply because the government attempted to demonstrate that its exclusion of members of the NCJ was justified on the test's grounds – that the NCJ 'did not constitute "employment" or any other comparable legal relationship',[30] and 'the subject-

[25] *Grzęda* v. *Poland*, para. 178.
[26] *Grzęda*, para. 184.
[27] *Grzęda*, para. 187.
[28] *Grzęda*, para. 254.
[29] *Grzęda*, para. 264.
[30] *Grzęda*, para. 178.

matter of the applicant's complaint related exclusively to the exercise of State power (*acta iure imperii*)'.[31]

It is at this second step that one can discern the Court shifting from the formalities of the test and elaborating, in substantive terms, on the importance of the judiciary in a democratic society:

> the Court considers that its examination of the second condition of the *Eskelinen* test must take due account of the fact that the present case is closely related to judicial independence, since the dispute at issue concerns a judicial member of the NCJ, which is the constitutional body with responsibility for safeguarding the independence of courts and judges.[32]

This then allows the Court to extend the judicial functions concerned by the principles of independence and impartiality: 'in this connection, the Court considers that judicial independence should be understood in an inclusive manner and apply not only to a judge in his or her adjudicating role, but also to other official functions that a judge may be called upon to perform that are closely connected with the judicial system'.[33] This extension also includes the requirement that no fewer than half of judicial council members should be chosen by judges themselves.

Furthermore, this elaboration highlights the more important role that proportionality can play in examining judicial reform. The Polish government claimed that the new mode of electing judges to the NCJ was a proportionate measure to implement the judgment of the Polish Constitutional Court. Yet the Court clarified that

> the Court is not persuaded by the Government's assertion that the implementation of the judgment of 20 June 2017 could not have been accomplished without the shortening of the terms of office of the sitting judicial members of the NCJ. Nor is it convinced that the introduction of a new system without such shortening would have both unduly extended that process over time and complicated it.[34]

At the same time, the Court had to reiterate the substance of its rule of law principles while preserving and demonstrating the principle of subsidiarity.[35] As with its findings on a 'tribunal established by law', the Court comes to terms with the fact that the government cannot be assumed to adhere to a law-making process that is substantively, and

[31] *Grzęda*, para. 184.
[32] *Grzęda*, para. 300.
[33] *Grzęda*, para. 303.
[34] *Grzęda*, para. 279.
[35] Including by direct reference to Protocol 15 at para. 324.

not just formally, valid. Towards the end of the judgment, the Court reiterates its supervisory mantra of 'shared responsibility' without which the Convention system cannot operate: 'the Court would emphasise that the Convention system cannot function properly without independent judges. The Contracting Parties' task of ensuring judicial independence is thus of crucial importance.'[36] In analogy to 'tribunal established by law', therefore, the Court stretched its account of the test device to essentially affirm and develop the scope of application of its substantive principles.

The open question that emerges from reconstructing this portion of the case law is whether the Court's understanding of judicial independence in an 'inclusive manner' to include judicial councils could also extend the reach of its principles of independence and impartiality to other oversight, supervisory, and regulatory bodies performing a similar function outside the strict judicial sphere – often called the 'fourth branch' institutions – whose function also requires independence (if not impartiality).[37] The body of case law just reviewed derived from a single article (Article 6) centred on the judicial function, but one may wonder about other offices within the judicial branch[38] and, considering the authoritarian populist logic contemplated in this investigation, one may also wonder if these guarantees could fall under Court's purview when it adjudicates other bodies in connection with other rights of the Convention. This also links up with the previous chapter centred on media oversight bodies and the next chapter where another such body, namely electoral commissions, will be addressed. Such bodies often present a hybrid character – executive, administrative, legislative, and (quasi-)judicial – with respect to constitutional, statutory, or just policy norms whose commonality is that they are 'non-self-enforcing', namely norms that 'powerful existing actors in the polity are likely to have reasons and capacity to frustrate'.[39] While the literature in constitutional theory suggests constitutionalizing these bodies, in the Court's context they could be anchored in the Court's 'democratic society' and inform its repertoire of 'democratic watchdogs' with added weight in the proportionality test.

36 *Grzęda* v. *Poland*, para. 324.

37 *Grzęda*, para. 300.

38 Kosař and Šipulová, 'The Strasbourg Court Meets Abusive Constitutionalism'; David Kosař, Katarína Šipulová, and Ondřej Kadlec, 'The Case for Judicial Councils as Fourth-Branch Institutions', *European Constitutional Law Review* 20, no. 1 (2024): 82–119.

39 Khaitan, 'Guarantor Institutions', 53.

7.2 Article 18 and the 'Pandora's Box' of the Convention

Having taken the vantage point of Article 6, in this second section I examine another provision of the Convention that bridges the 'rule of law'- and the 'democracy'-protecting equipment of the Court, namely Article 18. The article concerns the (ab)use of restriction or limitation clauses of rights – as the Convention specifies them – by governments. As the text of the provision states, 'an ulterior purpose is a purpose which is not prescribed by the relevant provision of the Convention and which is different from that proclaimed by the authorities (or the one which can be reasonably inferred from the context)'. Like Article 14 (the Convention provision against discrimination), Article 18 can be invoked only in conjunction with another qualified provision of the Convention. The reason why Article 18 bridges the 'rule of law' and 'democracy' values is that, in fact, its potential scope of application transcends these listed aims and more widely applies to purpose(s) of the Convention itself, as I suggest later (Chapter 9).

The text and function of Article 18 makes it a relatively special provision of the Convention and, allegedly, a quite unique one in the wider realm of international human rights law. The question is what exactly makes this provision special, and why. One angle is to focus on the function of the provision and its scope of application. As the previous paragraph makes clear, the function of Article 18 is *accessory*: it is conceived to raise further questions about the purpose of the interference, and therefore these questions can only be raised, again, in the context of the alleged violation of another qualified right of the Convention (esp. Article 5 and Articles 8–11, which all contain limitation or restriction clauses). The Court may also find ulterior purposes that are illegitimate but not predominant, in which case no violation is found. Of course, the Court does not examine purpose-centred questions if the applicant does not claim this specific right violation in the first place.

Article 18 also remains special in that the purpose questions can in addition be answered independently from the qualified right with which they are considered. Indeed, what grounds the illegitimacy of purposes is not only derived from the established list of legitimate aims of qualified rights (in particular, Articles 8–11), which broadly cover 'national security or public safety', 'the prevention of disorder or crime', 'the protection of health or morals', 'the protection of the rights and freedoms of others', or 'maintaining the authority and impartiality of the judiciary'. As the Court explains in various seminal cases, the prescribed purposes can also be derived from 'the Convention itself'.[40] As the Court's guide to Article 18 confirms, this article 'does not, however, serve merely to clarify the scope of the restriction clauses. It also expressly prohibits the High Contracting Parties from restricting the rights and freedoms enshrined in the Convention for purposes not prescribed by the Convention itself, and to this extent it is autonomous.'[41] This is where, in my view, the specialness lies: Article 18 opens an exceptionally wide, and so far unspecified, realm of normative concerns that could be subject to a bad faith test. That is also where considerations of subsidiarity matter: as argued in Chapter 4, the Court is structurally conditioned by subsidiarity at the interpretive stage, and the persistent history of assuming the governments' good faith. The idea that Article 18 opens unchartered territory has been advanced in the recent literature dedicated to that article. Çalı has pioneered the idea that 'given that bad faith is now out of the Pandora's box, however, the central challenge for the Court is to identify how this doctrine can have purchase across Convention rights and what consequences should follow from finding Article 18 violations'.[42]

The basic reason why Article 18 matters in the context of authoritarian populism specifically is that its distinctive features – the distortion of deliberation and representation, as explained in Chapter 4 – may help guide the Court in selecting which aspects of the respondent state are

[40] *Selahattin Demirtaş* v. *Turkey* (GC), 22 December 2020, Application No. 14305/17, para. 421.

[41] Registry of the European Court of Human Rights, 'Guide on Article 18 of the Convention – Limitation on Use of Restrictions on Rights', ECHR-KS, 28 February 2025 https://ks.echr.coe.int/documents/d/echr-ks/guide_art_18_eng#:~:text=This%20particular%20Guide%20analyses%20and%20sums%20up%20the,principles%20in%20this%20area%20and%20the%20relevant%20precedents.

[42] Başak Çalı, 'Coping with Crisis: Whither the Variable Geometry in the Jurisprudence of the European Court of Human Rights', *Wisconsin International Law Journal* 35, no. 2 (2018), 273. See also Joseph Finnerty, 'When Is a State's "Hidden Agenda" Proven? The Role of the Merabishvili's Three-Legged Evidentiary Test in the Article 18 Strasbourg Case Law', *European Convention on Human Rights Law Review* 4, no. 4 (2023): 447–72; Joseph Finnerty, 'How Should the European Court of Human Rights Remedy Violations of Article 18 ECHR? The Case for Remedial Realignment', *European Convention on Human Rights Law Review* 5, no. 3 (2024): 380–99; Tobias Mortier, 'Reprehensible or Legitimate Aims? A Proposal for a New Approach to Article 18 ECHR in Light of its Predominance Test', *European Convention on Human Rights Law Review* 4, no. 2 (2023): 133–78.

suitable for an Article 18 analysis (when invoked by the applicant). More precisely, in line with the conclusions of Chapter 5, the question is whether the Court is not only examining bad faith as applying to the coercive and individualistic plane, which would typically take place under Article 5 alleged violations. Indeed, authoritarian governments archetypically use the coercive powers of criminal law to silence opposition figures while invoking a Convention-authorized, but easily abusable, aim – for example, 'the protection of public order'. In fact, as we shall see, the majority of cases where the Court considered bad faith violations involved Article 5 with reference to coercive practice of the state under criminal law. It is true that the Court most recently extended the application of Article 18 to Article 6 cases (it did not previously, based on Article 6 not forming part of 'qualified rights' that do not include restriction clauses that can be abused). In the interstate case of *Ukraine* v. *Russia (re Crimea)*, the Court found an 'administrative practice' of grave human rights violations (including forced disappearances, killings, and torture) and that Crimean courts could be considered 'established by law'.[43] The use of Article 18 here highlighted how far a state party can go in claiming Convention compliance while systematically violating the most basic human rights. Yet, from a populist perspective, it is the more insidious forms of attack upon the democratic process and the rule of law that primarily matter, relying on infrastructural findings to corroborate evidence of an ulterior purpose.

As hypothesized in preceding chapters, the premise here is that there is terminological and normative indeterminacy around the purposes and legitimate aims for which Convention rights – in particular, its qualified rights – can be restricted in the first place. This does not only concern the overarching condition of 'necessary in a democratic society' as the balancing and last step of the proportionality test. This indeterminacy also concerns the specification of the 'legitimate aim' pursued by the government, which conventionally corresponds to the third stage of the proportionality test. At that stage, the Court already has an opportunity to review the purpose of the interference – and whether in fact there was another, ulterior but predominant purpose that the government did not disclose. The ensuing question is whether a revision of the 'legitimate aim' test, which is highlighted by the increasing recourse to Article 18, is

[43] *Ukraine* v. *Russia (re Crimea)* (GC), 25 June 2024, Application Nos. 20958/14 and 38334/18.

warranted for the Court to strengthen its interpretive equipment in the authoritarian populist context.

7.2.1 'Beyond Proof': Over What?

The emerging literature on the evolution of Article 18 in the Court's case law has emphasized that, initially and for a long time, the Court assigned an extremely high evidentiary burden to the applicant to prove the bad faith of the government's alleged aim for the restriction.[44] An example of the almost-insurmountable level of proof can be discerned in the case of *Khodorkovskiy* v. *Russia*, in which the applicant, one of the richest people in Russia and the major shareholder in one of Russia's formerly largest oil companies (Yukos), complained that his pre-trial detention by the Russian authorities was politically motivated:

> [I]t is not sufficient for this Court to conclude that the whole legal machinery of the respondent State in the present case was *ab initio* misused, that from the beginning to the end the authorities were acting with bad faith and in blatant disregard of the Convention. This is a very serious claim which requires an incontrovertible and direct proof.[45]

The standard of proof in effect implies that the applicant must 'convincingly rebut' the assumption of good faith. But that is not all. As we shall see later, the applicant must also show there was an ulterior and illegitimate motive, and that this motive was the *predominant* one if there were several purposes discernible. To pass the threshold, the applicant is required to have direct proof of the existence of that motive, or at the very least that this motive can be 'reasonably inferred from the context'. This is exemplified in the case of *Tymoshenko* v. *Ukraine*, in which the applicant, a former prime minister of Ukraine, contested the motive for her detention conditions by the Ukrainian authorities: 'an applicant alleging that his rights and freedoms were limited for an improper reason must

[44] Floris Tan, 'The Dawn of Article 18 ECHR: A Safeguard against European Rule of Law Backsliding?', *Goettingen Journal of International Law* 9, no. 1 (2018): 109–41; Corina Heri, 'Loyalty, Subsidiarity, and Article 18 ECHR: How the ECtHR Deals with Mala Fide Limitations of Rights', *European Convention on Human Rights Law Review* 1, no. 1 (2020): 25–61; Joseph Finnerty, 'When Is a State's "Hidden Agenda" Proven? The Role of the Merabishvili's Three-Legged Evidentiary Test in the Article 18 Strasbourg Case Law', *European Convention on Human Rights Law Review* 4, no. 4 (2023): 447–72; Finnerty, 'How Should the European Court of Human Rights Remedy Violations of Article 18 ECHR?'

[45] *Khodorkovskiy* v. *Russia*, 31 May 2011, Application No. 5829/04, para. 260.

convincingly show that the real aim of the authorities was not the same as that proclaimed or which could be reasonably inferred from the context'.[46] It appears that there is a larger spectrum of criteria spanning from 'direct' proof to a more indirect set of inferences being drawn from a wider set of sources that may describe an 'entire legal machinery' being abused. As Tan comments, 'the Court never explained on what basis it decided whether direct evidence was required, or whether circumstantial evidence sufficed'.[47] Moreover, the Court exercised discretion in zooming in on certain features of the case that could be subject to a bad faith test – a discretion that amounts to a normative choice as to which of the features matter, and why. In the same *Tymoshenko* v. *Ukraine*,

> the Court discerned several specific features of the applicant's pre-trial detention which allow it to look into the matter separately from the more general context of the allegedly politically motivated prosecution of the applicant as an opposition leader by instigating several criminal charges after the change of power and before the Parliamentary elections.[48]

This raises the question of which aspect of a violation is relevant for the purpose of Article 18, and what makes it normatively significant. Yet, since the seminal decision of *Merabishvili* v. *Georgia*, which concerned the pre-trial detention of a prominent Georgian opposition politician and former prime minister of Georgia, the Court has shown a clear openness to reversing the burden of proof onto the government and also specifying its governing criterion of a proof 'beyond reasonable doubt' in order to establish violations of Article 18: 'such proof can follow from the coexistence of sufficiently strong, clear and concordant inferences or similar unrebutted presumptions of fact'.[49] As pointed out by recent literature on Article 18, the Court came to establish a 'three-legged test' to which the new 'beyond proof' standard should apply, namely, the fundamental aspect of the case criterion, the identification of an ulterior purpose criterion, and the predominance criterion. Finnerty comments that 'his recalibration of the standard and burden of proof was motivated by the Court's recognition of the evidentiary difficulties faced by applicants in certain case contexts, particularly in those concerning Article 18'.[50] Yet

[46] *Tymoshenko* v. *Ukraine*, para. 294.
[47] Tan, 'The Dawn of Article 18 ECHR', 128–9.
[48] *Tymoshenko* v. *Ukraine*, para. 298.
[49] *Merabishvili* v. *Georgia* (GC), 28 November 2017, Application No. 72508/13, para. 314.
[50] Finnerty, 'When Is a State's "Hidden Agenda" Proven?', 452.

one can clearly observe that the Court gives itself exceptionally wide discretion for selecting and evaluating the evidence relevant to running the bad faith test; the Court even held that

> when assessing evidence, it is not bound by formulae and adopts the conclusions supported by the free evaluation of all evidence, including such inferences as may flow from the facts and the parties' submissions. It has also stated that it is sensitive to any potential evidentiary difficulties encountered by a party. The Court has consistently adhered to that position, applying it to complaints under various Articles of the Convention.[51]

However, what exactly ought to be included in widening evidence has not yet been clarified by the Court – as Finnerty explains, 'failure to do so will only preserve, or even exacerbate, the lack of clarity in the way in which the Court will weigh contextual evidence and result in more incoherencies in the case law'.[52]

More than the evidence itself and the use of inferences from the evidence available, the normative variables falling within the scope of the bad faith test are even more indeterminate. The normative question always comes before the empirical question – an enhanced bad faith test evidentially speaking, but over what? What counts as a 'fundamental aspect of the case', using the Court's own language? This is particularly salient when the Court assesses which purpose is actually predominant among several, as in *Merabishvili* v. *Georgia*:

> [I]n addition, the Court reiterates that in order to determine which purpose is predominant in a given case, bearing in mind that the Convention was designed to maintain and promote the ideals and values of a democratic society governed by the rule of law, it must also take into consideration factors such as the nature and degree of reprehensibility of the alleged ulterior purpose.[53]

Yet 'the ideals and values of a democratic society governed by the rule law' loom large. As I suggest in the next section, this grounds the claim that Article 18 in this sense only patches the severe deficiencies of the proportionality test and the poorly defined 'legitimate aim'.

For now, it seems fair to note that the Court's standard of proof has oscillated considerably in the Court's case law. Using Article 18 as an example of a broader trend of variability, Çalı cogently argues that

[51] *Merabishvili* v. *Georgia*, para. 315.
[52] Finnerty, 'When Is a State's "Hidden Agenda" Proven?', 468.
[53] *Merabishvili* v. *Georgia*, para. 304.

'the voice that the Court chooses to speak to states thus depends on how these states approach the Convention and its underpinning values. This is what we may call a realist turn in the case law of the Court as the Court develops an increasing awareness of whom it interacts with instead of imagining a homogenous nondescript audience.'[54] The question I raise in this context is whether this realistic turn includes a populist one. As we shall see below, the Court has been proactive under Article 18 with respect to bad faith from a rule of law standpoint, but it remains to be seen if that is enough to grasp the populist logic with respect to distinctively democratic infrastructure.

7.2.2 Delineating the Normative Domain of Article 18

Indeed, what is less discussed is the precise nature and scope of the threat to the Convention that Article 18 aims at detecting, which is a properly normative rather than evidentiary issue. Article 18 significantly expands the agency of the Court in uncovering, often inductively, the intentionality of the government when it adduces restrictions to Convention rights. While the literature flags that there is uncertainty as to the scope of application of Article 18, it does not explore what is the relevant normative realm of Article 18 as a matter of principle – that is, the purpose(s) in the light of which the evidence must be assessed. This question precedes the issue of whether, as a matter of concordant or inferential evidence, a violation of Article 18 occurred. From the perspective of populism surveyed in Chapter 3, the risk here is that the Court sees and limits the purposes to what I have called its 'minimalist' account of democracy and the rule of law. Judging from the recent case law, it is a characteristically rule-of-law concern, such as judicial independence, that has been subject to a bad faith test under Article 18. The rule-of-law character of these concerns is explicit not only in the series of cases pertaining to Article 5 but also, more recently, in cases pertaining to other qualified rights such as Article 8, as in *Juszczyszyn* v. *Poland*, which pertains to the suspension of a district court judge for having issued a court order asking about compliance with an EU law judgment. The Court found that the predominant aim behind the suspension was to sanction and dissuade the judge

[54] Çalı, 'Coping with Crisis', 270.

from verifying the lawfulness of the appointment process of judges via the recommendation of the reformed NCJ, as we saw earlier:

> The Court finds that to hold, as the Disciplinary Chamber did in its decision of 4 February 2020, that such a judicial decision amounted to a disciplinary offence which justified suspension from judicial duties should be regarded as contrary to the fundamental principles of judicial independence and the rule of law.[55]

Therefore, it seems that the normative domain of Article 18 is circumscribed by the Court's account of the rule of law that we discussed earlier in this chapter – the Court will therefore examine if governments acted in bad faith with respect to that domain primarily.

Yet I argue that there remains an enormous discrepancy between the Court's potential room for examining the government's purposiveness and the Court's current record, and I believe that this discrepancy is informed by a minimalist account of the overarching purposes of the Convention in the first place. This ties in with the claim advanced in Chapter 4 that the Court's 'democratic society' is still protected against external rather than internal threats of the populist kind. On the one hand, Article 18 allows the Court to grasp the intention of the government not just to interfere with one or several rights of one individual in bad faith. Based on its self-extended evidentiary basis, it can freely accumulate evidence to point to an infrastructural – that is to say, not individual – intentionality. In *Juszczyszyn*, the Court was keen to observe that 'in so far as the applicant's individual situation was concerned, the Court notes that his suspension was the culmination of a series of measures taken by the authorities following the issuance of his order of 20 November 2019'.[56] To that extent, Article 18 provides a unique room for grasping infrastructural factors underpinning individual violations – in other words, it can grasp the government's inferred intentionality pertaining not just to the sanctioning of individual actions but to the altering of its own infrastructure, the consequence of which is that individuals be (arbitrarily) sanctioned.

Indeed, on the other hand, most cases in the Court's case law of Article 18 concern restriction and deprivations of Article 5;[57] one could infer that the

[55] *Juszczyszyn* v. *Poland*, 6 October 2022, Application No. 35599/20, para. 334.

[56] *Juszczyszyn* v. *Poland*, para. 324.

[57] See, more recently, *Udaltsov* v. *Russia*, 6 October 2010, Application No. 76695/11; *Razvozzhayev* v. *Russia and Ukraine and Udaltsov* v. *Russia*, 19 November 2019, Application Nos. 75734/12, 2695/15, and 55325/15; *Sabuncu and Others* v. *Turkey*, 10 November 2020, Application No. 23199/17; and *Şik* v. *Turkey (No. 2)*, 24 November 2020, Application No. 36493/17.

nature of the threat engages criminal proceedings – the respondent party's government having brought the applicant under criminal prosecution. Given this correlation, one could understand why the relevant normative concern is the rule of law in that it concerns the use of coercive use of force by public authorities – most typically, the practice of pre-trial detention. This may explain why the Court has been keen to actually examine alleged Article 18 violations in conjunction with Article 5, because they represent the kind of coercive and individualistic attacks on political opposition. Çalı is therefore right that Article 18 aims at addressing 'a particular problem in decaying democracies, that of controlling or punishing opposition political movements or civil dissent'.[58] As I explained in Chapter 2, the protection of political opposition as part of the Court's account of 'democratic society' is indeed a foundational purpose of the Convention system.

But as I pointed out in Chapter 3 and Chapter 5, the populist threat points to a qualitatively distinct attack on that same opposition. It is not that populist governments use all the range of coercive tools at their disposal to silence it. As a result, it remains conceptually difficult to conclude that an ulterior purpose deemed illegitimate is tied to a normative concern that is rule-of-law-based only if, as I argued across the last chapters, corrupting the rule of law is in fact subordinated to the distortion of democracy. In other words, from an infrastructural perspective, the Court may very well miss the *relevant* infrastructural underpinnings when it concentrates on its own rule of law requirements under Article 18. It may miss the distinctively democratic values – such as deliberation and representation, as posited in Chapter 4 – concerning which bad faith may also be checked. In that sense, while Article 18 has been described as a relevant provision to combat 'democracy decay',[59] the basis upon which it operates may miss the populist target specifically.

7.3 Moving Forward

As far as the rule of law provisions are concerned, the intermediary conclusion here is that, while the Court has extended standards of independence and impartiality to some bodies at risk of infrastructural erosion under Article 6, such as judicial national councils, these are considered on ad hoc basis as opposed to identifying a typology that may be subject to infrastructural erosion based on their hybrid character

[58] Çalı, 'Coping with Crisis', 266.
[59] Tan, 'The Dawn of Article 18 ECHR'; Heri, 'Loyalty, Subsidiarity, and Article 18 ECHR'.

as executive, administrative, legislative, and (quasi-)judicial institutions. The guarantees of independence could apply to oversight, supervisory, and regulatory bodies attached to other rights of the Convention, as we shall also see in the next chapter. The claim here is that the Court has not yet delineated a distinct type of alteration to the infrastructure of democracy and the rule of law in its reasoning, one that would be tailored to the authoritarian populist logic. The most that the Court has done in the context of Poland and its national judicial council, for example, is to use the pilot judgment for addressing repetitive cases and to 'eliminate the source of the violation for the future and to provide a remedy for the past prejudice suffered not only by the individual applicant(s) in the pilot case but also by all other victims of the same type of violation'.[60] While the Court issued 'general measures',[61] it also held that 'it is not for the Court to elaborate further on what would be the most appropriate way to put an end to the systemic situation described above'.[62]

In turn, Article 18 establishes the conditions for the Court to reconsider the purposes of the Convention in a new light and empowers it to detect infrastructural deficiencies that ultimately explain the occurrence of an individual human rights violation. But the Court can still refine the relevant normative concern at it sees fit, since it is not tied to only examining the list of legitimate aims textually speaking. 'Legitimacy', in that sense, is a concept that covers a much broader set of normative variables from the Court's own standpoint. Still, the avenue for improving the utility of Article 18 may still lie with the proportionality stage of 'legitimate aim' that the Court routinely must examine when it scrutinizes the justification offered by governments for restricting rights. This step has historically been the one on which the Court spills the least ink when it conducts proportionality analysis. Very often, the Court presumes that the government pursued a legitimate aim and turns quickly to the last, balancing step of 'necessity in a democratic society'. This assumption is another expression of the Court's overall good faith presumption.

On this count, one cannot exclude that the recent rise of Article 18 cases in fact partially compensates for the indeterminacy of the 'legitimate aim' step cutting across most parts of the case law. Now, one avenue to address both the limitations of the general 'legitimate aim' test and the

[60] *Wałęsa* v. *Poland*, 23 November 2023, Application No. 50849/21, para. 318.
[61] *Wałęsa* v. *Poland*, paras. 328–32.
[62] *Wałęsa*, para. 332.

rule of law focus of Article 18 would be for the Court to further exploit the potential offered by proportionality at the 'legitimate aim' step to review the deliberative records of governments' decision-making. This is not only because of the risk posed by governments acting in bad faith generally, but also because the link between populism and the erosion of deliberation is a close one.

8

The Electoral Ecosystem

In this chapter, I turn to the third area of law and policy identified in Chapter 6 that populist rulers alter when they reach executive power, namely, electoral norms and processes. To recall the situational propositions advanced in Chapter 5, populists have a particularly twisted approach to elections: while celebrating the electoral trajectory that brought them to power, proclaiming that the elections allowed the 'true people to finally speak', their governmental record shows a sustained and insidious effort to prevent the opposition from competing equally in future bids. The twist is clear: the 'people' can only speak if populists win. However, the main effects observed – from the classic of gerrymandering to opportunistically moving (or not moving) the electoral agenda, from clientelist practices to capturing electoral bodies – are certainly not distinctive of populist rule. One may therefore again raise the concern that other and not only populist ideologies – in particular, (competitive) authoritarianism – distort the democratic process in a similar fashion. The major difference, as argued in Chapter 3, is that populism is attached to a (thin) ideology, while authoritarianism can be void of any ideology.

As explained in Chapter 5, however, it is true that the discourse of populism and the effects of populist rule may not coincide, which may be linked to the distortion of political representation conducive to more authoritarian practices. Nonetheless, how can one make populist sense of these effects? As explained in Chapter 3, elections are not conceived of as 'starting new' (in Nässtrom's sense) – and that applies to the elections bringing populists to power as well as elections once they are in power. Rather, populist representation again mobilizes its 'true people', which pre-exists the electoral process – the 'pre-political people'[1] – personified in the movement, party, or government leader. On these terms, the electoral process, among other things, becomes a plebiscitary exercise

[1] Blokker, 'Populism as a Constitutional Project', 542.

that suppresses the deliberative and representational requirements of democracy. In other words, on the populist view, elections do not create an additional and structured space for the process of pursuing consensus and compromise, ideas which are dear to the egalitarian ideal of mutual justifiability. To recall, as I suggested in Chapter 2, the extent of that damage depends on one's normative assumptions about the demands of democracy itself. On my account, the attack on deliberation, coupled with the attack on representation, are the two vantage points from which to measure the Court's equipment to respond to populism. While the Court's equipment via Articles 10–11 has the resources to detect and respond to the former, is the same true of the latter?

The Convention protects electoral norms and processes via Article 3 of Protocol 1, the right to free elections. P1-3 is the only right of the Convention that explicitly refers to political participation in its core text. However, the wording of this article is not just irremediably short and concise. In addition, it suggests that there is no self-standing right but simply a promise from state parties to run elections freely and regularly: 'the High Contracting Parties undertake to hold free elections at reasonable intervals by secret ballot, under conditions which will ensure the free expression of the opinion of the people in the choice of the legislature'. While there was no indication that drafting states wanted to exclude the rights to vote and to stand for election from the scope of P1-3, this article was not included in the Convention itself and was added only after renewed negotiation. One often-cited reason for this late addition is the perceived risk that this right would pose to the then-colonial possessions of several prominent states whose role was key in creating the Convention system in the first place. This concerned the right to education (Article 2 of Protocol 1) and the right to property (Article 4 Protocol 1).[2]

Even more importantly for our purposes, it is the primacy accorded to state parties in designing their electoral system that transpires from the preparatory works – and, as far as the Court's adjudication is concerned, it has led in practice to a multilayered judicial restraint that Ziegler has aptly termed 'Strasbourg's timidity'.[3] This primacy is ultimately grounded in considerations of democratic legitimacy (normatively construed) all the way down: an electoral system qua necessary and

[2] For a historical overview, see in particular Kovács, 'Parliamentary Democracy by Default'.

[3] Reuven Ziegler, 'Voting Eligibility: Strasbourg's Timidity', in *The UK and European Human Rights: A Strained Relationship?*, ed. Loveday Hodson, Liz Wicks, and Katja Ziegler 29/09/2025 11:48:00 AM (Hart, 2015): 165–91.

constitutive condition of the democratic process superimposed by a supranational judiciary such as the ECtHR is constructed as an intrusion in the autonomy of state parties. Therefore, the Court only intervenes when the very essence of the right is violated. When the Court does nonetheless intervene on behalf of P1-3, is it able to detect and respond to the distinct erosion of authoritarian populism?

This chapter therefore performs the same exercise as Chapters 6 and 7 do for expression, and assembly and the rule of law. As the Court defines it, Article P1-3 has two right-based constitutive components, the right to vote and the right to stand for election. For the purpose of our investigation, however, I shall concentrate on the interpretive principles that the Court deploys across these two facets. Furthermore, I shall pay particular attention to the complementarity between Article 3 Protocol 1 on the one hand and Articles 10 and 11 on the other. Indeed, the Court cannot insist enough that its 'democratic society' depends on this multi-rights complementarity. This is continuous with the methodological argument defended in Chapter 5, according to which the Court's 'democratic society' offers a vantage point to normatively evaluate the Court's interpretive equipment – generally but with particular emphasis on the threat that populism poses. As such, this chapter builds upon the points that have run through the book, yet with some specification relative to P1-3. This specification is the claim that while the Court celebrates the complementarity of Articles 10–11 and Article P1-3 and cannot insist more on their crucial contribution to the normatively construed 'democratic society', in practice, the level of scrutiny that the Court exercises varies widely between the two right-based components of that imagined society. While the Court places 'deliberative pluralism' on a pedestal in applying Articles 10–11, in the case of P1-3 the Court's default position is a deferential one reflected in the wide, and almost standardized, margin of appreciation offered to the state party. While the importance of political opposition at times makes its way into P1-3 cases, it does not drive the Court's scrutiny beyond a rather superficial level. This discrepancy, I argue, carves out a space that populism can exploit to advance its agenda, defined by democratic distortion and rule of law corruption.

Indeed, as I shall explain, the Court is ready to step out of its default retreat only when serious issues arise – in particular, when a pattern of arbitrariness results in violating the 'essential' obligations deriving from the provision such as universal suffrage – as the Court explains, when limitations imposed by national authorities 'curtail the rights in question to such an extent as to impair their very essence and deprive them of their effectiveness'.[4] Also, and correlatively, proportionality is not conducted with the same rigour and depth as other democratic rights, and the margin of appreciation abounds – thereby preventing the Court from scrutinizing, most importantly, the ecosystemic variables surrounding the electoral process. The procedural obligations that the Court attaches to P1-3 exist and overlap with Article 13 (the right to an effective remedy), but the Court takes their fulfilment at face value and/or places a high burden of proof on the applicant to show how deficient the electoral structures affect the applicant's exercise of P1-3. This corroborates the broader argument running through this investigation: the Court has been concerned with the strictly necessary conditions of the democratic process (their violations). To reuse the terminology of Chapter 4, the Court makes use of its power of scrutiny when there are existential threats to the democratic process. True, P1-3 is a largely positive provision in requiring that electoral institutions and processes are implemented, while Articles 10–11, the other facet of the Court's 'democratic society', mostly require state parties not to interfere with these freedoms. This objection is not only defective on its own terms: as shown in Chapter 6, Articles 10–11 have an inherently positive dimension anchored in their tenet of 'deliberative pluralism'. More importantly, if P1-3 is by its very nature positive, from a populist standpoint, that feature offers more room for alteration – and this should call for the utmost caution on the Court's part.

In that context, I argue that the Court should better calibrate its scrutiny to include the other right-based conditions of its sacrosanct 'democratic society' within the scope of P1-3. This ecosystemic argument holds not just because P1-3 and its reference to the 'will of the people' may prompt populist governments to justify their reforms using the Convention's terminology. It is also because populist rule may pay lip service to the electoral process while ravaging the other right-based conditions that sustain that same process, in particular, the media (under Articles 10–11) and the rule of law (under Articles 6 and 18). The Court could do so by systematically considering the other infrastructural alterations to the democratic process, without which elections become meaningless. Absent such a holistic approach, the Court may, in fact, fall prey to the populist distortion of democracy, which is to run the formal process of elections while having captured and distorted core democratic safeguards that make the electoral

4 *Mathieu-Mohin and Clerfayt* v. *Belgium*, 2 March 1987, Application No. 9267/81, para. 22.

process meaningful in the first place. What is more, the Court champions complementarity between expression and elections as a matter of principle (typically, in the initial paragraphs of its assessment) but not as a matter of the decisive part of its reasoning. It does not scrutinize, for instance, the legitimacy of the aim pursued by the interference. Yet populists do not necessarily target the electoral system if they do not need to – they first and foremost aim at disabling the prior stages of the democratic process, particularly the deliberative ones – to the point where, if these prior steps are distorted, the electoral stage loses its meaning entirely.

In what follows, I present the main principles, content, and scope of P1-3 and then point to the Court's striking discrepancy between the thick proportionality test and burden placed on state parties to guarantee 'deliberative pluralism' under Articles 10–11, on the one hand, and the thin proportionality test deprived of teleological and contextual analysis under P1-3, on the other hand. This analysis allows the identification of the serious blind spots in the Court's responses to attacks on electoral processes. It is imperative that the Court effectively examines – that is, it does not only suggest that it does so – alleged violations of P1-3 in a much more infrastructural and holistic fashion by consistently employing its core understanding of democracy, which I reconstructed under Articles 10–11.

8.1 P1-3 within the Court's 'Democratic Society'

As explained in Chapter 5, this investigation scrutinizes the Court's overarching notion of 'democratic society' as a vantage point from which to evaluate the Court's interpretive equipment. There are various ways to situate P1-3 in the wider group of rights that are essential to the Court's 'democratic society'. One is the general feature that, contrary to the other rights of the Convention, the right to free elections has a positive dimension at the core of its text, as already mentioned. In the Court's view,

> Article 3 of Protocol No. 1 differs from other rights guaranteed by the Convention and its Protocols as it is phrased in terms of the obligation of the High Contracting Party to hold elections which ensure the free expression of the opinion of the people rather than in terms of a particular right or freedom.[5]

[5] *Ždanoka* v. *Latvia*, para. 102.

What the Court underlines here is that a state party cannot fulfil the obligations of P1-3 only by *allowing* individuals to do or not to do something the way it would under Articles 10 and 11, for example. The level of positive obligations on the part of public authorities is therefore higher – not to necessarily meet some higher threshold defined by the Court, as we shall see, but to fulfil the necessary conditions for making the right(s) derived from P1-3 effective. This already indicates that 'the Court's approach reveals a certain caution or prudence in imposing a Strasbourg view of how the national constitutional order should function in place of that chosen by the "people" through national institutions'.[6] I do not find the positive versus negative distinction is helpful for our purposes. That is because the overarching principle of 'deliberative pluralism' entails both positive and negative obligations in the first place – and the precise contours of these obligations are not set in stone but vary depending on the Court assigning various societal actors a contributive role in realizing this society. The same applies to the scope of protection of P1-3: the Court's deferential attitude is a normative construct rather than a legally determinate analysis.

Another way to situate P1-3 within the Court's 'democratic society' for our purposes is how the Court from very early on defined and specified P1-3 as a necessary complement to the other quintessentially democratic rights of the Convention, Articles 10–11. The complementarity is intuitively clear: while Articles 10 and 11 protect the conditions of democratic debate prior to the elections, P1-3 protects the conditions for all subjects to have an equal say in the choice of representatives (the right to vote or the 'active' dimension of the right to free elections) and an equal opportunity to run for office (the right to stand for election or the 'passive' dimension of the right to free elections). But how else does the Court understand the place of P1-3 in its 'democratic society'? While the overall aim is built into the text of the provision itself – to ensure the free expression of the opinion of the people – the Court explained how the features of the provision apply to the two rights that the Court read into it, as in *Labita* v. *Italy*: '"free" elections at "reasonable intervals" "by secret ballot" and "under conditions which will ensure the free expression of the opinion of the people", are the subjective rights to vote and to stand for election'.[7]

[6] Michael O'Boyle, 'Electoral Disputes and the ECHR: An Overview', https://www.venice.coe.int/webforms/documents/default.aspx?pdffile=CDL-UD(2008)010rev-e.

[7] *Labita* v. *Italy* (GC), 6 April 2000, Application No. 26772/95, para. 201.

This wording, which remains intact today, suggests that P1-3 finds its autonomous role in the expression of the will of the people, not its formation. But this autonomy regarding expression does not loom large in the Court's reasoning, however. In that same first case, the Court started its interpretation of P1-3 by asserting that: 'fundamental human rights and freedoms are best maintained by an "effective political democracy". Since it enshrines a characteristic principle of democracy, Article 3 of Protocol No. 1 (P1-3) is accordingly of prime importance in the Convention system.'[8] More recently, the Court has used similar wording with a similar emphasis on an 'effective and meaningful democracy': 'The rights guaranteed under Article 3 of Protocol No. 1 are crucial to establishing and maintaining the foundations of an effective and meaningful democracy governed by the rule of law and are accordingly of prime importance in the Convention system'.[9]

This definition suggests that 'effective' refers to the running of the formal aspects of the electoral procedure only – it does not extend to the preconditions of the same procedure despite the Court systematically pointing to their conceptual linkage at the beginning of its review of P1-3 cases. Indeed, at the level of principle the Court cannot insist enough on the interdependence between freedom of expression (and assembly), on the one hand, and the right to free elections, on the other, in guaranteeing the conditions of its 'democratic society', thereby pointing to a consonance of purpose – in particular, when the Court evokes what I have described in Chapter 7 as 'deliberative pluralism':

> free elections and freedom of expression, particularly freedom of political debate, together form the bedrock of any democratic system [...]. The two rights are inter-related and operate to reinforce each other: for example, as the Court has observed in the past, freedom of expression is one of the 'conditions' necessary to ensure the free expression of the opinion of the people in the choice of the legislature.[10]

It clearly appears that, for the Court, freedom of expression (and one can include freedom of assembly for that purpose) is a necessary condition for elections to be free and for the opinion of the people to be expressed. Yet, in practice, the key concern of the Court does not pertain to that interrelation. Rather, as we shall see, the Court's most active role in that

[8] *Matthews* v. *United Kingdom* (GC), 18 February 1999, Application No. 24833/94, para. 47.

[9] *Guðmundur Gunnarsson and Magnús Davíð Norðdahl* v. *Iceland* (GC), 1 December 2020, Application No. 26374/18, para. 57.

[10] *Bowman* v. *United Kingdom* (GC), 19 February 1998, Application No. 24839/94, paras. 18 and 22.

regard is an assessment of the procedural aspects of the provision. As the Court repeated in recent cases,

> the concept of free elections would be put at risk only if there was evidence of procedural breaches that would be capable of thwarting the free expression of the opinion of the people, and where such complaints received no effective examination at domestic level.[11]

This should allow us to draw some parallels between the Court's procedural focus under Articles 1–11 and P1-3. As we shall see later, the Court has recently developed a test for evaluating allegations of procedural unfairness under P1-3, which offers a further window into the Court's interpretive equipment.

In other words, defining the basic purpose of P1-3 and establishing its content is one thing; defining the grounds for its restriction in practice is another. That is where a troubling dissonance appears – and where our investigation shall concentrate. In conformity with our approach in the previous chapters, in what follows I shall reconstruct the Court's approach to proportionality testing under P1-3. While this article does not form part of the qualified rights of the Convention with similar restriction clauses, the Court has developed an approach that is relatively similar to Articles 8–11, but without a list of predetermined legitimate aims. We already saw in Chapter 6 how the Court focuses on proportionality *stricto sensu* – via the 'necessary in a democratic society' step – at the expense of looking at the purpose of the restriction. Under P1-3, the Court operates the same bifurcation and favours an approach based on instances of arbitrariness in assessing disenfranchisement. This is seen in the Court's emphasis that the restriction should not curtail the exercise of the right so as to impair its 'very essence' and its 'effectiveness'. Inferring from the Court's reasoning, one may posit that the Court understands this essence as universal suffrage in all its dimensions (universal, secret, free, equal, direct). Yet, in finding such instances, the Court limits its scrutiny to thin rule of law criteria such as blanket bans and the lack of individualized restrictions and sanctions qua the criterion of proportionality. As a result, the purpose of the interference, and the wider democratic conditions prevailing in that state, are only superficially examined. Is this approach apt to detect and respond to populist attacks in the infrastructural sense?

[11] *Davydov* v. *Russia*, 30 May 2017, Application No. 75947/11, paras. 283–7.

8.2 The Right to Vote and the Right to Stand for Election

Let us now see how the Court's minimalism is more concretely reflected in the two right-based components of P1-3. As far as the active dimension of the article – the right to vote – is concerned, the vast majority of P1-3 cases before the Court concern patent exclusions of persons or groups of persons from participating in electoral life as in the cases of *Matthews* v. *UK* (for voters located in Gibraltar)[12] and of *Aziz* v. *Cyprus* (for Turkish-Cypriot residents located in the non-occupied territory of Cyprus).[13] In terms of the criteria used for establishing violations, the Court predominantly relies on apparent arbitrariness and basic proportionality standards (in particular, blanket bans or the lack of reasoned decisions). Beyond these approximate thresholds, however, the Court only rarely explores why and how restrictions occur. As a result, the ecosystem of elections – for example, whether a restriction may reflect a wider distortion of the democratic process prior, during, or after the election – does not fall within the Court's conventional ambit – and this reflects the Court's democratic minimalism in the electoral domain.

Certainly, there are instances of disenfranchisement that may seem benign, yet only when they are placed again within the ecosystem inclusive of the wider conditions of the democratic process can the Court effectively assess their significance. Granting a margin of appreciation as the default, as the Court repeatedly does, makes such assessment more difficult. For example, how long an individual should reside in a country to hold the right to vote, for example, has remained within the margin of appreciation of states. In the case of *Py* v. *France*, the Court held that a ten-year residency requirement to qualify for the right to vote was acceptable without much thought as to the democratic implications of it.[14] As a result, state parties are not obliged to ensure that expatriates, for example, can vote or, if they do, to provide expatriates with the means to vote from abroad. More worryingly, allowing nationals without a residence in the state in question to vote to strengthen an electoral base, or adjusting – increasing or lowering – the percentage of votes necessary for party representation in national parliament to create a likely divided opposition landscape are unlikely to be comprehensively examined by the Court. It is true that the Court may scrutinize residency requirements further when such requirements are imposed on

[12] *Matthews* v. *United Kingdom*.

[13] *Aziz* v. *Cyprus*, 22 June 2004, Application No. 69949/01.

[14] *Py* v. *France*, 11 January 2005, Application No. 66289/01.

a vulnerable minority, such as prisoners.[15] The Court has tended to find violations when a blanket ban prevents any individualized decision, as we shall see later. What is more, the Court in fact argues as a matter of principle that 'any electoral legislation must be assessed in the light of the political evolution of the country concerned, so that features that would be unacceptable in the context of one country may be justified in the context of another'.[16] But again, this emphasis does not translate into questioning the purpose of the restriction in a wider context – rather, it operates as a justification in relativist terms for not doing so. Only rarely does the Court examine whether restrictions on the right to vote may serve to tame political opposition.[17]

By deliberately drawing back from addressing these questions, the Court creates interstices that authoritarian populist governments are likely to exploit. The issue that emerges in this context is whether the Court's approach would still apply if, as we saw in Chapter 4, the legislative process were infrastructurally stripped of its deliberative and representative functions. The Court may catch rule of law deficiencies when it focuses its assessment on the proportionality of a ban on voting rights of a defined group of the population – but at the cost of failing to detect and address infrastructural erosion of the democratic process that may be entrenched by the time people turn out at the polling station. In effect, the Court only superficially inspects whether the disenfranchisement has any place in its 'democratic society' as a matter of principle. In this domain, the Court further restricts its scrutiny to proportionality *stricto sensu*. Now, as we explained in Chapter 4, the Court has established a procedural approach that allows state parties to benefit from a margin of appreciation if the right-interfering legislation has been properly debated in parliament and the Convention standards – including proportionality itself – were duly considered by domestic courts. The same approach applies here with respect to proportionality *stricto sensu*.

As far as the right to stand for election is concerned, the discretion afforded to state parties, and margin of appreciation is even wider. For example, state parties can restrict the right of public officials to stand for elections for the purpose of maintaining the impartiality of the public office as in *Alajos Kiss* v. *Hungary*.[18] Again, only when there is a blanket ban on standing for election for an entire class of former public officials,

15 *Mironescu* v. *Romania*, 30 November 2021, Application No. 17504/18.
16 *Yumak and Sadak* v. *Turkey* (GC), 8 July 2008, Application No. 10226/03, para. 111.
17 *Selahattin Demirtaş* v. *Turkey*, para. 390.
18 *Alajos Kiss* v. *Hungary*, 22 May 2010, Application No. 38832/06.

for example, does the Court step in and find a violation, as in the case of a former KGB officer in Latvia.[19] In that case, the Court held that 'the Court's test in relation to the passive aspect of the above provision has been largely limited to a check on the absence of arbitrariness in the domestic procedures leading to disqualification of an individual from standing as a candidate'.[20] As mentioned earlier, 'arbitrariness' as forming the key criterion under P1-3 reflects the very limited supervisory role that the Court gives to itself, and the one that calls for review in the populist context. An arbitrary restriction may seem less arbitrary and a lot more rational when its purpose is ascertained.

If, proportionality is already watered down, it remains to be seen how the Court understands 'arbitrariness'. Looking for principled statements of the Court does not help much: the criteria must at the very least 'reflect, or not run counter to, the concern to maintain the integrity and effectiveness of an electoral procedure aimed at identifying the will of the people through universal suffrage'.[21] Looking at cases helps a bit more but only provides further evidence of minimalism. Indeed, the 'interference with the free expression of the people' implicitly refers to a quasi-coercive understanding of 'interference' in that it concerns the formal and practical conditions of participating in the electoral process. In the context of the right to stand for election, this would typically amount to a government arbitrarily disqualifying an individual from standing, as was the case in *Ždanoka* v. *Latvia*[22] and in *Melnychenko* v. *Ukraine*.[23] It is the refusal by the national authority to register the applicant as a candidate that forms the object of scrutiny. And the 'cautious' assessment of the Court even increases as far as the right to vote, as in *Communist Party of Russia and Others* v. *Russia*, which also quotes *Yumak and Sadak* v. *Turkey*:

> The Court recalls that this case is primarily about the applicants' participation in the elections as candidates, i.e. about the passive electoral right. In the context of the 'passive' aspect of the rights guaranteed by Article 3 of Protocol No. 1, the Court has stressed that it would be even more cautious in its assessment of restrictions in that context than when it has been called upon to examine restrictions on

[19] *Ždanoka* v. *Latvia*.
[20] *Ždanoka*, para. 40.
[21] *Ždanoka*.
[22] *Ždanoka*, para. 115.
[23] *Melnychenko* v. *Ukraine*, 19 October 2004, Application No. 17707/02, para. 57.

> the right to vote, that is, the so-called 'active' element of the rights under Article 3 of Protocol No. 1.[24]

Formal criteria of participation are, to use the adjective employed throughout our investigation, existential – without them, the democratic process simply ceases to exist. So, when the Court holds that the respondent state's electoral arrangement should 'reflect, or not run counter to, the concern to maintain the integrity and effectiveness of an electoral procedure aimed at identifying the will of the people through universal suffrage', it is primarily the very formal and practical requirement of universal suffrage that the Court ultimately examines – implying that the 'integrity' and 'effectiveness' of the electoral procedure actually extends to the requirement of universal suffrage only. This conflation makes it clear that the Court does not seek to assess elections through its more encompassing notion of 'democratic society' despite, again, celebrating their complementarity in principle and having grounding principles – in particular, what I have called 'deliberative pluralism' – to guide its scrutiny throughout. Using the distortion of deliberation and representation as a heuristic device again here, it appears that Court's interpretive reach, before and for the purpose of the 'free expression of the will of the people', remains ill-equipped to consider the conditions of that will's formation and the potential attack(s) on it.

This approach is warranted if and only if the Court understands its own role as minimal in reviewing the electoral records of states, which is underpinned by its historical mandate of protecting against categorical threats. If the Court were to understand its 'democratic society' holistically, and therefore if other right-based conditions were built into its approach to elections – as the Court itself insists, these other right-based conditions are particularly important 'in the period preceding an election that opinions and information of all kinds are permitted to circulate freely'[25] – the equipment of the Court to detect and counter typically populist attacks would be strengthened. In the recent case of *Bakirdzi* v. *Hungary*,[26] the Court found the minority list system implemented by the government in violation of P1-3 on the grounds that it arbitrarily restricts the freedom of minority voters (they cannot vote for another list than the minority one) and violates their secrecy (their electoral preferences are revealed as a result). Yet nowhere did the

[24] *Yumak and Sadak* v. *Turkey*, para. 109.
[25] *Bowman* v. *United Kingdom*, para. 42.
[26] *Bakirdzi* v. *Hungary*, 10 November 2022, Application Nos. 49636/14 and 65678/14.

Court assess whether this legislation reflects, or can be inferentially associated with, other alterations to the Hungarian electoral system, including practices of gerrymandering, as we saw in Chapter 5. Rather, the Court reiterated that its task is only 'to determine whether the effects of the rules governing parliamentary elections is to exclude some persons or groups of persons from participating in the electoral life of the country'.[27] To appreciate this risk in greater depth, I suggest exploring the Court's practice of proportionality testing under P1-3 in more detail.

8.3 Minimalism in Proportionality Analysis

As explained in Chapter 4, the vantage point from which to measure the Court's equipment in the face of populism more precisely is to examine how proportionality testing is conducted. In the text of P1-3, as already mentioned, there is not much attention paid to scrutinizing the aim(s) that the respondent state party invokes to justify an interference with that provision: 'Contracting States are therefore free to rely on an aim not contained in that list to justify a restriction, provided that the compatibility of that aim with the principle of the rule of law and the general objectives of the Convention is proved in the particular circumstances of a case.'[28] As stipulated in Chapter 6, proportionality sheds clear light on the Court's ambiguous approach to components of its right-based democratic society: while celebrating the complementarity between Articles 10–11 and P1-3 in principle, in practice the Court strikingly distinguishes its approach regarding both restriction grounds and principles of interpretation:

> However, where an interference with Article 3 of Protocol No. 1 is in issue the Court should not automatically adhere to the same criteria as those applied with regard to the interference permitted by the second paragraphs of Articles 8 to 11 of the Convention, and it should not necessarily base its conclusions under Article 3 of Protocol No. 1 on the principles derived from the application of Articles 8 to 11 of the Convention'.[29]

This distinction results in the Court overlooking not just the purpose of the interference – by the same token, it fails to replace the restriction

[27] *Bakirdzi* v. *Hungary*, para. 45.
[28] *Yumak and Sadak* v. *Turkey*, para. 106.
[29] *Ždanoka* v. *Latvia*, para. 115.

within its overall 'democratic society' both normatively and descriptively. Normatively, the Court fails to assess the justification given as a matter of principle. Descriptively, it does not examine the wider institutional context of these restrictions, namely whether restrictions correlate with a broader and systemic attack on democracy and the rule of law – even though the Court does that when it engages with Article 18, as we saw in Chapter 7. In other words, restrictions on the right to vote are examined in isolation conceptually and empirically. The Court's 'democratic society' becomes a lot less of a 'society' altogether.

One of the most salient examples of this is seen in the practice of denying the right to vote based on a person's criminal conviction. Irrespective of whether the Court ultimately finds a violation of P1-3,[30] this restraint applies. It is true that in the decisive part of the judgment the Court usually starts by explaining that the scrutiny will be threshold-based as opposed to proportionality-based – an approach that one finds with respect to many other rights. The Court examines that the interference does 'not curtail the rights in question to such an extent as to impair their very essence and deprive them of their effectiveness' when their essence is again understood by the Court as 'the free expression of the people in the choice of the legislature'.[31]

This does not mean, however, that the Court ignores all the proportionality criteria that usually apply. What matters to the Court in this context is proportionality qua rationality and necessity – namely, whether the measure taken by the national authority is rationally connected and strictly necessary to serve the aim pursued. But as students of proportionality will know, it is only sensible to determine the issues of necessity and rationality if the aim of the interference has been established (and deemed 'legitimate') in the first place. Taking the government aim at face value in fact straightforwardly deprives the Court of further room for inspecting and even contemplating more insidious and infrastructural erosion of the electoral process prior and after the process was formally completed. The emphasis on proportionality qua rationality and necessity is most famously evident in the case in *Hirst* v. *United Kingdom (No. 2)* where the Court found that the United Kingdom's measure – depriving *all* convicted felons from voting rights – was *indiscriminate* and therefore excessive:

> such a general, automatic and indiscriminate restriction on a vitally important Convention right must be seen as falling outside any acceptable

[30] It did in *Hirst* v. *United Kingdom*, while it did not in *Scoppola* v. *Italy (No. 3)* (GC), 22 May 2012, Application No. 126/05.

[31] *Mathieu-Mohin and Clerfayt* v. *Belgium*, para. 22.

> margin of appreciation, however wide that margin might be, and as being incompatible with Article 3 of Protocol No. 1.[32]

Note how the assumption of a thick margin of appreciation is the claim to be outweighed, rather than to be argued for in the first place. It clearly appears that holding a particular law or policy to be disproportionate under P1-3 does not entail questioning its aim. In fact, the stage of purpose was passed earlier in the Court's review when it examined whether the law or policy pursued a legitimate aim (in this case, 'preventing crime and enhancing civic responsibility and respect for the rule of law'). This is again premised on the view that limitations to the right to free actions are adduced in good, 'democratic' faith. The question that emerges here is whether this holds true when deliberation and representation have been captured. The overall result to bear in mind for now is that the Court does not discuss the aim of disenfranchisement practices and their compatibility with its sacrosanct 'democratic society' in principled and normative terms.

The same kind of reasoning is found in *Scoppola* v. *Italy (No. 3)* although the measure taken by the respondent state party was deemed proportionate and therefore Convention-compliant: 'in the circumstances the Court cannot conclude that the Italian system has the general, automatic and indiscriminate character that led it, in the *Hirst (no. 2)* case, to find a violation of Article 3 of Protocol No. 1'.[33] The point has been well noted in the literature, most clearly by Ziegler: 'without further analysis, the judgment proceeded on the assumption that the *Hirst* judgment (No. 2) is legitimate and applicable, here, too'.[34] He also rightly mentions that the Court invokes democracy to ground the respondent state party's aim of 'ensuring the proper functioning and preservation of the democratic regime'.[35] This reveals the Court's attachment to minimal democracy understood as procedural and majoritarian, which seems to fit uncomfortably the Court's substantive approach to Articles 10–11 driven by deliberative pluralism, as I shall explain later (below).

Indeed, the Court rather employs consensus among state parties, rather than any normative principle, to calibrate its scrutiny and thicken the margin of appreciation attached to P1-3 anyway. As I explained in

[32] *Hirst* v. *the United Kingdom*, para. 82.
[33] *Scoppola* v. *Italy*, para. 82.
[34] Ziegler, 'Voting Eligibility', 166.
[35] *Scoppola* v. *Italy*, para. 92.

Chapter 4, consensualism and the existence of a wide margin of appreciation often go in concert in the Court's practice. This becomes patent in the proportionality test in *Scoppola*, for example:

> since the Convention is first and foremost a system for the protection of human rights, the Court must have regard to the changing conditions within the respondent State and within Contracting States generally and respond, for example, to any evolving convergence as to the standards to be achieved.[36]

In that respect, the Court observed that:

> only nineteen of the States examined impose no restrictions on the voting rights of convicted prisoners. Of the remaining twenty-four States, which do apply restrictions to varying degrees, eleven require a decision of the criminal court on a case-by-case basis (with some exceptions where the most serious sentences are concerned – as in Greece and Luxembourg).[37]

In more recent cases, the Court appealed to consensus along the same lines to find a violation against Romania about prisoners being unable to vote if their place of detention is outwith the electoral constituency attached to their place of residence. While often this empirical justification is coupled with the Court finding a failure of national courts 'to provide relevant and sufficient reasons to demonstrate that the restriction of the applicant's right to vote was proportionate',[38] the same absence of assessing the aim of the interference applies.

The Court's assumption seems to be that whatever the respondent state intends to achieve with its legislation on disenfranchisement, it only matters that decisions are individualized, which itself does require proportionate decisions in terms of rationality and necessity. As Bates notes in the *Hirst* case, 'arguably the reference to proportionality suggested that the specific conduct ("crime committed") had to match the "sanction" (disenfranchisement) for the individual prisoner concerned, the intervention of a judge being best suited for that'.[39] Yet again, requiring sentences to be proportionate in the thin sense is very different from any teleological examination, which would first require scrutinizing the aim pursued by the legislation itself. Therefore, the approach based on thin rule of law criteria and European consensus replaces the teleological

[36] *Scoppola*, para. 94.
[37] *Scoppola*, para. 101.
[38] *Mironescu* v. *Romania*, para. 52.
[39] Ed Bates, 'Analysing the Prisoner Voting Saga and the British Challenge to Strasbourg', *Human Rights Law Review* 14, no. 3 (2014), 509.

approach on the question of the legitimate aim. The proportionality test takes places between the state party's legitimate aim and the measure adopted, without the legitimate aim being balanced against the Court's wider idea of 'democratic society' that plays such an important role under Articles 10–11, as we have seen. The rest 'is for each Contracting State to mould into their own democratic vision', as the Court repeatedly holds. The discretion systematically afforded to state parties poses a pregnant risk that allows the advancement of the populist distortion of democracy.

8.4 Minimalism in Procedural Terms

The Court's minimalism under P1-3 does not only pertain to proportionality analysis and to the absence of a teleological assessment that would again place restrictions upon the right within the Court's celebrated 'democratic society' – a link that prevails under other provisions. In addition to the content of the two aspects of P1-3, the Court has also been stunningly silent on extending what counts as the object of the elections (the national parliament), and on the kind of electoral system that meets the demands of the Court's 'democratic society' in the first place.

Concerning the latter, the Court has been very clear that P1-3 does not prescribe a particular type of electoral system. This means that deciding over a 'first-past-the-post' system or a proportional system remains within the margin of appreciation.[40] This is because of the inherent tension, the Court holds, between 'on the one hand, reflecting faithfully the opinions of the people, and on the other hand, to channel currents of thought as to promote the emergence of a sufficiently clear and coherent political will' that the Court has invoked since the seminal case of *Mathieu-Mohin and Clerfayt* v. *Belgium*.[41] But while the Court emphasizes the emergence of a democratic will, it does not investigate how, for the purpose of exercising the right to free elections meaningfully, this will has been effectively formed – and this is despite having the interpretive equipment derived from Articles 10–11 at its disposal.

With respect to the former, for example, the Court has rejected putting referenda within the scope of P1-3 on admissibility grounds *rationae materiae*, which means that the subject matter at issue, the referendum, is not even contemplated as part of the Court's review. As the Court

[40] *Matthews* v. *United Kingdom*, para. 64.
[41] *Matthews*, para. 54.

explained in *Moohan and Gillon* v. *the United Kingdom* pertaining to the independence referendum in Scotland, however, the Court has not excluded the possibility that 'a democratic process described as a "referendum" by a Contracting State could potentially fall within the ambit of Article 3 of Protocol No. 1 [. . .]'.[42] However, in order to do so, the process would need to take place 'at reasonable intervals by secret ballot, under conditions which will ensure the free expression of the opinion of the people in the choice of the legislature', as we have seen. This implies that state parties are not prevented from having referenda, but that referenda should then be subject to P1-3 protections. As such, the Court avoids the question of the democratic significance of referenda. The same reasoning applies to presidential elections, as reflected in the recent decision of *Călin Georgescu* v. *Romania*.[43]

A key final angle to shed light on the Court's minimalism is to zoom in on the procedural obligations of P1-3 – that is, which procedural safeguards are in place for individuals for challenging election-related decisions, typically in the post-electoral context. This angle reflects the procedural turn explored in Chapter 8 with application to elections: provided that the basic procedural guarantees obtain, the Court is likely to afford a wide margin of appreciation (as we have seen, the proportionality requirement is accordingly basic too). This angle is particularly interesting because it epitomizes 'the structure within the structure': if populism attacks structures and processes from within, rather than individuals directly, and if the right to free elections is a quintessential example of a structural right, then it becomes crucial to study the procedural guarantees attached to the right – that is, the remedy in place for individuals to complain about alleged violations of the right using the Convention.

Here again, the Court's minimalism is striking. In *Communist Party of Russia and Others* v. *Russia*, in which the applicants claimed that the media coverage leading to the presidential election in 2003 – and the wider Russian media system – were manipulated by the government. On the substantive grounds, the Court conducted a strikingly cursory and approximative review and established that:

> the applicants did obtain some measure of access to the nation-wide TV channels; thus, they were provided with free and paid airtime, with no

[42] *Moohan and Gillon* v. *the United Kingdom*, 6 July 2017, Application Nos. 22962/15 and 2334/15.

[43] 11 February 2025, Application No. 37327/24.

> distinction made between the different political forces. The amount of airtime allocated to the opposition candidates was not insignificant. The applicants did not claim that the procedure of distribution of airtime was unfair in any way. Similar provisions regulated access of parties and candidates to regional TV channels and other mass media. In addition, the opposition parties and candidates were able to convey their political message to the electorate through the media they controlled.[44]

Note the approximate wording used, but also how the burden of proof, again, is placed upon the applicants to substantiate claims of government interference. In fact, while they brought evidence pointing to suspicious alterations to electoral legislation the year preceding the election, the Court simply did not review these aspects and only pointed to the absence of evidence demonstrating how the restriction affected applicants directly:

> As to the first point raised by the applicants, the Court considers that, as such, countries are free to amend and modify their legislation on elections, provided that they remain within their margin of appreciation under Article 3 of Protocol No. 1. In the present case the applicants (both individual and party candidates) did not demonstrate how the changes to the legislation they mentioned had directly affected them or the parties they represented.[45]

Even when applicants brought evidence of the practice of seat forfeiture – 'in the aftermath of the elections 37 freshly elected members had renounced their mandates. Most of them had been high-level public officials who had thus kept their positions in the executive while ceding their places in the parliament to candidates not known to the voters'– the Court showed a striking level of self-restraint:

> The Court expresses concern in respect of the practice of coordinated forfeiture of a great number of mandates obtained by a political party. However, the Court will not analyse the dangers inherent in such a practice in the abstract. In the case at hand, the Court confines itself to observing that the rule allowing forfeiture of parliamentary mandates was not as such contrary to the concept of free elections [. . .].[46]

This illustrates the steady reluctance of the Court to examine electoral processes in a holistic fashion.

44 *Communist Party of Russia and Others* v. *Russia*, para. 126.
45 *Communist Party of Russia*, para. 135.
46 *Communist Party of Russia*, para. 136.

On procedural grounds, the Court has derived the obligation according to which there should be a 'domestic system for effective examination of individual complaints and appeals in matters concerning electoral rights',[47] which highlights the overlap between P1-3 and Article 13 (the right to an effective remedy – applicants often allege violations of both, but the Court tends to focus on P1-3). Yet, as in *Communist Party of Russia and Others* v. *Russia*, the Court simply held that the Russian judicial system – in particular, the Supreme Court – met 'basic procedural safeguards': 'it is sufficient to note that the applicants' complaint about unequal media coverage of the elections was examined by an independent body in a procedure which afforded the basic procedural guarantees, and that a reasoned judgment was given',[48] which the Court established in its separate review (in the same case) of an alleged violation of Article 13. The Court's procedural minimalism is also embedded in relativism – and this is illustrated by how it reviews administrative bodies such as electoral commissions. Here again, while the Court may investigate and analyse how these structures may lack sufficient procedural safeguards, it still does not examine the restriction beyond basic rule of law and proportionality criteria. Where is the Court's 'democratic society', one may ask?

Furthermore, the Court tends to place the burden of evidence onto the applicant to show how infrastructural deficiencies, if any, directly affect the exercise of rights in the applicant's specific case. In *Georgian Labour Party* v. *Georgia*, the applicant party complained about the president of Georgia's power to appoint seven of the fifteen members of the electoral commission (including the president). The Court acknowledges that:

> a proportion of seven members out of fifteen-member electoral commissions, including the chairmen who have the casting votes (Article 22 § 8 of the EC) and are appointed by the President of Georgia and his party, is particularly high in comparison to other legal orders in Europe,[49]

and

> that the contested composition of electoral commissions at all levels indeed lacked sufficient checks and balances against the President's power and that those commissions could hardly enjoy independence from the outside political pressure. However, in the absence of any proof of particular acts of abuse of power or electoral fraud committed

[47] See *Namat Aliyev* v. *Azerbaijan*, 8 April 2010, Application No. 18705/06, para. 81.
[48] *Communist Party of Russia and Others* v. *Russia*, para. 124.
[49] *Georgian Labour Party* v. *Georgia*, 8 July 2008, Application No. 9103/04, para. 106.

> within the electoral commissions to the applicant party's detriment, no breach of the latter's right to stand for election can be established.[50]

As I explain in the final section of this chapter, the dismissive attitude regarding the infrastructural conditions of the electoral process (pre- or post-) is worrying. This concerns both the object of scrutiny (e.g., appeals and complaints bodies) and the kind and degree of scrutiny via a thicker account of proportionality (e.g., the place of P1-3 within its 'democratic society').

Now, this minimalism does not necessarily imply that P1-3 is void of any development as far as procedural guarantees are concerned. In recent years, the Court has developed a framework for when a procedural issue pertaining to P1-3 is sufficiently serious and how to adjudicate it. Indeed, several cases have brought up the issue of elections bodies composed of members of parliament that have to adjudicate post-election disputes where issues of impartiality and independence arise. For example, a candidate for election contests the recounting of the votes and brings their case to an appeals committee or an electoral commission composed of members of (the new) parliament who may have failed to get elected if the applicant's claims were found to be correct.[51]

These cases give us another vantage point onto the Court's specification of impartiality and independence standards, this time in the electoral context. Most importantly, they show that the Court can engage with aims and purposes within the electoral context. Furthermore, these cases concern distinctively infrastructural matters pertaining to democratic representation when the electoral body scrutinized is a parliamentary body. Indeed, as we saw in Chapter 6 with respect to interferences with parliamentary autonomy, the Court has been deferential to the latter when it comes to oversight and appeal bodies. Unlike most cases under P1-3 analysed so far, the Court is scrutinizing state parties that are conventionally considered established or 'old' democracies.

Historically, the Court had consistently held that 'a mere mistake or irregularity in the electoral process would not, per se, signify unfairness of the elections if the general principles of equality, transparency, impartiality and independence in the organisation and management of

[50] *Georgian Labour Party* v. *Georgia*, para. 110.

[51] See *Mugemangango* v. *Belgium* (GC), 10 July 2020, Application No. 310/15 and *Guðmundur Gunnarsson and Magnús Davíð Norðdahl* v. *Iceland*.

elections were complied with'.[52] Yet the Court has now elaborated more specific impartiality and rule of law standards that domestic bodies reviewing electoral disputes should follow. In *Mugemangango* v. *Belgium*, for example, the applicant contested the procedural safeguards of independence and impartiality of the relevant parliament's committee in the regional constituency of Wallonia, whose mode of resolving the dispute was a simple majority vote. In particular, the MPs who were the applicant's opponents in the election were include in that vote. The Court found that this insufficiently protected the impartiality of the body in question. As the Court explained, 'the decision was therefore taken by a body that included members of parliament whose election could have been called into question if the applicant's complaint had been declared well-founded and whose interests were directly opposed to his own'.[53]

In coming to that conclusion, the Court relied other human rights bodies' case law that a parliamentary body reviewing electoral disputes necessarily runs the risk of political and partisan decisions and that individuals appealing to this kind of body should have access to judicial review in the last instance. Citing guidance from the Venice Commission, the Court held that:

> Appeals to Parliament, as the judge of its own elections, could lead to political decisions, and that appeals of that kind were acceptable at first instance where they were long established, but that in such cases a judicial appeal should then be possible at last instance. It [the Venice Commission] emphasised that there should be adequate institutional and procedural safeguards against political and partisan decisions.[54]

In addition to this risk pertaining to independence, the Court also invoked the lack of clarity ('the criteria that could be applied by the Walloon Parliament in deciding on complaints such as the one lodged by the applicant were not laid down sufficiently clearly in the applicable provisions of domestic law') and accessibility and foreseeability ('in the absence of a procedure laid down in the applicable regulatory instruments, those safeguards were the result of ad hoc discretionary decisions taken by the Credentials Committee and the plenary Walloon Parliament').[55]

52 *Davydov and Others* v. *Russia*, para. 287.
53 *Mugemangango* v. *Belgium*, para. 106.
54 *Mugemangango* v. *Belgium*, para. 99.
55 *Mugemangango* v. *Belgium*.

8.5 Moving Forward

The overall takeaway of this review of the Court's case law is the following ambivalence. On the one hand, the Court proclaims that electoral norms and process form an inherent part of its 'democratic society'. What is more, the Court emphasizes how the circulation and exchange of ideas matter prominently during the pre-electoral period. In that sense, the very integrity of the electoral process depends not only on the election taking place and meeting minimal standards, but on the deliberative and representative record of the pre-electoral moment. That is where I detect the link between the Court's principle of 'deliberative pluralism', which guides the Court's review of Articles 10–11 and P1-3: 'the free expression of the opinion of the people in choice of the legislature' cannot obtain without having a thorough and deliberative process involving the range of safeguards that the Court has routinely identified as the 'watchdogs of a democratic society' in civil society (journalists and the media, NGOs, scientists and intellectuals, etc.). Because of this intuitively clear link, one would expect this corollary to be the cornerstone of the Court's review under P1-3. The Court would pay the utmost attention to the multiples disruptions and distortions that may *in fine* compromise the electoral process. More simply put, Articles 10–11 should guarantee deliberation and representation. Strikingly, the Court does not bridge the two.

Now, the argument pervading this investigation resonates even louder: the generalized restraint observed under P1-3 (both in terms of the right's general content and intensity of review in proportionality) is a further and even more striking illustration of the minimal account of 'democratic society'. While this finding has independent value in revealing the internal inconsistency of the Court's 'democratic society', what matters more for our endeavours is the systemic risk that such a finding poses in creating particularly fertile room for the populist distortion of deliberation and representation to take effect. The risk is simply that, under such a minimal account, populist governments' array of anti-democratic practices fall within Convention compliance. This minimalism is again both content- and process-based. The latter prevents the Court from even starting to grasp the erosion while remaining within Convention compliance with respect to P1-3.

9

Proportionality as Anti-populist Detector and Responder

Chapters 6, 7, and 8 offered a deep dive into the Court's practice of adjudicating those rights that were prima facie identified as vulnerable to populist erosion. It is now opportune to zero in and reposition the various findings in the previous chapters within the overall investigation. This shall lay down the basis for articulating a more general and systematic way forward as to how the Court could better respond to authoritarian populism. The driving argument supporting the reconstruction of the case law has been that the Court's approach to democracy has been minimal and inadequate to grasp the specifically infrastructural erosion orchestrated by populists. This minimalism is multifaceted, and the location in the Court's reasoning where this minimalism manifests itself depends on the provision in question. As far Articles 10–11 are concerned, the Court in a nutshell has the equipment to detect the distortion of democracy as far as deliberation in the public arena is concerned. Its relentless scrutiny of whether a certain view pertains to a public interest, also reflected in the positive requirement of 'deliberative pluralism' as I put it in Chapter 6, ensures the adequacy of the Court's interpretive equipment in the populist context.

However, the procedural requirements of the Court's 'democratic society' under Articles 10–11 are noticeably poor and show the limits of the Court's approach to procedural review summarized in Chapter 4. Indeed, the Court only examines whether the procedural guarantees offered by the domestic legislation meet some basic availability, effectiveness, and fairness criteria. The Court does not scrutinize how an appeal procedure for disciplining a journalist, for example, is *actually* operated: how is the judicial or administrative body in charge of the decision-making composed? Infrastructural erosion does not concern the mere existence and availability of these procedures to a particular individual, but *how* these procedures are fulfilled – that is, the infrastructure itself. Despite celebrating it as the watchdog of its 'democratic society', the Court pays very little attention to the infrastructure of the media system as the background against which individual violations occur, as we established in Chapter 6. The distinct logic of infrastructural erosion in the media market, the key role of oversight bodies, and their distortive impact on democratic deliberation, as surveyed in Chapter 5, do not feature prominently in the Court's reasoning and are absent from its interpretive equipment more generally. The positive duty of pluralism seems the most relevant where there is quasi-total absence of it, rather than when it is seeming pluralistic but *in fine* distorted.

As far as the rule of law provisions are concerned, the analysis concluded that while the Court has extended standards of independence and impartiality to some bodies at risk of infrastructural erosion under Article 6, such as judicial councils, these are considered on an ad hoc basis as opposed to identifying a typology of oversight, regulatory, and supervisory bodies that may be subject to infrastructural risk. The same procedural guarantees could apply to appeal bodies in the media or electoral domains, for example. The claim here is that the Court has not yet delineated a distinct type of alteration to the infrastructure of democracy and the rule of law in its reasoning, one that the authoritarian populist process of capture highlights. As a result, the Court has not recalibrated its demands to the respondent state party accordingly. For example, the Court could shift the burden of proof onto the respondent state party to demonstrate that infrastructural change is not an attempt to erode the separation of powers, considering concomitant and wider indicators of such a manoeuvre in the domestic sphere. Again, the same could apply to distorting the infrastructural parameters of a media oversight body or an electoral commission. As we saw in Chapter 7, it remains that the burden of proof falls onto the applicant, albeit with some notable and slowly emerging exceptions.

In this context, the rise of Article 18 cases in recent years raises both hope and concern. To recall, this provision helps the Court investigate whether the aim presented by the government in the proportionality test is the actual one – that is, whether the actual aim is presented in good faith or whether it is hidden. There is hope that when the Court scrutinizes the purpose of the interference, it conducts precisely the holistic assessment required to depict the infrastructural erosion, notably by drawing a web of concordant inferences. When the Court surgically scrutinizes the interference in that holistic manner, it is able to identify distinctively infrastructural issues of the kind highlighted in Chapter 5. The Court could again rely on such inferential evidence to heighten the burden of proof that the respondent state party must consider in demonstrating the legitimacy of the interference's aim. However, the grounds used by the Court and the relevant domains of application considered in conducting such a review are under-inclusive and under-systematized. The normative domain of Article 18 needs to be calibrated to reach beyond rule of law issues (under Article 5 and, more recently, under Article 6) to include distortions to democracy proper, so that the Court's interpretive equipment cuts across the wide array of populist targets.

Now, while the Court exercises agency under Article 18, the opposite is true when it comes to the right to free elections. I argued in Chapter 8 that the Court's reasoning is not only minimal in the grounds used for finding a violation, which centre around arbitrary disenfranchisement. These violations again reflect categorical violations of democracy – those requirements without which democracy, in particular political participation, ceases to exist at all. More importantly, I showed that the Court is inattentive to the aim pursued by the government in justifying interferences under P1-3. While cherishing the interdependence of its democratic provisions as a matter of principle, the Court displays a staggeringly asymmetrical approach between Articles 10–11 and P1-3 when it comes to the depth and scope of its scrutiny. The procedural obligations under P1-3 are also poor: echoing Articles 10–11 in that sense, it is enough to comply with the Court's standards that there is an available avenue for remedy, a minimal approach which misses the core of the populist logic that institutional safeguards are maintained but turned against their dedicated purpose. This notably prevents the proportionality analysis consistently operating throughout the various stages of the democratic process from the deliberative arena to the voting booth. To recall, populism entails a distortion of democratic representation – and if the deliberative stage of the process is infrastructurally captured, the electoral process loses its purpose and meaning altogether.

In taking stock of these jurisprudential findings, and in measuring the adequacy of the Court's interpretive equipment, the critical role of proportionality is made apparent. Yet the level and depth of scrutiny is by far not uniform across the portions of case law examined. While it supports the Court's efforts in scrutinizing the deliberative stage of the democratic process in deploying the Court's principles to the maximum of their detective and responsive potential, the same is not true of the electoral process, for example. The adjustment variable of the margin of appreciation still appears prominently – and when it does, its grounds and scope are far from being clearly delimited. Rather, as explained in Chapter 4, these are assumed rather than demonstrated.

9.1 Towards a More General Argument

In this conclusive chapter, I systematize the argument that the Court should and can calibrate its proportionality test to the infrastructural dimension of the populist attack on democratic and rule of law provisions – and, as such, operate the test as 'anti-populist detector'. I outlined this argument in Chapter 4 when I presented 'democratic society' as playing a decisive role not only in informing the values from which interpretive principles are drawn but also in resolving cases in the proportionality test specifically.

By 'anti-populist detector', I imply that proportionality can effectively detect and counter the distortion of democracy and the corruption of the rule of law that are distinctive of the infrastructural erosion of populism. There are a few important steps and qualifiers to this argument that I will develop throughout the chapter. First, the argument is not only and not primarily about effectiveness. It could be that, empirically, proportionality performs or can perform such a detective and responsive function. As outlined in Chapter 4, proportionality and democracy are continuous at the level of normative principle. Each stage of the test embodies democratic and rule of law values to a different extent – and the Court's actual practice of operating the test adds a layer of variation and specification in how these values are embodied and translated into operational principles. In other words, proportionality cannot be confined to considerations of legal validity or empirics but engages substantive normative reasoning. As scholars have established, the rise of proportionality in rights adjudication precisely reflects 'a turn from authority to justification'.[1] While the empirics crucially matter to operating all the stages of the test, the normative point of these stages is not empirical. The key claim here is that the stages of the test all have a normative point that is directly and principally relevant to the populist distortion democracy and the corruption of the rule of law. But how?

Second, not all the stages of the proportionality test are equally relevant for detecting the relevant infrastructural erosion. It is true that

[1] Cohen-Eliya and Porat, *Proportionality and Constitutional Culture*; Etienne Mureinik, 'A Bridge to Where? Introducing the Interim Bill of Rights', *South African Journal on Human Rights* 10, no. 1 (1994): 31–48.

authoritarian populists are prone to proportionality failure generally. This is because, proportionality being a standard rather than a rule, all stages amount to a structured exercise of justification and deliberation based on a complex set of facts and arguments, and these are precisely tasks that authoritarian populists generally avert. As saw in Chapter 5, populist governments may erode rule of law standards that form part of the general and widely accepted requirements of legality – for example, the generalizability and/or foreseeability of their rights-interfering norm. This is detected at the stage of 'prescribed by law' under the Convention. At the balancing stage, populist governments are likely to insist that they should benefit from a margin of appreciation, as we saw in Chapter 6. They may very well instrumentalize the Court's trend of procedural review that entails removing the Court's own review of the balancing, as we saw in Chapter 4.

However, these stages cannot be conducted independently of the prior stages, in particular the stage of purpose, 'legitimate aim' in the Convention's text, the third stage of the test. Here, the central claim is that authoritarian populism cannot account for the independent role of democratic procedures in forming the will of the people – these only have an instrumental and opportunistic value, as explained in Chapter 3. I argue that the same applies to the proportionality test, and this aversion makes it distinctively valuable from a detective and responsive standpoint. In other words, if there is a portion of the Court's review where the populist distortion comes to the fore, and one where the Court may have the agency to detect infrastructural deficiencies, the proportionality test appears to be a primary locus of interpretive intervention. But where in the test exactly, and how should the current interpretive framework used by the Court be amended?

The formation of the will of the people within the democratic arena and the proportionality assessment of the Court are very different stages of the democratic process. Yet it is crucial to account for the continuity between the two: as much as elections involve a vacuum as to the locus of political power, as we saw in Chapter 3, proportionality involves a vacuum as to the justifiability of interferences with rights. All the stages of proportionality assessment introduce elements of contingency, uncertainty, opposability, and fallibility that are all equally toxic to the logic of populism. In that sense, there is a general case that proportionality can operate as an anti-populist detector and responder. But again, one may object that this general function equally applies to a range of anti-democratic threats. The general case does not track proportionality's role in detecting the infrastructural erosion of democracy specifically. Consequently, one needs to be specific about which contribution the various stages make to detecting infrastructural erosion, which has guided the analysis from Chapter 5 through to Chapter 8. One may think that the stages of rationality and necessity, for example, are closer to the rule of law than to democracy proper, as their operation itself relies on empirical, rather than normative, criteria.[2] Which stage is therefore most relevant to detecting the infrastructural erosion of democracy?

Third, I argue that the Court should revise its approach to the initial stage of the proportionality assessment, namely the purpose or 'legitimate aim' of the interference. The Convention includes a list of 'legitimate aims', a list that varies slightly depending on the provision in question. Conventionally, the Court has not insisted on scrutinizing the actual aim or its legitimacy in substantive terms. This stage has been largely formalistic and classificatory – with some exceptions, as we shall see later in the Chapter. The Court often even reconstructs the government submission to read one of the listed aims into it.[3] This again reflects the Court's subsidiary and supervisory role: the Court leaves it to the government to indicate, rather than substantiate and demonstrate, the aim(s) pursued by the interference on the usual grounds of epistemic privilege and democratic legitimacy. The key claim here is that, as a result, the Court has not utilized its normative account of 'democratic society' (developed in understanding the rights themselves) to inform the screening of the aims that the government presents. The understanding of the right's purpose in such a society, on the one hand, and the purpose test, on the other hand, are disentangled. Because populist governments are prone to maintaining the facade of institutional safeguards while operating them in ways that contradict their purpose and values, they are likely to do the same when they need to justify the purpose of their interferences before the Court. For sure, they may fail to pass the further stages of the test – yet paying lip service to the purpose presented by the

[2] Aharon Barak, 'Limitation of Constitutional Rights', in *Proportionality: Constitutional Rights and Their Limitations* (Cambridge University Press, 2012): 99–106; Gerards, 'The Prism of Fundamental Rights'; Gerards, 'Procedural Review by the ECtHR'.

[3] Necdet Umut Orcan, 'Legitimate Aims, Illegitimate Aims and the ECtHR: Changing Attitudes and Selective Strictness', *University of Bologna Law Review* 7, no. 1 (2022): 7–40, 7; Anne Carter, *Proportionality and Facts in Constitutional Adjudication* (Hart Publishing, 2023); Jonas Christoffersen, *Fair Balance: Proportionality, Subsidiarity and Primarity in the European Convention on Human Right* (Brill Nijhoff, 2009).

government deprives the Court of enquiring into the infrastructural patterns developing in concomitance with the alleged violation.

The purpose stage structures the rest of the assessment: the rationality, necessity, and balancing stages are operated in relation to the purpose having been deemed legitimate. The purpose stage is therefore crucial. But the detective value rather arises from the Court's task of identifying the purpose of the government behind the interference. Indeed, the Court does not have the epistemic access necessary to grasp the intent of the respondent state party and its government. Rather, depicting the aim of the interference is a holistic process of drawing inferences from a range of relevant pointers that can be qualified as infrastructural. But that is not all – if the purpose stage was only an epistemic enterprise, it would not address the concern of legitimacy, which is an inherently normative one. Establishing the legitimacy of the aim amounts to specifying its justifiability in a normative sense. As Möller puts it, the point 'is to filter out reasons that are impermissible, so that the remainder of the proportionality inquiry can assess the strength of the permissible reasons'.[4] This exercise is categorically different from finding the aim of the interference. In disregarding this normative aspect, the Court has created a vacuum that needs remedy and which authoritarian populism highlights. I therefore argue that the Court should ground its account of legitimacy in the two higher principles that form the cornerstone of its 'democratic society', namely deliberation and representation, and identify the infrastructure relevant to the Convention article in question. In this sense, the detective and responsive role of the purpose stage is twofold. On the one hand, it allows the Court to exercise agency in placing the interference in a wider social, political, and legal context of the respondent state party and to draw on the infrastructural erosion that underpins individual violations. On the other hand, the Court can exercise agency in evaluating the aim normatively using an 'upgraded' understanding of 'democratic society'.

9.2 The Structure and Meaning of Proportionality

Let me first recall the basic structure of the proportionality assessment as presented in Chapter 4. In the specific case of the Convention, the Court follows a four-pronged test and must determine if there was indeed an

[4] Kai Möller, 'Authority and Intent in U.S. Constitutional Culture', *Jerusalem Review of Legal Studies* 10, no. 1 (2014), 125.

interference with rights (first stage), whether this interference was 'prescribed by law' (second stage), whether it pursued 'a legitimate aim' (third stage), and, finally, whether it was 'necessary in democratic society' (fourth stage). As a matter of practice, the last stage operates against the presence of a 'social pressing need'. It usually includes the sub-steps of suitability and necessity in addition to the final balancing stage or 'proportionality *stricto sensu*', where the existence of a 'pressing social need' is weighed against the impact on the individual to establish whether the interference was indeed 'necessary in a democratic society'. While every step must be fulfilled by the respondent state, it is widely established that the Court's reasoning gets increasingly adversarial and substantive when it reaches the balancing stage.[5] The balancing stage is also where the Court conducts an overall discussion inclusive of all the prior stages.

Indeed, having to consider a protected provision (duly interpreted) and to weigh it against competing reasons advanced by the respondent state generally requires the Court to reassert, and potentially revisit, the rights' foundations, content, and scope in the specific circumstances of a case. For example, the Court's level of protection of freedom of expression heavily depends on the Court's finding that the views expressed constituted a matter of public interest, as we saw in Chapter 6. This implies that while the stages of proportionality are conceptually independent from each other, in the Court's practice the answers to these questions are not – rather, the principles pertaining to the right's content travels through to the balancing stage. Moreover, the Court does not always clearly establish which answer responds to which stage of the test. While the Court addresses these steps separately, there is no strict distinction between, say, the 'legitimate aim' of pursuing 'the protection of public morals' and the collective (and democratic) interest underlying it, which may be unpacked and discussed at the last step of 'necessity in a democratic society'.

9.3 Proportionality and Democratic Deliberation

The first step of the argument is that the proportionality test has a normative meaning that is highly relevant to the populist distortion

[5] Zysset, 'Searching for the Legitimacy of the European Court of Human Rights'; Zysset, 'Freedom of Expression, the Right to Vote, and Proportionality at the European Court of Human Rights'; Zysset, 'Calibrating the Response to Populism at the European Court of Human Rights'.

of democracy and the corruption of the rule of law – and therefore should be privileged to enhance the Court's responsive equipment. This normative meaning centres on the value of democratic deliberation. In Chapter 4, I developed the argument that populists strip the democratic process of its deliberative and representative requirements. In Chapter 6–8, we saw in the practice of the Court that populist governments indeed attempt to subvert the requirements of proportionality using references to democracy – and, since it is allocated at that stage, abuse the request for a margin of appreciation that can be accorded to them based on these credentials. As we shall see later (below), not all the stages of proportionality are equally vulnerable to populist distortion. Furthermore, the question is whether the Court makes use of the interpretive and detective room that proportionality affords it. The hypothesis here is that the Court's record of scrutiny remains highly reflective of its democratic minimalism highlighted across this investigation – a minimalism that underpins its understanding of the rights themselves and the default deference, namely through the margin of appreciation; that the Court affords in its subsidiary position.

I believe that the risk of proportionality abuse is no coincidence. Rather, the continuum is that populists aim to subvert deliberation equally at all the junctures of the legal process, legislative, executive, and judicial, requiring that the law be justifiable to the many, rather than the 'real' or 'authentic' people – whether in the informal setting of the open democratic arena or in the formal setting of responding to the Court's demand for justifying an interference with rights. As democratic deliberation and representation are premised on a vacuum of power and representation, as we saw in Chapter 3, proportionality involves a vacuum as to the justifiability of interferences – in fact, the respondent government must go through considerable norm- and fact-based deliberation to offer reasons that match the Court's demands. This is why one needs to attend to the nature of this demand and explore the Court's criteria attached to it. The populist facade-building here operates along the same line of maintaining the appearances of (proportionality) compliance with the Convention-allowed grounds for restricting rights while hollowing out their substance – one of which being democratic deliberation. But unlike other forms of rights, the populist distortion is significantly more difficult for judges to ascertain because it is often disguised as a necessary infrastructural project justified on grounds that seem as justifiable to all, as we shall see.

In analytic terms, the upshot here is that if proportionality's underpinning value is centrally, but not only, democratic deliberation, it follows that proportionality can directly engage with the democratic distortion of populism. Again, one may say that all stages of the assessment introduce elements of contingency, uncertainty, opposability, and fallibility that are all equally toxic to the logic of populism. In that sense, there is a general case that proportionality can operate as an anti-populist detector. This argument, however, remains normative. The question remains whether the Court actually operates the test so as to respond to this potentiality. While proportionality may have an inbuilt requirement for deliberation, not all systems of rights adjudication necessarily have a proportionality test geared towards *democratic* deliberation, and not every stage of the test, taken in isolation, can be conferred a democratic meaning either.[6] For example, the steps of suitability or necessity, taken in isolation, may require governments to deliberate as to which measure is necessary and rational without involving any democratic element. The rule of law defined in a thin sense – for example, clarity, efficacy, foreseeability – may suffice to detect potential forms of rule of law corruption.

The argument obtains when proportionality is contemplated as an interconnected framework. Once it is established that the stages of suitability, necessity, and balancing are analytically subordinated to the purpose of the interference, the normative realm of the latter becomes key – that is, when ascertained empirically, whether an aim counts as 'legitimate' aim (third stage of the test) depends on the prior question of the normative basis of 'legitimacy', which is 'derived from the values on which society is founded'.[7] The key task before us is therefore to explicate the nexus between proportionality and democratic deliberation by identifying at which stage(s) of the test this democratic value can and should operate in response to infrastructural erosion, and then evaluate whether Court could and should enhance its practice accordingly.

[6] On the point of contingency, see for example Moshe Cohen-Eliya and Iddo Porat, 'Proportionality in the Age of Populism', *The American Journal of Comparative Law* 69, no. 3 (2021): 449–77.

[7] Barak, *Proportionality: Constitutional Rights and Their Limitations*, 245; Carter, *Proportionality and Facts in Constitutional Adjudication*.

9.4 The Grounding Value: Justifiability among Free and Equal Moral Agents

The normative link between proportionality as a defined framework for evaluating rights' restrictions, on the one hand, and the value of democratic deliberation, on the other hand, has been ascertained in the literature at the intersection of political philosophy and theories of human rights and right-based adjudication. Rainer Forst's account of the 'right to justification', on the one hand, and Mattias Kumm's account of proportionality as operating a 'test of public reason' in the Rawlsian tradition, on the other, can shed light on the nexus in the context of the Court.[8] In what follows, I point to the key features of these accounts and then explain how my argument centred on the populist context borrows from, modifies, and develops these features. Generally, these joint accounts can explain how proportionality responds to a demand of justification that builds into a broader philosophical view of human beings construed as free and equal moral agents. On such a view, the Court operating the proportionality test effectively evaluates reasons and grounds compatibility within that construction.

At the core of such a nexus lies the overarching 'right to justification' that sustains the conventional list of established human rights. Rather than tying human rights to a rich and teleological notion of normative agency,[9] Forst links it to the ability to give and receive justifiable reasons – 'a notion of respecting an other's autonomy which is neither attached to a reasonable contestable notion of the good nor requires a translation of a prudential ethical value "for me" to a moral reason "for all"'.[10] Now, it should be borne in mind that Forst's account initially responds to the philosophical issue of identifying which rights count as human rights, which occupies a distinct debate in normative theory.[11] For the sake of our investigation, it suffices to recall the definition the definition of the right to justification:

> The moral basis for human rights, as I reconstruct it, is the respect for the human person as an autonomous agent who possesses a right to

[8] Zysset, 'The Right to Justification in the Context of Proportionality'.

[9] James Griffin, *On Human Rights* (Oxford University Press, 2008).

[10] Forst, 'The Justification of Human Rights and the Basic Right to Justification', 724.

[11] Adam Etinson, ed., *Human Rights: Moral or Political?* (Oxford University Press, 2018); Rowan Cruft, S. Matthew Liao, and Massimo Renzo, eds., *Philosophical Foundations of Human Rights* (Oxford University Press, 2015); Zysset, *The ECHR and Human Rights Theory*.

> justification, that is, a right, to be recognized as an agent who can demand acceptable reasons for any action that claims to be morally justified and for any social or political structure or law that claims to be binding upon him or her. Human rights secure the equal standing of persons in the political and social world, based on a fundamental moral demand of respect.[12]

For Forst, as a result, human rights are generally conceived as a precondition of any legitimate political and legal order: 'they are moral rights of a specific kind which are directed to a political-legal authority and have to be secured in a legally binding form'.[13] In addition, Forst identifies a legal and institutional task, namely determining 'how this can be realized in such a way that the moral status of being a justificatory equal acquires the best possible legal and political expression'.[14] Forst does not, however, specifically examine conflicts of rights – an issue that the proportionality test crystallizes.

Kumm's seminal contribution has been to specify how the overarching right to justification operates in rights adjudication with specific application to the proportionality test, endorsing the view that 'we should think of human rights as constituting a particular conception of law and politics: a conception of law and politics as justice-seeking among free and equals'.[15] The right to justification, as built into the proportionality test, implies the right of individuals to contest the justifiability of the reasons offered by a public authority to restrict the exercise of rights – 'human rights norms empower rights-holders to challenge existing power relationships by insisting that those relationships be susceptible to justification in terms of public reason'.[16] When the Court scrupulously examines possible grounds for infringing one or several Convention rights, it is equally examining the mutual justifiability of the interference: 'when courts apply the proportionality test, they are in fact assessing whether or not legislation can be justified in terms of public reasons, reasons that every citizen might reasonably accept'.[17] While it is beyond the scope of this investigation to delve into the Rawlsian concept of

[12] Forst, 'The Justification of Human Rights and the Basic Right to Justification', 719.

[13] Ibid., 736.

[14] Ibid., 736.

[15] Kumm, 'The Idea of Socratic Contestation and the Right to Justification', 157.

[16] Mattias Kumm, 'The Turn to Justification: On the Structure and Domain of Human Rights Practice', in *Human Rights: Moral or Political?*, ed. Adam Etinson (Oxford University Press, 2018), 251.

[17] Kumm, 'The Idea of Socratic Contestation and the Right to Justification', 168–9.

'public reason'[18] or the notion of 'fairness' in the Dworkinian tradition,[19] as Möller suggests,[20] it suffices here to concentrate on how the normative value of mutual justifiability feeds into the structure of the proportionality test.

How is the normative value of justifiability and its role in proportionality assessment prima facie relevant to the populist distortion of democracy and the corruption of the rule of law? In Chapter 3, I argued that populism strips the democratic process of its deliberative and representative requirements. In that chapter, I assumed that deliberation implies a reliance on reasons, rather than predetermined wills or interests, as the relevant currency for defining the shared terms under which free and equal individuals ought to live. In Chapters 5–8, I showed that the effects of populism chiefly amount to the erosion of the infrastructure of democratic and rule of law rights. The implication was not that these rights cannot be exercised individually because of infrastructural erosion – as we saw, expressing opposition in the open democratic arena is still allowed – but rather that, under the populist predicament, the exercise of these rights loses its point or meaning. While infrastructural erosion does not target any individual agent, it surely has agential consequences in terms of disabling the pursuit of mutual justifiability. I showed with support from the case law that the Court's 'democratic society' centres on the superstructure of an open and pluralistic debate, rather than on the infrastructure of the rights.

I therefore argue here that it is precisely the preconditions for reason-giving required by justifiability that is eroded by populist forces, albeit originating in the infrastructural domain. This argument helps corroborate the view that the Court's overarching principle of deliberative pluralism under Articles 10–11 reviewed in Chapter 6 is an asset against populism but falls short of tracking the infrastructural erosion of the media system, the justice system, and the electoral system. Justifiability requires the Court to assess both the super- and the infrastructure in tandem in each system. Our critique of the right to elections as understood by the Court, which we reviewed in Chapter 8, is pertinent at this point. Without a coherent and infrastructurally centred account of the

18 Rawls, *Political Liberalism*; Silje Langvatn, Mattias Kumm, and Wojcieh Sadurski, *Public Reason and Courts* (Cambridge University Press, 2020).

19 Ronald Dworkin, *Law's Empire* (Belknap Press, 1988).

20 Möller, *The Global Model of Constitutional Rights*; Kai Möller, 'Dworkin's Theory of Rights in the Age of Proportionality', *The Law & Ethics of Human Rights* 12, no. 2 (2018): 281–99.

Court's 'democratic society', justifiability cannot be pursued. Absent a holistic account of its 'democratic society', the Court adjudicates the infrastructure of democracy without addressing the infrastructural conditions that make the pursuit of justifiability even possible. The fragmented and minimalist approach to the electoral system under P1-3 best illustrates this deficiency.

9.5 The Purpose Test and Democratic Infrastructure

The upshot so far is that proportionality, defined as pursuing the normative horizon of mutual justifiability, can restore the infrastructural steps that are necessary – if not sufficient – for this condition to obtain. It is this condition that effectively underpins the value of democratic deliberation as built into the proportionality framework. When governments are interrogated about the proportionality of their interference, they are asked to offer reasons that are justifiable to free and equal moral agents. Two final questions follow from this. One is whether the populist erosion of democratic infrastructure changes anything about the general argument in the previous section. I believe that infrastructural erosion should redirect scholarly attention to the purpose stage of proportionality analysis, that of 'legitimate aim'. The other question is whether the Court's practice of proportionality aligns with this modified argument – that is, whether the Court is equipped to fulfil the detective and responsive roles advocated here. I argue that the Court's equipment has been historically deficient in that regard – a shortcoming that authoritarian populism highlights and which requires systematic attention in calibrating the response. To illustrate this deficit, I return to select portions of the case law surveyed in Chapters 6–8.

9.6 Mutual Justifiability and the Purpose Test

Having laid down the grounding value of justifiability and its relevance to proportionality generally, one can turn to the various stages of the test to identify which stage(s) are relevant to detecting and countering the infrastructural erosion specifically. Here, I argue that the purpose stage of finding a 'legitimate aim' should be prioritized and needs recalibration in the overall framework of proportionality as practised by the Court. This is because it can liaise between the alleged individual violation and the infrastructural conditions without which the right loses much of its purpose and relevance. In other words, the purpose test allows the Court to establish whether there is a wider and infrastructural erosion that renders the purpose presented by the government questionable, requiring demonstration that the government is not actually attempting to erode infrastructure. Typically, the Court could examine and link between the infrastructure of deliberation (the erosion of the media) and the infrastructure of representation (the erosion of the electoral system) as far as the link between Articles 10–11 and Article 3 Protocol 1 is concerned. The purpose test offers room for both normative and empirical enquiry whose results can inform the following stages of the test, from suitability to necessity and ultimately balancing. As Carter more generally explains, 'while the question of legitimacy is ultimately a normative one, and one that will differ between jurisdictions, the identification of the relevant purpose may be seen to involve empirical issues'.[21]

The mutual justifiability condition has been applied first and foremost to justifications by public authorities that reflect a particularist or comprehensive moral view, or a particularist interest incompatible with mutual justifiability among free and equal moral agents. More precisely, Kumm targets a range of 'political pathologies' that fail the condition of mutual justifiability. For example, the justification of religion for treating homosexuality as sin: 'this type of reason, a reason relating to what it means to live a good, authentic life, might not generally count as legitimate reasons to restrict someone's right'.[22] More generally, the deontological basis of the right to justification is at odds with any particularist, perfectionist, or consequentialist justifications (including tradition, convention, or simply preference) that typically fail the first, purpose stage of the test. Note that in response to Kumm, Möller has argued in favour of a harm-based argument that centres on the overarching value of autonomy. On that view, a particularist justification should only be deemed impermissible when actual harm results from the interference – 'rather, the question must be whether the demonstration involves an independent harm to their autonomy, for example an attack on their sense of self-worth'. So, ethical disapproval is by itself not sufficient: 'when goals are offered which are about protecting others from a certain harm to their autonomy – such as the harm flowing from offence – we must ask whether this harm rests on ethical disapproval. When it does, the goal is impermissible.'[23]

[21] Carter, *Proportionality and Facts in Constitutional Adjudication*, 32.
[22] Kumm, 'The Idea of Socratic Contestation and the Right to Justification', 159.
[23] Möller, *The Global Model of Constitutional Rights*, 190.

Kumm also registers 'hyperbolic' or 'ideological' justifications, which are typically invoked to increase governmental discretion in response to an inflated threat, for example, in response to a threat to national security. While seemingly legitimate at first sight, these reasons do not survive the rational connection and necessity stages. In the same vein, Kumm lists 'the capture of the democratic process by rent-seeking interest groups',[24] when governments muddy their justification in technicalities that favour a specific group at the expense of others, typically in the domain of socio-economic redistribution. Yet both Kumm and Möller do not specifically contemplate the scenario where it is the infrastructure of democracy itself (its erosion) that is aimed at, and how this plays out in the proportionality framework (and the practice of the Court specifically). The distinct feature of infrastructural erosion is not its particularism, but precisely its genuine justifiability in furthering the equal rights of all – or, as we shall see later (below), in the Court's parlance, 'the rights of others'. The populist context calls not for a charitable reconstruction of the aim considering the means used – 'whether there are any interests which are candidates for justifying the interference in the sense that it is not entirely implausible that they will at least be rationally connected to the policy' – but rather for investigating the aim itself using a wider range of infrastructural variables that are equally relevant to the Court's 'democratic society' under the relevant Convention article.

Considering this background, I argue that the populist context singles out yet another type of justification for interfering with democratic and rule of law rights that needs a calibrated scrutiny, an infrastructural one. As suggested throughout the investigation, populist governments do not necessarily attack the superstructure of the democratic arena – and the Court's 'democratic society' remains robust in that domain. Rather, it is concerned with the infrastructural conditions that, together, make the exercise of democratic rights agentially meaningful, enabling the pursuit of mutual justifiability at the level of the superstructure.

On the one hand, governments following the populist logic are likely to contend that an infrastructural justification affords them a high level of discretion in the means and resources to achieve the infrastructural aim – this is generally the case as far as the positive obligations of the Convention are concerned, together with the default margin of

24 Kumm, 'The Idea of Socratic Contestation and the Right to Justification', 163.

appreciation. The means and resources are quintessentially subject to subsidiarity considerations in the Court's practice for both empirical and normative reasons, as we saw in Chapter 4. Normatively, governments are even more likely to invoke their democratic credentials as part of or in addition to the margin of appreciation that applies in the infrastructural domain, overplaying the card of subsidiarity. Epistemically, they are likely to claim that that 'they are best placed' to assess their own needs. In fact, Möller takes these reasons to be rather dismissive of the purpose stage of the test 'because in almost all circumstances the realization of those rights requires scarce resources; therefore, any limitation will always further the legitimate goal of saving resources and will always be suitable and necessary to the achievement of that goal. The only meaningful test would be the balancing stage.'[25]

The authoritarian populist logic requires the Court to investigate whether any practical justification, cost-effective or otherwise, disguises an attempt to bypass deliberative and representative requirements of the democratic process as a matter of infrastructural prerequisites, not only in terms of the agential effects of the interference. Conventionally, when it comes to its 'positive' rights and obligations, the Court has limited its scrutiny to rule of law criteria such as 'prescribed by law' (first stage of the test), as we saw in the example of the positive obligation of media pluralism in Chapter 6.[26] This allows the situating of another intersecting body of literature that focuses on the place of proportionality and 'reasonableness' in economic, social, and cultural rights' adjudication: where the latter prevails, it has been shown that the interpretation of the right's content is collapsed in an incremental, and context-driven inquiry,[27] meaning that 'reasonableness review develops in a normative vacuum'.[28] The claim is that democratic and rule of law infrastructure, as relevant to the three Convention domains examined in this investigation, cannot be subject to resource considerations that would trigger the aspirational dimension often associated with positive human rights.

25 Möller, *The Global Model of Constitutional Rights*, 179.

26 On this point, see also Gardbaum, 'Human Rights as International Constitutional Rights'.

27 Katharine G. Young, 'Proportionality, Reasonableness, and Economic and Social Rights', in *Proportionality: New Frontiers, New Challenges*, ed. Mark Tushnet and Vicki C. Jackson (Cambridge University Press, 2017), 26.

28 David Bilchitz, *Poverty and Fundamental Rights: The Justification and Enforcement of Socio-economic Rights* (Oxford University Press, 2007), 143. For a critique, see Alain Zysset and Antoinette Scherz, 'Proportionality as Procedure: Strengthening the Legitimate Authority of the UN Committee on Economic, Social and Cultural Rights', *Global Constitutionalism* 10, no. 3 (2021): 1–23.

On the other hand, the infrastructural justification is significantly more likely to match the Convention-authorized aim(s) which, as we already mentioned, are strikingly easy to meet if the Court does not pay particular attention to them. It is true that the last years have witnessed an increase of violations found at the third stage of 'legitimate aim' and under various grounds at that stage,[29] when the government does not present any aim[30] (or when the Court identifies a legitimate aim instead of the government but finds a violation);[31] when the Court rejects the legitimate aim present by the government;[32] or when it finds that the government did not pursue the aim invoked but another one.[33] Yet, again, this jurisprudence refers to the largely empirical issue of aim-finding based on the Court's established account of legitimate aims.

This is relevant to the condition of mutual justifiability: reforming a judicial council, an electoral system, or a media oversight body – or invoking them to distort deliberation and representation – can very conveniently fit the rationale of the interference ultimately serving the (democratic or rule of law) rights of others equally, including the applicant themselves. As a result, the Court will face severe difficulties in discerning the infrastructural erosion by examining the agential violation and its justification in isolation. This is also where our analysis of the portions of the case law in Chapter 6–8 matters: in the infrastructural domain, the Court is likely to ensure that procedural guarantees are in place for individuals to contest the interference and claim the relevant Convention right(s), in accordance with the minimalism that characterizes its approach to democratic infrastructure generally. This therefore concerns the entire catalogue of obligations of the Court under the relevant Convention article, either substantive or procedural. Yet, as already mentioned, both types of obligations are subject to

29 Orcan, 'Legitimate Aims, Illegitimate Aims and the ECtHR'.

30 See for instance *Bochev* v. *Bulgaria*, 13 November 2008, Application No. 73481/01, para. 97; *Mihal* v. *Slovakia*, 5 July 2011, Application No. 22006/07, para. 55; *Kostadin Mihaylov* v. *Bulgaria*, 27 March 2008, Application No. 17868/07, para. 42.

31 See for example *Young, James and Webster* v. *the United Kingdom*, para. 60; *Ciubotaru* v. *Moldova*, 27 April 2010, Application No. 27138/04, para. 55; *Frodl* v. *Austria*, 8 April 2010, Application No. 20201/04, para. 28.

32 See, for example, *Maširević* v. *Serbia*, 11 February 2014, Application No. 30671/08, para. 51; *Karajanov* v. *The 'Former Yugoslav Republic of Macedonia'*, 6 April 2017, Application No. 2229/15, para. 75.

33 For the finding that the government did not pursue the aim invoked, see Umut Orcan, 'Legitimate Aims, Illegitimate Aims and the ECtHR', 15; in general, *Baka* v. *Hungary*, para. 123; *Emin Huseynov* v. *Azerbaijan*, 7 May 2015, Application No. 59135/09, para. 87; *Tkachevy* v. *Russia*, 14 February 2012, Application No. 35430/05, para. 39.

a proportionality assessment. It is therefore important to return to select portions of the case law to evaluate if a more structured approach to the purpose test could help to detect and respond to infrastructural cracks that are relevant to the pursuit of mutual justifiability and to remedy them.

9.7 The Court's Record of Infrastructural Reasoning

Let us therefore proceed to the second issue identified in the first section of this chapter, namely whether the Court's practice of proportionality aligns with this modified argument – that is, whether the Court is equipped to fulfil the detecting and countering at the level of the purpose test. The argument here is not that infrastructural elements do not feature into the Court's assessment of an individual situation. Rather, the Court does not have a systematic approach to detecting and determining whether a wider and infrastructural attack is developing because it does not link up the various components of its 'democratic society' that are spread in various (and right-specific) portions of its jurisprudence. The purpose test can and should be used to ascertain this considering that infrastructural conditions are essential to the pursuit of mutual justifiability – and, therefore, the meaningful exercise of democratic rights protected by the Convention. True, the Court has shown willingness to address infrastructural considerations when examining an alleged individual violation. Let us recall, as we saw in Chapter 7, the case of *Grzęda* v. *Poland* pertaining the removal of a judge at the Polish Supreme Court from the National Council of the Judiciary (NCJ) before the end of his tenure and the absence of access to a court to review the decision (under Article 6):

> The Court notes that the whole sequence of events in Poland (see paragraphs 14–28 above) vividly demonstrates that successive judicial reforms were aimed at weakening judicial independence, starting with the grave irregularities in the election of judges of the Constitutional Court in December 2015, then, in particular, remodelling the NCJ and setting up new chambers in the Supreme Court, while extending the Minister of Justice's control over the courts and increasing his role in matters of judicial discipline [. . .]. As a result of the successive reforms, the judiciary – an autonomous branch of State power – has been exposed to interference by the executive and legislative powers and thus substantially weakened. The applicant's case is one exemplification of this general trend.[34]

[34] *Grzęda* v. *Poland*, para. 349.

This passage illustrates how the illegitimate purpose of the interference is ascertained through a widened detection range pointing to infrastructural pattern of erosion of the independence of justice. It suggests that it is only by a holistic and inferential process in which one interference (the justification thereof) examined by the Court is replaced within a larger spectrum of infrastructural 'reform' and its justification that the erosion is identified.

Moreover, there also is emerging evidence that the Court can place a higher burden of demonstration onto the government to substantiate the actual aim (the purpose test) and the means (suitability and necessity) using a wider set of evidential contributions from various observers (NGOs, international organizations, and advisory bodies) pointing to patterns of wider infrastructural erosion. In *Reczkowicz* v. *Poland*, which also pertained to the new election model of judges by the Sjem, the Court went to on to isolate the position of the Polish Constitutional Court by directly referring to these inputs: 'The Constitutional Court appears to be isolated in its perception and assessment of the necessity and legitimacy of the change in the procedure for election of the judicial members of the NCJ.'[35] In particular, the Court cited the distortion of democratic deliberation in the undertaking the reform:

> The UN Special Rapporteur on the Independence of Judges and Lawyers, in his report of 5 April 2018 following his mission to Poland, noted that the reorganisation of the Polish judicial system had been 'undertaken by the governing majority in haste and without proper consultation with the opposition, the judiciary and civil society actors' and recommended that the 2017 Amending Act be 'amended to bring it into line with the Constitution and international standards relating to the independence of the judiciary and separation of powers'.[36]

Now, we saw in Chapter 7 that finding a violation ultimately relies on expanding the content and scope of the Court's cherished principles of impartiality and independence within Article 6, requiring, however, that governments demonstrate the purpose of the interference – in this case, the purpose of the reform – against the evidence of a much wider infrastructural erosion. The purpose test therefore opens a conceptual and empirical horizon for the Court to detect the concerted nature and gravity of that erosion. Indeed, as our analytical framework has

[35] *Reczkowicz* v. *Poland*, para. 239.
[36] *Reczkowicz* v. *Poland*, para. 244.

suggested, the very meaning of such infrastructural erosion – the gravity of it – is hardly grasped without incorporating not only attacks on the rule of law, but also distortions of the democratic process itself, in particular deliberation and representation, which underpin the Court's overarching account of 'democratic society'. It is this fuller and holistic assessment that can enable the Court to calibrate its response to populism for what it is – not only one instance but concerted instances of democratic distortion in the infrastructural domain.

In that regard, the current role of the purpose test is irremediably falling short of its detective and evaluative potential with respect to other key rights covered in this investigation. Rather, the Court pays lip service to the purpose, suitability, and necessity stages and ignores the ravages that populism inflicts on democratic infrastructure. As we have already mentioned, the Court failing to discuss the aim makes the scrutiny of the suitability and necessity stages largely incomplete. Recall the case of *Karácsony and Others* v. *Hungary* under Articles 10–11 that we reviewed in Chapter 6. The case pertains to the fines – termed 'ex post facto disciplinary sanctions' – imposed on opposition members in the Hungarian parliament who had used a placard, banners, and megaphone on the floor of the parliament to express their fierce objection to the government's policies on tobacco trading. Unsurprisingly, and as already mentioned, the Court itself 'finds' the legitimate aim of the interference in a way that meets the mutual justifiability condition, namely, the effective functioning of parliament, which matched both 'the prevention of disorder' and the 'the rights of others':

> The Court is satisfied that the interference pursued two legitimate aims within the meaning of Article 10 § 2 of the Convention. Firstly, it was aimed at preventing disruption to the work of Parliament so as to ensure its effective operation and thus pursued the legitimate aim of the 'prevention of disorder'. Secondly, it was intended to protect the rights of other members of parliament, and thus pursued the aim of the 'protection of the rights of others'.[37]

This passage not only makes it clear how the Court eventually only classifies claims presented by Hungarian authorities into the available boxes of the Convention. By doing so, it also forecloses the inclusion of such argumentation – and the actions of the public authorities it refers to – into an overarching and contextualized discussion of its 'democratic society'. If the Court were to do so at the purpose stage, it could have

[37] *Karácsony and Others* v. *Hungary*, para. 129.

asked the state party to demonstrate that the interference is not another attempt to distort deliberation and representation as a matter of infrastructure – in this case, the parliamentary one. Rather, the Court concluded that the interference was rationally connected to the aim and necessary without much substantive analysis:

> Furthermore, having regard to the circumstances of the present case, the Court finds no reason to doubt that the impugned disciplinary sanctions which were imposed on the applicants were supported by reasons that were relevant for the legitimate aims pursued, namely, the prevention of disorder and the protection of the rights of other members of parliament. However, it sees no need to rule on whether, bearing in mind the State's wide margin of appreciation, those reasons as such were also sufficient to show that the disputed interference was 'necessary'.[38]

This passage illustrates how the Court's lack of engagement with the purpose test in a substantive and contextualized manner precludes a meaningful engagement with the subsequent stages of suitability and necessity, making proportionality's function of restoring the horizon of mutual justifiability largely ineffective. As explained earlier in the chapter, there is analytical interdependence between these stages, so that if the purpose is superfluously classified – for example, as 'the prevention of disorder' – the rationality and necessity of the specific action(s) undertaken by the Hungarian authorities are equally superfluous – how else could it be? Again, if the purpose stages were substantively addressed, the meaning of the rationality and necessity of the interference in light of that aim may look very different. That is, if the Court were to engage in infrastructural reasoning by examining whether these state actions were instances of a wider trend consolidating the erosion of deliberation, representation, or the rule of law – along the lines of the Polish cases just examined, the suitability and necessity stages would need to be contextualized too. Note also that the margin of appreciation is assumed rather than demonstrated, as we pointed to in Chapter 4.

In another, almost-identical Hungarian case, the Court addresses the infrastructural issue – both the deliberative and representative distortion – alleged by the applicants but places the burden of demonstration onto the applicants to show that disrupting parliament with images was necessary to inform the public. The case pertains to opposition MPs having shown posters with photographs from before and after what they alleged was environmental degradation resulting from governmental development

[38] *Karácsony*, para. 129.

plans. While the applicants claimed that 'the only way to express their opinion effectively had been by drawing the media's attention to it. Having regard to the political situation in Hungary, in particular the government's control of national television and radio and its overrepresentation in the media in general, the applicants were not in a position to perform their legitimate role as elected representatives with a reasonable chance of success by using ordinary means of communication',[39] the Court does formally address the concern but immediately places the burden of demonstration onto them:

> The Court must also address the applicants' argument that their intention in using the posters was to attract media attention, in view of their otherwise limited access to the audiovisual media in Hungary [...]. Having said that, the Court would note, without prejudice to the applicants' argument concerning the opposition's allegedly limited access to the audiovisual media in Hungary, that the applicants did not provide sufficient information to show that potentially interested members of the public could not have been informed of the images in question other than by their display during the interpellation.[40]

This passage quintessentially illustrates one of the key arguments running through our investigation, namely, the Court's narrow and minimalist horizon of its 'democratic society' with specific reference to parliamentary infrastructure. Indeed, the premise of the Court's reasoning is that the 'fairness' of parliamentary deliberation can be established based on whether dissenting views are included in such proceedings, without again the infrastructural conditions that make these proceedings meaningful. This speaks to the 'deliberative pluralism' principle discussed in Chapter 6. The deliberative and representative distortion of populism requires the Court to examine the infrastructural conditions that are necessary to the pursuit of mutual justifiability. Scrutinizing the purpose stage of the proportionality test affords the Court such an opportunity in a structured manner – the suitability, necessity, and balancing stages will be accordingly informed by the expanded analysis, all contributing to the overarching purpose of mutual justifiability.

Yet, as far as the purpose stage is concerned, the Court's infrastructural record is meagre – it does not satisfy itself with the 'efficiency of the

[39] *Ikotity and Others* v. *Hungary*, 5 October 2023, Application No. 50012/17, para. 23.
[40] *Ikotity and Others* v. *Hungary*, para. 43.

democratic process' and the formal inclusion of dissent as far as parliamentary proceedings are concerned:

> The Court notes that the orderly conduct of parliamentary debate is aimed at ensuring the authority and effective functioning of Parliament and hence the efficiency of the democratic process. The use of non-conventional means of communication – though perhaps effective in attracting media attention – could reasonably be regarded as carrying a risk of obstructing that aim. In the present case the opposition MP was free to deliver her interpellation speech and there is no indication that the restriction imposed on the use of posters amounted to unequal or unfair treatment of the applicants as members of the opposition.[41]

This passage precisely reflects the difficulty outlined earlier about depicting and contextualizing the purpose of the interference when the aim of the interference and its justification is infrastructural. Surely the democratic process – on the Court's own account – cannot be subsumed under efficiency considerations. This would play right into the hands of the populist distortion, considering their talent for putting up only the facade of democratic infrastructure. It is exactly when democratic deliberation takes place in the infrastructural domain that the Court should be the most vigilant and attentive, and without engaging in a holistic and contextualized analysis of the purpose stage, it simply fails to enforce the tenets of its sacrosanct 'democratic society'. The purpose test affords the Court the framework to do so – not only to adduce evidence of wider infrastructural distortions, but also to then place the burden of proof on the government to justify the interference. There is in fact little evidence that the Court can operate that switch – for example, when the Court adduced sufficient evidence to suggest that the dismissal of a judge could not be said to pursue the legitimate aim of maintaining the authority of the judiciary.[42] This again shows that that purpose stage of the proportionality test is crucial for detective and evaluative purposes, but also that it is not currently systematized.

9.8 'Procedural Safeguards' and Article 18: Symptom or Remedy?

Now, as we discussed at length in Chapters 6–8, it would be unfair to say that the Court has ignored other dimensions of infrastructure available in its interpretive equipment. The Court has indeed championed procedural safeguards – or, as it sometimes calls it, the 'procedural arm' of this

[41] *Ikotity and Others* v. *Hungary*, para. 43.
[42] *Baka* v. *Hungary*, para. 149.

or that Convention provision – which are included in the mixture of considerations subject to the proportionality test. Often, we have seen, the Court even substitutes the substantive arm with the procedural one in terms of adjudicatory focus. This speaks to one aspect of procedural review analysed in Chapter 4: provided that these safeguards are in place and meet minimal standards, the Court is far less likely to revisit the proportionality test performed by domestic authorities and substitute its own substantive assessment for it.

One could view the procedural arm of a Convention as reflecting the right to justification mobilized earlier in the chapter: the normative point of having, say, a parliamentary committee examining complaints following sanctions imposed on MPs, or the point of an electoral commission for examining post-electoral complaints, is for public authorities to offer reasons that are justifiable in terms of the freedom and equality of democratic subjects in pursuit of mutual justifiability. However, procedural review, as also illustrated in Chapters 6–8, has the effect of relying on the reasons offered by the government rather than scrutinizing them. Rather than expanding on the purpose (or suitability and necessity stages) of the interference on its own terms, the Court deliberatively concentrates on these basic guarantees as the decisive criteria for finding a (non-)violation. The argument here is that, since the purpose stage largely remains a 'tick-box' exercise, the Court has hardly any substantial basis to proceed with the suitability and/or necessity stages. In other words, while both proportionality and procedural review have at their core the demand of justification and mutual justifiability, they do not respond to this demand to the same extent, if at all.

Indeed, in both *Karácsony and Others* v. *Hungary* (violation of Article 10) and *Ikotity and Others* v. *Hungary* (non-violation of Article 10), the Court satisfies itself with the mere existence of the domestic authority – in that case, the parliamentary committee in charge of disciplinary sanctions and the parliamentary committee for immunities, respectively – having a procedure in place that guarantees the inclusion of the appellant ('the right to be heard') and the obligation of state basic reasons for the decision to interfere with the Convention. Importantly, and following the model of procedural review, it does not assess the necessity determination of the domestic authority in its own terms. In *Karácsony*, which concerned ex-post disciplinary sanction by a parliamentary committee, the Court held that:

> it sees no need to rule on whether, bearing in mind the State's wide margin of appreciation, those reasons as such were also sufficient to show that the

> disputed interference was 'necessary'. The Court finds it more appropriate to concentrate its review on whether the restriction on the applicants' right to freedom of expression was accompanied by effective and adequate safeguards against abuse.[43]

These include the 'right to be heard'[44] and the obligation to 'state basic reasons, thus not only enabling the MP concerned to understand the justification for the measure but also permitting some form of public scrutiny of it'.[45] Here again, if the Court had engaged in infrastructural reasoning beyond recording the mere existence of these procedural safeguards, the necessity of the interference would have looked very different. By opting for a procedural review, the Court refrains from examining the distortions of democracy, particularly the deliberative ones, strikingly assuming that there can be 'some form of public scrutiny' in a Hungarian society riddled with deliberative and representative distortions. Here again, the Court could have repositioned the interference within an infrastructural analysis, paying utmost attention to the holistic nature of its celebrated 'democratic society'.

In *Ikotity and Others* v. *Hungary*, the Court goes one step further in endorsing the government's own determination of the necessity of the interference. This determination of government is presented in the text of the case as follows:

> [. . .] the use of the illustration requested by the LMP leader was 'not necessarily required' in order to understand the content of the interpellation and to expand on its meaning [. . .]

and that

> the purpose of the . . . illustration in this case was, contrary to what is stated in the application for redress, clearly not to properly express and substantiate the opinion of the interpellant, but [to use it] as a means of protest and political confrontation.[46]

In its assessment, the Court does not review such a determination on its own terms – terms that could be informed by much larger infrastructural considerations. Rather, it relies on the margin of appreciation and the fact that the applicants knew they were breaching the applicable rules of

43 *Karácsony and Others* v. *Hungary*, para. 151.
44 *Karácsony*, para. 157.
45 *Karácsony*, para. 158.
46 *Ikotity and Others v. Hungary*, para. 12.

conduct in parliament – and, places the burden of demonstration onto them:

> The Court, having regard to the margin of appreciation afforded to the national bodies in this respect, will confine itself to noting that the applicants – being aware that their request for permission to use the posters had been refused – knowingly acted in breach of the applicable rules of conduct, which aggravated the nature of the disciplinary breach [. . .]. The applicants did not argue, let alone show, that the sanctions they had received were more severe than those imposed for disciplinary breaches on the MPs from the ruling party alliance.[47]

Yet there is no domain analysed in this investigation that better reflects the ill-equipment of the Court to respond to populism than its scrutiny of electoral systems and, within them, the review of post-election complaints and appeals. On the substantive front, I made the argument in Chapter 8 that the Court's standards for finding a violation of Article P1-3 are strictly limited to arbitrary instances of disenfranchisement, reducing the right to free and fair election to the formal inclusion in the majoritarian voting process. While it celebrates complementarity between the deliberative stage (via Articles 10–11) and the electoral stage (via Article P1-3), in effect, the Court decidedly disentangles the two in adjudicatory routine, in particular in proportionality assessment. As argued in Chapter 8, the heightened risk is that the electoral stage becomes largely cosmetic and the meaning of democratic rights structured around the pursuit of mutual justifiability largely vacuous when the deliberative distortion has materialized.

To illustrate this discrepancy further, one only needs to look at the Court's practice of shifting the burden of evidence and demonstration to the applicant. I have made the argument that while the Court should systematically add evidence of infrastructural erosion that the government needs to rebut as part of the purpose stage review, in the electoral domain that burden of evidence strikingly falls upon the applicant – and this applies to the procedural arm of P1-3 specifically. Indeed, while it has started to do so in relation to alleged violations of Article 10 using inferential reasoning, under P1-3 the Court strictly requires a direct causal link between infrastructural erosion and the alleged violation of the right to stand for election. Recall the case of *The Georgian Labour Party* v. *Georgia*, in which the applicant party complained about the role of the president of Georgia's power to appoint seven of the fifteen

[47] *Ikotity*, para. 44.

members of the electoral commission (including the president). The Court acknowledged that:

> the contested composition of electoral commissions at all levels indeed lacked sufficient checks and balances against the President's power and that those commissions could hardly enjoy independence from the outside political pressure. However, in the absence of any proof of particular acts of abuse of power or electoral fraud committed within the electoral commissions to the applicant party's detriment, no breach of the latter's right to stand for election can be established.[48]

Now, this analysis allows us to draw a distinction between the Court's deficient analysis of infrastructural erosion generally, on the one hand, and the expanded review of such erosion when it engages in reviewing a similar factual presentation with the added purview of Article 18, on the other hand. In the latter case, the Court has indeed engaged in precisely the kind of inferential reasoning that widens the evidence span, which then allows the Court to shift the burden of demonstration onto the government. Recall the seminal case of *Merabishvili* v. *Georgia*, in which the Court showed a clear openness to reversing the burden of proof onto the government and specified its governing criterion of a proof 'beyond reasonable doubt' in order to establish violations of Article 18: 'when assessing evidence, it is not bound by formulae and adopts the conclusions supported by the free evaluation of all evidence, including such inferences as may flow from the facts and the parties' submissions'.[49] Also recall, more recently, *Juszczyszyn* v. *Poland*, which pertained to the suspension of a district court judge for having issued a court order asking about compliance with an EU law judgment. In that case, the Court goes further in defining its mode of reasoning: 'In this context, circumstantial evidence means information about the primary facts, or contextual facts or sequences of events which can form the basis for inferences about the primary facts.'[50]

Conversely, such expanded review only highlights the deficiency of the Court's proportionality test routinely applied by the Court – deficiencies that are even more salient in the context of populist infrastructural erosion. The question raised here is whether there is anything that is categorically distinct in Article 18 that the Court could not generalize if it were to revise its proportionality test along the lines proposed in this investigation. The answer is no. On the one hand, it is not just that Article

[48] *Georgian Labour Party* v. *Georgia*, para. 110.
[49] *Merabishvili* v. *Georgia*, para. 315.
[50] *Juszczyszyn* v. *Poland*, para. 316.

18 remedies the pre-existing deficiencies of the Court's proportionality test, in particular the purpose stage. Article 18 performs this task in a remedial manner in the Court finding a predominant or ulterior purpose other than the one presented by the government. There is nothing in the task of purpose finding that the generic test, when duly and consistently applied, could not perform. In other words, the added value of Article 18 is potentially built into a systematic revision of the purpose stage. At the very least, this is required to detect and counter the distortion of democracy orchestrated of the populists. It is not only that the Court's record of applying Article 18 is on its own terms deficient. It is also that, as I suggested in Chapter 7, while Article 18 has entailed the expansion of the agency of the Court in uncovering infrastructural erosion, the normative domain of Article 18 remains highly indeterminate. In practice, the Court's history has addressed distinctively rule of law concerns, which have typically taken the form of Article 5 (and recently, Article 6) violations. As suggested in Chapter 5, while authoritarian governments typically use the coercive powers of criminal law to silence opposition figures while invoking a Convention-authorized, but easily abusable, aim – for example, 'the protection of public order' – populist times have come, and it is equally time that the Court adapts its interpretive equipment to that specific form of erosion.

10

Conclusion

In Chapter 1, I set the goal of the investigation to bring in closer contact the new realities of the populist age with the Court's interpretive record of protecting democracy and the rule of law through the medium of rights, with a view to calibrating the Court's interpretive equipment to respond to this phenomenon. This project had a methodological and substantive component: methodologically, it required crafting an interdisciplinary framework to analyse the phenomenon of (authoritarian) populism in theoretical, social scientific, and legal terms, ensuring that the analysis is the most appropriate for and specific to this phenomenon. Substantively, the project aimed at evaluating the Court's equipment in a comprehensive, yet focused and structured, manner, identifying not only where the Court could do more and better, but also explaining why it should do so and where its current limitations could originate. It is now time to recapitulate the milestones achieved in a succinct and compact manner, to consider potential objections to the core arguments, and to draw the main conclusions for subsequent research on the theme.

The first and preliminary stage of our inquiry, reached in Chapter 2, was to highlight the lack of Court-centred analysis of the Court's role and practice considering the more specific threat of authoritarian populism as distinct from the totalitarianism(s) that the Court's initial mandate was focused on. Indeed, the limitations of the literature on the legal response to authoritarian populism are twofold: one, it is often challenging to discern if the response specifically applies to populism as opposed to a more general mechanism to respond to anti-democratic threats, as reflected in the literature on 'militant democracy'. This justified exploring the concept of populism, both descriptively and normatively, also considering that such an exploration cannot be evaluated without involving one's assumptions and premises about what constitutes a normatively compelling political and legal order, including the place and limits of (democratic) rights in it. The central claim in that regard is that authoritarian populism is a severe distortion of democratic deliberation and representation as overarching values, which I take to be normatively central to the legitimacy of the democratic process. The (thin) rule of law, which I envisaged to be the consequence of democratic distortion, is attacked directly – it is therefore corrupt – but in a multifaceted manner that resists generalization. I took this analysis to offer insights as to *why*, ultimately, one should care about the rise of authoritarian populism in the first place, adducing the methodological requirement that one should rationally link, as much as possible, the discourse and the manifestations of populism to that specific ideational and normative basis.

Two, the conceptual, normative, and methodological framework that underpins the legal response in the current literature is archetypically constitutional, as argued in Chapter 3. By 'constitutional', I implied a basic framework of shared and balanced authority between constituted powers in a hermetically sealed domestic sphere that can be comprehensively reviewed and recalibrated to prevent overreach, particularly the executive. Whether the Convention and the Court can play a role within this framework has not been studied in great depth. An example of this has been the revival of interest in the enhanced account of judicial review by J. H. Ely, giving rise to a flurry of recent contributions that identify the blind spots of conventional accounts, which can stretch to conferring an enhanced role and responsibility to *any* domestic (constitutional) institution or actor in the constitutional framework whose function has systematic effects on the democratic process.[1] This constitutional approach has its own valid motivations: authoritarian populists in power have a clear tendency to alter, if not dismember, the positive constitutional framework it inherits, with a strong emphasis on constitutional court packing. And a response that prevents, rather than remedying, the constitutional alterations of populism and its ensuing damage appears prudent. Yet translating this framework onto the plane of a regional human rights court comes at the cost of side-stepping what makes human rights distinct across the legal and judicial realm, affecting the relevance and applicability of the research design.

My challenge to the constitutionalist approach is not only that the Court's jurisdiction is constrained by its international and subsidiary jurisdictions and limited subject matter, the Convention rights, and, therefore, any readjustment or 'recalibration' of the Court's scrutiny in

[1] Gardbaum, 'Human Rights as International Constitutional Rights'; Gardbaum, 'Comparative Political Process Theory II'; Gardbaum, 'Comparative Political Process Theory'; Dixon and Landau, '1989–2019'; Dixon and Landau, *Abusive Constitutional Borrowing*.

principled terms must take these parameters into account. In fact, subsidiarity at the interpretive level has reached new heights through the rise of 'procedural review', which further highlights whether such doctrine, as it emerges in the Court's case law, remains warranted in the populist context, considering the populists' talent for running procedures and preserving institutions while operating them against their very purpose. The fact that authoritarian populists still operate within the familiar forms of the law casts doubt on whether a formal review, even informed by the substantive standards of the Convention and the Court, is sufficient.

More fundamentally, I argued that democracy, rather than constitutionalism, is a more insightful framework conceptually, normatively, and methodologically for the purpose of examining the Court's response to authoritarian populism. Democracy matters not only because it can bridge from the jurisdictional question of subsidiarity – that is, to explain when the supranational level of the Court's jurisdiction is engaged in the first place – to the substance of democratic rights themselves, namely, to explain the Court's reliance on its 'democratic society' to modulate its level of scrutiny, including by allocating the margin of appreciation. It is also because, again, authoritarian populism, from the perspectives of its discourse and practical effects, can itself be viewed as a distortion of democracy, including by the means of corrupting the rule of law. More simply put, I argued that democracy should have conceptual priority in addressing the claims of populism, on the one hand, and has more currency in the context of the Court's practice, on the other. This democratic nexus can enhance, I believe, our understanding of (the pathologies of) populism also to ground the claim that there exists a close relationship between this phenomenon, on the one hand, and the role and practice of the Court, on the other – one that is amenable to an in-depth and mutually informative investigation about the response and the role, actual and potential, of the Court in the populist age.

The immediate constraints adduced to this project, of course, were that the Convention only protects certain democratic and rule of law rights, and therefore the reflection from a democratic perspective should apply first and foremost to these rights as they are defined and interpreted by the Court. Yet rights do not exhaust our democratic imagination. Rather than just rights, democratic values – via democratic theory – must be mobilized to enable a genuinely critical perspective on the Court's records. In Chapter 3, I argued that authoritarian populism distorts two cardinal values of the democratic process, deliberation and representation. On the one hand, the antagonistic horizon of authoritarian populism disables the role of deliberation as the mediating procedure for justifying political authority (or attempting to do so). By its exclusionary nature, authoritarian populism exacerbates deliberative and representative inequalities. On the other hand, while elections remain essential to populist representation, their normative role is peripheral if not epiphenomenal: elections confirm and celebrate a pre-existing and evident embodiment of the people into a person, the leader. In both cases, authoritarian populism compresses the necessary vacuum that is distinctive of democratic deliberation and representation. This explains why authoritarian populists can operate democratically while hollowing out what is substantively 'democratic' about the democratic process, including (failing to grant) an independent normative value to democratic procedures and the rule of law substantively understood. This theoretical foundation allowed for measuring the gravity of the erosion in question.

In crafting the framework, I also brought further angles that have important democratic meaning in the Court's context. Historically, by retrieving the idea that while the 'alarm bell' function of the Convention system has today consolidated and grown into a system of individual justice that ramifies into (limiting) the day-to-day exercise of any public authority in the forty-six state parties to it, history lingers. And as far as the lineaments of the Court's understanding of democracy and the rule of law are concerned, one can discern a clear and continuous emphasis on the rights of political opposition, and the imperative of protecting a vibrant democratic arena – for every voice to find a place in a democratic arena, which I labelled 'deliberative pluralism'. Jurisprudentially, as I argued more conclusively in Chapter 10, democracy also concerns one of the core functions of the Court's review, namely the proportionality assessment of the interferences with Convention rights, which can be reconstructed as an assessment of the deliberative records of governments, the normative basis of which is the justifiability to free and equal moral agents. By establishing the normative foundations in Chapter 3 and in returning to them in Chapter 9, I aimed at closing a circle in a conceptually and methodologically consistent manner. What was included between Chapter 4 and Chapter 8 are more fact-dependent (empirically or legally) and therefore needed to be delineated as such in the structure of the book.

The reason why this investigation paid utmost attention to research design and methodology is that authoritarian populism has been predominantly explored as an ideational construct by political and constitutional theorists, less as a practice of governments and its implications for rights.[2] To bridge the gap between the practice of the Court and an ideational construct, one needs to have at least an overview of what populist governments do when in power and identify which rights may be implicated in these practices, which then allows for evaluating whether the Court is aptly responding to it. To address that concern, a more social scientific perspective was needed to specify *how* democracy and the rule of law are eroded by authoritarian populism in Chapter 5. This component, I have emphasized, is certainly only indicative and heuristic – the claims held in that chapter were situational in approximating the areas and domains in which authoritarian governments in Europe have shown activity in recent years, helping with the subsequent identification not just of the relevant Convention rights, but of the relevant aspects of these rights that should be more closely examined.

Reflecting on these effects, I argued and illustrated throughout Chapters 5 to 8 that authoritarian populism indeed erodes democratic deliberation and democratic representation and corrupts the rule of law – albeit in a distinctively infrastructural manner, which allowed for specifying which aspects of the Convention rights that need particular attention. The media, the justice system, and the electoral system are the key domains of democratic and rule of law infrastructure whose erosion can make the individual exercise of associated rights lose their meaning and purpose. Infrastructural erosion, distinct from coercive attack, does not target individuals specifically. But since infrastructure reflects the point or purpose of the rights, eroding infrastructure indirectly affects these rights. I offered the further philosophical interpretation that infrastructural erosion indirectly, but deliberately, targets the background norms that make the pursuit of mutual justifiability possible. To summarize just one domain covered in Chapter 6, I illustrated how infrastructural erosion takes place in Hungary and Poland. On the one hand, it concerns the capture of key monitoring, regulatory, and oversight bodies with the power to discipline the activities of the press (in print or online), radio, and television alike without attacking the freedom of press coercively. As far as deliberation is concerned, captured bodies that typically fail to give reasoned decisions are more generally prone to expedite processes altogether. This could concern the licensing

[2] See the contributions in Andreas Føllesdal, Jan Petrov, and Alain Zysset, 'The ECtHR's Response to Illiberal and Authoritarian Practices', *ECHR Law Review*, forthcoming 2026.

of channels, the review of complaints pointing to government propaganda dressed as public information campaigns, or the practice of mergers and acquisitions in public and private and media markets. As far as representation is concerned, captured bodies with seats occupied by ruling party members only and accountable only to the government that appointed them blatantly fail to include political opposition and dissensus.

Democratic infrastructure is the weak point of the Court's equipment for interpreting the relevant Convention rights. The Court may be well equipped to protect the open, public, and deliberative arena – but that concentration is at odds with the populist modality of eroding the very background and norms required by and for democratic deliberation. This is seen not only in reviewing the general principles of interpretation associated with rights, but also in the operation of proportionality, where the Court often fails to assess the point and purpose of the restriction of these rights in the infrastructural domain, as I showed in Chapter 6. For example, in the former case, while the Court does adduce a duty of 'positive pluralism' to Article 10, requiring that state parties put in place a pluralistic media system, the violations found on these grounds concern situations where the very existence of any kind of pluralism is at risk, or when a media oversight body fails *at all* to represent political forces, in particular the opposition. In the latter case, I showed how the Court not engaging with purposive analysis under its proportionality review disables the very possibility of considering the infrastructural breadth of the populist capture of the media. The Court could object that it does have a dedicated category of 'procedural safeguards' deployed to limit the effects of the capture on individuals, but it has remained a largely formalistic, box-ticking exercise. Moreover, often the Court again reviews these obligations at the expense of the purpose of the necessity of the interference in the first place. This jurisprudential analysis reflected the wider, cross-perspectival point running through the investigation, that the Court has been focused on what I have called 'existential' threats to democracy.

As far as the rule of law provisions are concerned, the analysis in Chapter 7 concluded that while the Court has extended standards of independence and impartiality to some bodies at risk of infrastructural erosion under Article 6, such as judicial councils, these are considered on ad hoc basis as opposed to identifying a typology of oversight, regulatory, and supervisory agencies that may be subject to erosion. The guarantees could apply to appeal bodies in the media or electoral domains, for example. The claim here is that the Court has not yet delineated a distinct type of alteration to the infrastructure of democracy and the rule of law in its reasoning, one that the authoritarian populist process of capture highlights. As a result, the Court has not recalibrated its demands and requirements to the respondent state party accordingly. In this context, I also claimed that the rise of Article 18 in recent years raises both hope and concern. There is hope that when the Court scrutinizes the purpose of the interference, it conducts precisely the holistic assessment required to depict infrastructural erosion, notably by drawing a web of concordant inferences observable in the state party. However, the normative domain of Article 18 needs to be calibrated and reach beyond rule of law issues (under Article 5 and, more recently, under Article 6) to include distortions to democracy proper, so that the Court's interpretive equipment cuts across the wider array of populist targets. It seems, however, difficult to address purposive issues systematically without including the wider purpose stage under the more general regime of proportionality analysis.

But there is no other domain relevant to the Court's 'democratic society' that is more thinly protected from authoritarian populism than the electoral ecosystem under Article 3 Protocol 1. In Chapter 8, I showed how the Court proclaims that electoral norms and processes form an inherent part of its 'democratic society'. What is more, the Court emphasizes how the circulation and exchange of ideas matter prominently during the pre-electoral period. In that sense, the very integrity of the electoral process depends not only on the election taking place and meeting minimal standards, but on the deliberative and representative record of the pre-electoral moment. That is where I detect the link between the Court's principle of 'deliberative pluralism', which guides the Court's review of Articles 10–11, and P1-3 – it cannot obtain without having a thorough and deliberative process involving the range of agents that the Court has routinely identified as the 'watchdogs of a democratic society'. Because of this intuitively clear link, one would expect this corollary would be the cornerstone of the Court's review under P1-3. The Court would pay the utmost attention to the infrastructural distortions that may *in fine* compromise the purpose and meaning of the electoral process. Strikingly, the Court does not bridge the two. The limited scope of its interpretive principles, both substantive and procedural, have remained the same almost since the Court's founding. Protecting individuals against isolated instances of arbitrary disenfranchisement remains the norm and misses the infrastructural landscape – again, a requirement without which there is no democracy to speak of.

While the Court may investigate 'procedural safeguards' here too, it still does not examine the restriction beyond basic rule of law and proportionality criteria. The margin of appreciation abounds.

In the conclusive Chapter 9, I argued that one central tool at the Court's disposal that speaks both to the triad of democratic deliberation, democratic representation, and the rule of law and to the observed limitations of the Court's record is an enhanced proportionality assessment. There is not only an affinity between democracy and the rule of law and proportionality. I argued that they also normatively cohere in principle. As much as deliberation and representation involve a vacuum as to the locus of political power, proportionality involves a vacuum as to the justifiability of interferences with rights. More precisely, proportionality requires democratic deliberation and representation in that the Court evaluates the reasons that are justifiable to free and equal moral agents and ensures that minorities are not un- or misrepresented. In that sense, there is a general case that proportionality can operate as an anti-populist detector and responder. The specific case pertains to *where* in the Court's review the Court could practically enhance its equipment while mobilizing its account of 'democratic society' along the calibration connecting the infrastructural and superstructural levels. I argued that infrastructural erosion highlights and exacerbates the deficiencies of the Court's assessment of the legitimate aim pursued by the respondent state party. The growing case law on Article 18 not only corroborates this assessment in leaving open the normative grounds for which a 'bad faith' test should be warranted but also paves the way for the Court to identify the (predominant) purpose by reasoning holistically and inferentially – a form of reasoning that attracts the multifaceted infrastructural erosion of authoritarian populism.

Is the implication of this final argument that states parties are by default suspected of 'bad faith' when their records are reviewed by the Court – an implication that may trigger backlash? The argument resists such an implication on two grounds. First, the Court has found violations of the Convention under the legitimate aim stage without involving the addition of Article 18, and increasingly so. The distinct obstacle here is not the application of the purpose test, but the normative and empirical basis upon which it ought to proceed. To proceed empirically, the revised test requires principled pointers that can inform its inferential and holistic reasoning. The balancing exercise still needs to be performed, implying that the purpose stage remains informative, rather than decisive, in the Court's review. Second, and as a result, reviewing the purpose stage cannot be completed without revising the Court's 'democratic society' in a substantive and principled sense. Here, the argument is not that such a society, looking at it from a principled perspective, is ill equipped, but rather that the populists' distortions of it, which are predominantly infrastructural, are not well identified and systematized. Third, while this investigation aimed at delivering a practice-informed and practicable account, its core contribution remains interdisciplinary and reflective in that sense, rather than designing guidelines for judicial methodology. It seeks to strengthen a philosophically informed yet situated account not just of the Convention, but of the Court's role and practice – one that can overcome the disciplinary silos that persistently clog the reflective and academic space on human rights law and institutions.

BIBLIOGRAPHY

Books

Albertazzi, Daniele, and McDonnell, Duncan. *Populists in Power* (Routledge, 2015).

Barak, Aharon. *Proportionality: Constitutional Rights and Their Limitations* (Cambridge University Press, 2012).

Bates, Ed. *The Evolution of the European Convention on Human Rights: From Its Inception to the Creation of a Permanent Court of Human Rights* (Oxford University Press, 2010).

Bilchitz, David. *Poverty and Fundamental Rights: The Justification and Enforcement of Socio-economic Rights* (Oxford University Press, 2007).

Carter, Anne. *Proportionality and Facts in Constitutional Adjudication* (Hart Publishing, 2023).

Christoffersen, Jonas. *Fair Balance: Proportionality, Subsidiarity and Primarity in the European Convention on Human Right* (Brill Nijhoff, 2009).

Cohen, Joshua. *Rousseau: A Free Community of Equals* (Oxford University Press, 2010).

Cohen-Eliya, Moshe, and Porat, Iddo. *Proportionality and Constitutional Culture* (Cambridge University Press, 2013).

Council of Europe, *Collected Edition of the 'Travaux préparatoires' of the European Convention on Human Rights / Recueil des travaux préparatoires de la Convention européenne des droits de l'homme* (Martinus Nijhoff, 1975).

Cruft, Rowan, Liao, Matthew, and Renzo, Massimo, eds. *Philosophical Foundations of Human Rights* (Oxford University Press, 2015).

de Morree, Paulien. *Rights and Wrongs Under the ECHR: The Prohibition of Abuse of Rights in Article 17 of the European Convention on Human Rights* (Intersentia, 2016).

Dixon, Rosalind. *Responsive Judicial Review: Democracy and Dysfunction in the Modern Age* (Oxford University Press, 2023).

Dixon, Rosalind, and Landau, David. *Abusive Constitutional Borrowing* (Oxford University Press, 2021).

Duranti, Marco. *The Conservative Human Rights Revolution: European Identity, Transnational Politics, and the Origins of the European Convention* (Oxford University Press, 2017).

Dworkin, Ronald. *Law's Empire* (Belknap Press, 1988).

Dzehtsiarou, Kanstantsin. *Can the European Court of Human Rights Shape European Public Order?* (Cambridge University Press, 2021).

Ely, John Hart. *Democracy and Distrust: A Theory of Judicial Review* (Harvard University Press, 1980).

Finchelstein, Federico. *From Fascism to Populism in History* (University of California Press, 2019).

Forst, Rainer. *The Right to Justification: Elements of a Constructivist Theory of Justice*, trans. Jeffrey Flynn (Columbia University Press, 2011).

Fuller, Lon L. *The Morality of Law* (Yale University Press, 1969).

Griffin, James. *On Human Rights* (Oxford University Press, 2008).

Kirshner, Alexander, and Malkopoulou, Anthoula. *Militant Democracy and Its Critics: Populism, Parties, Extremism* (Edinburgh University Press, 2021).

Laclau, Ernesto. *On Populist Reason* (Verso, 2007).

Langvatn, Silje, Kumm, Mattias, and Sadurski, Wojcieh. EDS *Public Reason and Courts* (Cambridge University Press, 2020).

Lautenbach, Geranne. *The Concept of the Rule of Law and the European Court of Human Rights* (Oxford University Press, 2013).

Lefort, Claude. *Democracy and Political Theory* (University of Minnesota Press, 1989).

Levitsky, Steven, and Ziblatt, Daniel. *How Democracies Die* (Viking, 2018).

Martinico, Giuseppe. *Filtering Populist Claims to Fight Populism: The Italian Case in a Comparative Perspective* (Cambridge University Press, 2021).

Moffitt, Benjamin. *The Global Rise of Populism: Performance, Political Style, and Representation*, 1st ed. (Stanford University Press, 2016).

Möller, Kai. *The Global Model of Constitutional Rights* (Oxford University Press, 2012).

Müller, Jan-Werner. *What Is Populism?* (University of Pennsylvania Press, 2016).

Norris, Pippa. *Why Electoral Integrity Matters* (Cambridge University Press, 2014).

Näsström, Sofia. *The Spirit of Democracy Corruption, Disintegration, Renewal* (Oxford University Press, 2021).

Rawls, John. *Political Liberalism* (Columbia University Press, 1993).

Raz, Joseph. *The Morality of Freedom* (Clarendon Press, 1979).

Rostbøll, Christian. *Democratic Respect: Populism, Resentment, and the Struggle for Recognition* (Cambridge University Press, 2023).

Rousseau, Jean-Jacques. *The Social Contract and Other Later Political Writings*, ed. Victor Gourevitch (Cambridge University Press, 2019).

Roznai, Yaniv. *Unconstitutional Constitutional Amendments: The Limits of Amendment Powers* (Oxford University Press, 2019).

Sadurski, Wojciech. *A Pandemic of Populists* (Cambridge: Cambridge University Press, 2022).

Sadurski, Wojciech. *Poland's Constitutional Breakdown* (Oxford University Press, 2019).

Sajó, András. *Ruling by Cheating: Governance in Illiberal Democracy* (Cambridge University Press, 2021).

Schmitt, Carl. *The Concept of the Political*, expanded ed., trans. George Schwab (University of Chicago Press, 2007 [1932]).

Simpson, Alfred W. B. *Human Rights and the End of Empire: Britain and the Genesis of the European Convention* (Oxford University Press, 2004).

Tushnet, Mark. *The New Fourth Branch: Institutions for Protecting Constitutional Democracy* (Cambridge University Press, 2021).

Tushnet, Mark, and Bugaric, Bojan. *Power to the People: Constitutionalism in the Age of Populism* (Oxford University Press, 2022).

Tyulkina, Svetlana. *Militant Democracy: Undemocratic Political Parties and Beyond* (Routledge, 2015).

Urbinati, Nadia. *Me the People: How Populism Transforms Democracy* (Harvard University Press, 2019).

Vidmar, Jure. *European Populism and Human Rights* (Brill Nijhoff, 2020).

Waldron, Jeremy. *Law and Disagreement* (Oxford University Press, 1999).

Young, Alison. *Unchecked Power: How Recent Constitutional Reforms Are Threatening UK Democracy*, abridged ed. (Bristol University Press, 2023).

Zysset, Alain. *The ECHR and Human Rights Theory: Reconciling the Moral and Political Conceptions* (Routledge, 2017).

Edited Books

Belavusau, Uladzislau, and Gliszczyńska-Grabias, Aleksandra, eds. *Law and Memory: Towards Legal Governance of History* (Cambridge University Press, 2017).

Closa, Carlos, and Kochenov, Dimitry, eds. *Reinforcing Rule of Law Oversight in the European Union* (Cambridge University Press, 2016).

Etinson, Adam, ed. *Human Rights: Moral or Political?* (Oxford University Press, 2018).

Sajó, András, Uitz, Renáta, and Holmes, Stephen, eds. *Routledge Handbook of Illiberalism* (Routledge, 2021).

Chapters in Edited Books

Arai-Takahashi, Yukata. 'The Margin of Appreciation Doctrine: A Theoretical Analysis of Strasbourg's Variable Geometry', in *Constituting Europe: The European Court of Human Rights in a National, European and Global Context*, ed. Andreas Føllesdal, Birgit Peters, and Geir Ulfstein (Cambridge University Press, 2013): 62–105.

Bates, Ed. 'The Birth of the European Convention on Human Rights and the European Court of Human Rights', in *The European Court of Human Rights between Law and Politics*, ed. Jonas Christoffersen and Mikael Rask Madsen (Oxford University Press, 2011): 17–42.

Blokker, Paul. 'Populist Constitutionalism', in 'Global Populism Histories, Trajectories, Problems, and Challenges', in *Routledge Handbook of Global Populism*, ed. Carlos de la Torre (Routledge, 2018): 147–62.

Bodnár, Eszter. 'Disarming the Guardians: The Transformation of the Hungarian Constitutional Court after 2010', in *Anti-constitutional Populism*, ed. Martin Krygier, Adam Czarnota, and Wojciech Sadurski (Cambridge University Press, 2022): 254–94.

Brems, Eva. 'Procedural Protection: An Examination of Procedural Safeguards Read into Substantive Convention Rights', in *Shaping Rights in the ECHR: The Role of the European Court of Human Rights in Determining the Scope of Human Rights*, ed. Eva Brems and Janneke Gerards (Cambridge University Press, 2014): 137–61.

Brzozowski, Wojciech. 'Whatever Works: Constitutional Interpretation in Poland in Times of Populism', in *Populist Challenges to Constitutional Interpretation in Europe and Beyond*, ed. Fruzsina Gárdos-Orosz and Zoltán Szente (Routledge, 2021): 174–93.

Çalı, Başak. 'International Judicial Review', in *Handbook on Global Constitutionalism*, ed. Anthony F. Lang and Antje Werner (Edward Elgar Publishing, 2017): 291–303.

Chambers, Simone. 'Proceduralising the People: Deliberative Democracy, Majority Rule and the Rule of Law', in *Rule of Law vs Majoritarian Democracy*, ed. Giuliano Amato, Benedetta Barbisan, and Cesare Pinelli (Hart, 2021): 109–20.

Cohen, Joshua. 'Deliberation and Democratic Legitimacy', in *Deliberative Democracy: Essays on Reason and Politics*, ed. James Bohman and William Rehg (MIT Press, 1998): 67–92.

Cohen, Joshua. 'Procedure and Substance in Deliberative Democracy', in *Deliberative Democracy: Essays on Reason and Politics*, ed. James Bohman and William Rehg (MIT Press, 1998): 407–26.

Damiani, Marco. 'Radical Left-Wing Populism and Democracy in Europe', in *Routledge Handbook of Global Populism*, ed. Carlos de la Torre (Routledge, 2018): 473–85.

Diehl, Paula. 'Twisting Representation', in *Routledge Handbook of Global Populism*, ed. Carlos de la Torre (Routledge, 2018): 129–43.

Enyedi, Zsolt, and Whitefield, Stephen. 'Populists in Power: Populism and Representation in Illiberal Democracies', in *The Oxford Handbook of Political Representation in Liberal Democracies*, ed. Robert Rohrschneider and Jacques Thomassen (Oxford University Press, 2020): 582–98.

Fox, Gregory H., and Nolte, Georg. 'Intolerant Democracies', in *Democratic Governance and International Law*, ed. Gregory H. Fox and Brad R. Roth (Cambridge University Press, 2000): 389–435.

Gamper, Anna. 'An "Instrument of Government" or "Instrument of Courts"? The Impact of Political Systems on Constitutional Interpretation and the Case of Populism', in *Populist Challenges to Constitutional Interpretation in Europe and Beyond*, ed. Fruzsina Gárdos-Orosz and Zoltán Szente (Routledge, 2021): 47–63.

Gerards, Janneke. 'Procedural Review by the ECtHR: A Typology', in *Procedural Review in European Fundamental Rights Cases*, ed. Eva Brems and Janneke Gerards (Cambridge University Press, 2017): 127–60.

Halmai, Gábor. 'Illiberalism in East Central Europe', in *Routledge Handbook of Illiberalism*, ed. András Sajó, Renáta Uitz, and Stephen Holmes (Routledge, 2021): 813–21.

Halmai, Gábor. 'The Making of "Illiberal Constitutionalism" with or without a New Constitution: The Case of Hungary and Poland', in *Comparative Constitution Making*, ed. David Landau and Hanna Lerner (Edward Elgar Publishing, 2019): 302–23.

Hawkins, Kirk A. 'The Ideational Approach', in *Routledge Handbook of Global Populism*, ed. Carlos de la Torre (Routledge, 2018): 57–71.

Helfer, Lawrence. 'Populism and International Human Rights Law Institutions: A Survival Guide', in *Human Rights in a Time of Populism: Challenges and Responses*, ed. Gerald Neuman (Cambridge University Press, 2021): 218–49.

Krygier, Martin. 'Illiberalism and the Rule of Law', in *Routledge Handbook of Illiberalism*, ed. András Sajó, Renáta Uitz, and Stephen Holmes, 1st ed. (Routledge, 2021): 533–53.

Krygier, Martin. 'Tempering Power', in *Constitutionalism and the Rule of Law: Bridging Idealism and Realism*, ed. Maurice Adams, Anne Meuwese, and Ernst Hirsch Ballin (Cambridge University Press, 2017): 34–59.

Kumm, Mattias. 'Is the Structure of Human Rights Practice Defensible? Three Puzzles and Their Resolution', in *Proportionality: New Frontiers, New Challenges*, ed. Mark Tushnet and Vicki C. Jackson (Cambridge University Press, 2017): 30–50.

Kumm, Mattias. 'The Turn to Justification: On the Structure and Domain of Human Rights Practice', in *Human Rights: Moral or Political?*, ed. Adam Etinson (Oxford University Press, 2018): 238–61.

Kumm, Mattias, and Walen, Alec D. 'Human Dignity and Proportionality: Deontic Pluralism in Balancing', in *Proportionality and the Rule of Law: Rights, Justification, Reasoning*, ed. Bradley W. Miller, Grant Huscroft, and Grégoire Webber (Cambridge University Press, 2014): 67–89.

Madsen, Mikael Rask. 'From Boom to Backlash? The European Court of Human Rights and the Transformation of Europe', in *The European Court of Human*

Rights, ed. Helmut Aust, Esra Demir-Gürsel, and Georg Forster (Edward Elgar Publishing, 2021): 21–42.

Mahoney, Paul. 'The Changing Face of the European Court of Human Rights', in *Trends in the International Law of Human Rights: Studies in Honour of Professor Antônio Augusto Cançado Trindade*, ed. S. A. Fabris, vol. 2 (forthcoming 2025).

Manucci, Luca. 'Populism and the Media', in *The Oxford Handbook of Populism*, ed. Cristóbal Rovira Kaltwasser, Paul Taggart, Paulin Ochoa Espejo, and Pierre Ostiguy (Oxford University Press, 2019): 467–88.

Mazzoleni, Gianpietro. 'Populism and the Media', in *Twenty-First Century Populism: The Spectre of Western European Democracy*, ed. Daniele Albertazzi and Duncan McDonnell (Palgrave Macmillan UK, 2008): 49–64.

Mudde, Cas. 'Populism: An Ideational Approach', in *The Oxford Handbook of Populism*, ed. Cristóbal Rovira Kaltwasser, Paul Taggart, Paulin Ochoa Espejo, and Pierre Ostiguy (Oxford University Press, 2017): 1–26.

Mudde, Cas, and Rovira Kaltwasser, Cristóbal. 'Populism and (Liberal) Democracy: A Framework for Analysis', in *Populism in Europe and the Americas: Threat or Corrective for Democracy?*, ed. Cas Mudde and Cristóbal Rovira Kaltwasser (Cambridge University Press, 2012): 1–26.

Müller, Jan-Werner. 'Militant Democracy', in *The Oxford Handbook of Comparative Constitutional Law*, ed. Michel Rosenfeld and András Sajó (Oxford University Press, 2012): 1253–69.

Müller, Jan-Werner. 'Protecting the Rule of Law (and Democracy!) in the EU', in *Reinforcing Rule of Law Oversight in the European Union*, ed. Carlos Closa and Dimitry Kochenov (Cambridge University Press, 2016): 206–24.

Müller, Jan-Werner. 'Stronger Together? Populist (and Non-populist) Politics of Peoplehood', in *Rule of Law vs Majoritarian Democracy*, ed. Giuliano Amato, Benedetta Barbisan, and Cesare Pinelli (Hart Publishing, 2021): 157–70.

Neuman, Gerald L. 'Subsidiarity', in *The Oxford Handbook of International Human Rights Law*, ed. Dinah Shelton (Oxford University Press, 2015): 360–78.

Norris, Pippa. 'The Populist Challenge to Liberal Democracies', in *The Oxford Handbook of Political Representation in Liberal Democracies*, ed. Robert Rohrschneider and Jacques Thomassen (Oxford University Press, 2020): 544–62.

Nussberger, Angelika. 'Procedural Review by the ECHR: View from the Court', in *Procedural Review in European Fundamental Rights Cases*, ed. Eva Brems and Janneke Gerards (Cambridge University Press, 2017): 161–76.

Peruzzotti, Enrique. 'Laclau's Theory of Populism', in *Routledge Handbook of Global Populism*, ed. Carlos de la Torre, 1st ed. (Routledge, 2018): 29–43.

Rovira Kaltwasser, Cristóbal. 'Militant Democracy versus Populism', in *Militant Democracy and Its Critics: Populism, Parties, Extremism*, ed. Anthoula Malkopoulou and Alexandra Kirshner (Edinburgh University Press, 2019).

Rummens, Stefan. 'Populism as a Threat to Liberal Democracy', in *The Oxford Handbook of Populism*, ed. Cristóbal Rovira Kaltwasser, Paul Taggart, Paulin Ochoa Espejo, and Pierre Ostiguy (Oxford University Press, 2017): 554–70.

Sadurski, Wojciech. 'European Court of Human Rights in Pursuit of Public Reason? A Study of Lost Opportunities', in *Public Reason and Courts*, ed. Mattias Kumm, Silje A. Langvatn, and Wojciech Sadurski (Cambridge University Press, 2020): 231–55.

Sadurski, Wojciech. 'Institutional Populism, Courts, and the European Union', in *Anti-constitutional Populism*, ed. M. Krygier, A. Czarnota, and W. Sadurski (Cambridge University Press, 2022): 506–42.

Sadurski, Wojciech. 'Populism and Human Rights in Poland', in *Human Rights in a Time of Populism: Challenges and Responses*, ed. Gerald L. Neuman (Cambridge University Press, 2020): 60–80.

Stambulski, Michał. 'Constitutional Populism and the Rule of Law in Poland', in *Anti-constitutional Populism*, ed. Martin Krygier, Adam Czarnota, and Wojciech Sadurski (Cambridge University Press, 2023): 336–65.

Štětka, Václav, and Mihelj, Sabina. 'The Rise of the Illiberal Public Sphere', in *The Illiberal Public Sphere: Media in Polarized Societies*, ed. Václav Štětka and Sabina Mihelj (Springer, 2024): 25–59.

Szente, Zoltán. 'Populism and Populist Constitutionalism', in *Populist Challenges to Constitutional Interpretation in Europe and Beyond*, ed. Fruzsina Gárdos-Orosz and Zoltán Szente (Routledge, 2021): 3–28.

Taggart, Paul. 'Populism in Western Europe', in *The Oxford Handbook of Populism*, ed. Cristóbal Rovira Kaltwasser, Paul Taggart, Paulin Ochoa Espejo, and Pierre Ostiguy (Oxford University Press, 2017): 248–64.

Tóth, Gábor Attila. 'Illiberal Rule of Law? Changing Features of Hungarian Constitutionalism', in *Constitutionalism and the Rule of Law: Bridging Idealism and Realism*, ed. Maurice Adams, Anne Meuwese, and Ernst Hirsch Ballin (Cambridge University Press, 2017): 386–416.

Townend, Judith. 'Freedom of Expression and the Chilling Effect', in *The Routledge Companion to Media and Human Rights*, ed. Howard Tumber and Silvio Waisbord (Routledge, 2017): 73–82.

Vincze, Attila. 'Hungary: Regulatory Bodies in an Illiberal Democracy', in *Governance and Constitutionalism*, ed. Bogdan Iancu and Elena Simina Tănăsescu (Routledge, 2018): 119–33.

Wyrzykowski, Mirosław, and Ziółkowski, Michał. 'Illiberal Constitutionalism and the Judiciary', in *Routledge Handbook of Illiberalism*, ed. András Sajó, Renáta Uitz, and Stephen Holmes (Routledge, 2021): 517–32.

Young, Katharine G. 'Proportionality, Reasonableness, and Economic and Social Rights', in *Proportionality: New Frontiers, New Challenges*, ed. Mark Tushnet and Vicki C. Jackson (Cambridge University Press, 2017): 221–47.

Ziegler, Reuven. 'Voting Eligibility: Strasbourg's Timidity', in *The UK and European Human Rights: A Strained Relationship?*, ed. Loveday Hodson, Liz Wicks, and Katja Ziegler (Hart, 2015): 165–91.

Zysset, Alain. 'A Culture of Justification or a Culture of Presumption? The Turn to Procedural Review and the Normative Function of Proportionality at the European Court of Human Rights', in *Theory and Practice of the ECHR*, ed. Stephanie Schiedermair, Alexander Schwarz, and Dominik Steiger (Nomos/Hart Publishing, 2021): 215–32.

Zysset, Alain. 'The Right to Justification in the Context of Proportionality: A Plea for Determinacy and Stability', in *Public Reason and Courts*, ed. Mattias Kumm, Silje Langvatn, and Wojciech Sadurski (Cambridge University Press, 2020): 256–80.

Journal Articles

Albert, Richard. 'Constitutional Amendment and Dismemberment', *The Yale Journal of International Law* 43, no. 1 (2017): 1–84.

Arnardóttir, Oddný Mjöll. 'The "Procedural Turn" under the European Convention on Human Rights and Presumptions of Convention Compliance', *International Journal of Constitutional Law* 15, no. 1 (2017): 9–35.

Arnardóttir, Oddný Mjöll. 'Res Interpretata, Erga Omnes Effect and the Role of the Margin of Appreciation in Giving Domestic Effect to the Judgments of the European Court of Human Rights', *European Journal of International Law* 28, no. 3 (2017): 819–43.

Bajomi-Lázár, Péter. 'The Party Colonisation of the Media: The Case of Hungary', *East European Politics and Societies* 27, no. 1 (2012): 69–89.

Bánkuti, Miklós, Halmai, Gábor, and Scheppele, Kim Lane. 'Disabling the Constitution', *Journal of Democracy* 23, no. 3 (2012): 138–46.

Bates, Ed. 'Analysing the Prisoner Voting Saga and the British Challenge to Strasbourg', *Human Rights Law Review* 14, no. 3 (2014): 503–40.

Bellamy, Richard. 'The Democratic Legitimacy of International Human Rights Conventions: Political Constitutionalism and the European Convention on Human Rights', *European Journal of International Law* 25, no. 4 (2014): 1019–42.

Bermeo, Nancy. 'On Democratic Backsliding', *Journal of Democracy* 27, no. 1 (2016): 5–19.

Besson, Samantha. 'Subsidiarity in International Human Rights Law: What Is Subsidiary about Human Rights?', *The American Journal of Jurisprudence* 61, no. 1 (2016): 69–107.

Blokker, Paul. 'Populism as a Constitutional Project', *International Journal of Constitutional Law* 17, no. 2 (2019): 536–53.

Bugarič, Bojan. 'Could Populism Be Good for Constitutional Democracy?', *The Annual Review of Law and Social Science* 15, no. 1 (2019): 41–58.

Çalı, Başak. 'Coping with Crisis: Whither the Variable Geometry in the Jurisprudence of the European Court of Human Rights', *Wisconsin International Law Journal* 35, no. 2 (2018): 237–76.

Canovan, Margaret. 'Populism for Political Theorists?', *Journal of Political Ideologies* 9, no. 3 (2006): 241–52.

Canovan, Margaret. 'Trust the People! Populism and the Two Faces of Democracy', *Political Studies* 47, no. 1 (1999): 2–16.

Capoccia, Giovanni. 'Militant Democracy: The Institutional Bases of Democratic Self-Preservation', *The Annual Review of Law and Social Science* 9 (2013): 207–14.

Carozza, Paolo G. 'Subsidiarity as a Structural Principle of International Human Rights Law', *American Journal of International Law* 97, no. 38 (2003): 38–79.

Castillo-Ortiz, Pablo. 'The Illiberal Abuse of Constitutional Courts in Europe', *European Constitutional Law Review* 15, no. 1 (2019): 48–72.

Cohen-Eliya, Moshe, and Porat, Iddo. 'Proportionality in the Age of Populism', *The American Journal of Comparative Law* 69, no. 3 (2021): 449–77.

Corrias, Luigi. 'Populism in a Constitutional Key: Constituent Power, Popular Sovereignty and Constitutional Identity', *European Constitutional Law Review* 12, no. 1 (2016): 6–26.

Cumper, Peter, and Lewis, Tom. 'Blanket Bans, Subsidiarity, and the Procedural Turn of the European Court of Human Rights', *International & Comparative Law Quarterly* 68, no. 3 (2019): 611–38.

Daly, Tom Gerald. 'Democratic Decay: Conceptualising an Emerging Research Field', *Hague Journal on the Rule of Law* 11, no. 1 (2019): 9–36.

Dixon, Rosalind, and Landau, David. '1989–2019: From Democratic to Abusive Constitutional Borrowing', *International Journal of Constitutional Law* 17, no. 2 (2019): 489–96.

Doyle, Oran. 'Populist Constitutionalism and Constituent Power', *German Law Journal* 20, no. 2 (2019): 161–80.

Dragomir, Marius. 'Control the Money, Control the Media: How Government Uses Funding to Keep Media in Line', *Journalism* 19, no. 8 (2018): 1131–48.

Finnerty, Joseph. 'How Should the European Court of Human Rights Remedy Violations of Article 18 ECHR? The Case for Remedial Realignment', *European Convention on Human Rights Law Review* 5, no. 3 (2024): 380–99.

Finnerty, Joseph. 'When Is a State's "Hidden Agenda" Proven? The Role of the Merabishvili's Three-Legged Evidentiary Test in the Article 18 Strasbourg Case Law', *European Convention on Human Rights Law Review* 4, no. 4 (2023): 447–72.

Fomina, Joanna, and Kucharczyk, Jacek. 'Populism and Protest in Poland', *Journal of Democracy* 27, no. 4 (2016): 58–68.

Forst, Rainer. 'The Justification of Human Rights and the Basic Right to Justification: A Reflexive Approach', *Ethics* 120, no. 4 (2010): 711–40.

Føllesdal, Andreas. 'Subsidiarity and International Human-Rights Courts: Respecting Self-Governance and Protecting Human Rights – or Neither?', *Law and Contemporary Problems* 79, no. 2 (2016): 147–63.

Føllesdal, Andreas. 'Survey Article: Subsidiarity', *Journal of Political Philosophy* 6, no. 2 (1998): 190–218.

Føllesdal, Andreas. 'The Principle of Subsidiarity as a Constitutional Principle in International Law', *Global Constitutionalism* 2, no. 1 (2013): 37–62.

Føllesdal, Andreas, Petrov, Jan, and Zysset, Alain. 'The ECtHR's Response to Illiberal and Authoritarian Practices', *ECHR Law Review*, forthcoming 2026.

Freeden, Michael. 'Ideology and Political Theory', *Journal of Political Ideologies* 11, no. 1 (2006): 3–22.

Gardbaum, Stephen. 'Comparative Political Process Theory', *International Journal of Constitutional Law* 18, no. 4 (2020): 1429–57.

Gardbaum, Stephen. 'Comparative Political Process Theory II', *Global Constitutionalism* 14, no. 2 (2025): 219–37.

Gardbaum, Stephen. 'Human Rights as International Constitutional Rights', *The European Journal of International Law* 19, no. 4 (2008): 749–68.

Gerards, Janneke. 'The Prism of Fundamental Rights', *European Constitutional Law Review* 8, no. 2 (2012): 173–202.

Giannopoulos, Christos. 'The Reception by Domestic Courts of the Res Interpretata Effect of Jurisprudence of the European Court of Human Rights', *Human Rights Law Review* 19, no. 3 (2019): 537–59.

Grabowska-Moroz, Barbara, Grogan, Joelle, Kochenov, Dimitry V., and Pech, Laurent. 'Reconciling Theory and Practice of the Rule of Law in the European Union', *Hague Journal on the Rule of Law* 14, no. 2 (2022): 101–5.

Greer, Steven, and Wildhaber, Luzius. 'Revisiting the Debate about "Constitutionalising" the European Court of Human Rights', *Human Rights Law Review* 12, no. 4 (2012): 655–87.

Grimm, Dieter. 'Proportionality in Canadian and German Constitutional Jurisprudence', *The University of Toronto Law Journal* 57, no. 2 (2007): 383–97.

Guzek, Damian, and Grzesiok-Horosz, Agnieszka. 'Political Will and Media Law: A Poland Case Analysis', *East European Politics and Societies* 36, no. 4 (2022): 1245–62.

Hailbronner, Michaela, and Kujus, Lisa. 'Representation Reinforcement in the European Court of Human Rights', *Global Constitutionalism* 1 (2025): 1–23.

Halmai, Gábor. 'Populism, Authoritarianism and Constitutionalism', *German Law Journal* 20, no. 3 (2019): 296–313.

Heri, Corina. 'Loyalty, Subsidiarity, and Article 18 ECHR: How the ECtHR Deals with Mala Fide Limitations of Rights', *European Convention on Human Rights Law Review* 1, no. 1 (2020): 25–61.

Howse, Robert. 'Epilogue: In Defense of Disruptive Democracy – A Critique of Anti-populism', *International Journal of Constitutional Law* 17, no. 2 (2019): 641–60.

Issacharoff, Samuel. 'Fragile Democracies', *Harvard Law Review* 120, no. 6 (2007): 1405–67.

Issacharoff, Samuel. 'The Corruption of Popular Sovereignty', *International Journal of Constitutional Law* 18, no. 4 (2020): 1109–35.

Jackson, Miles. 'Judicial Avoidance at the European Court of Human Rights: Institutional Authority, the Procedural Turn, and Docket Control', *International Journal of Constitutional Law* 20, no. 1 (2022): 112–40.

Kaltwasser, Cristóbal Rovira. 'The Ambivalence of Populism: Threat and Corrective for Democracy', *Democratization* 19, no. 2 (2012): 184–208.

Kalyvas, Andreas. 'Popular Sovereignty, Democracy, and the Constituent Power', *Constellations* 12, no. 2 (2005): 223–44.

Kenny, Paul D. '"The Enemy of the People": Populists and Press Freedom', *Political Research Quarterly* 73, no. 2 (2020): 261–75.

Kerpel, Aron. 'Pole and Hungarian Cousins Be? A Comparison of State Media Capture, Ideological Narratives and Political Truth Monopolization in Hungary and Poland', *Slovo* 29 (2017): 68–93.

Khaitan, Tarunabh. 'Guarantor Institutions', *Asian Journal of Comparative Law* 16, no. 1 (2021): 40–59.

Kleinlein, Thomas. 'The Procedural Approach of the European Court of Human Rights: Between Subsidiarity and Dynamic Evolution', *International & Comparative Law Quarterly* 68, no. 1 (2019): 91–110.

Klimkiewicz, Beata. 'State, Media and Pluralism: Tracing Roots and Consequences of Media Policy Change in Poland', *Publizistik* 62, no. 2 (2017): 197–213.

Kosař, David, and Šipulová, Katarína. 'The Strasbourg Court Meets Abusive Constitutionalism: Baka v. Hungary and the Rule of Law', *Hague Journal on the Rule of Law* 10, no. 1 (2018): 83–110.

Kosař, David, Šipulová, Katarína, and Kadlec, Ondřej. 'The Case for Judicial Councils as Fourth-Branch Institutions', *European Constitutional Law Review* 20, no. 1 (2024): 82–119.

Kovács, Kriszta. 'Parliamentary Democracy by Default: Applying the European Convention on Human Rights to Presidential Elections and Referendums', *Jus Cogens* 2 (2020): 242–58.

Krekó, Péter, and Enyedi, Zsolt. 'Explaining Eastern Europe: Orbán's Laboratory of Illiberalism', *Journal of Democracy* 29, no. 3 (2018): 39–51.

Krygier, Martin. 'The Challenge of Institutionalisation: Post-communist "Transitions", Populism, and the Rule of Law', *European Constitutional Law Review* 15, no. 3 (2019): 544–73.

Kumm, Mattias. 'The Idea of Socratic Contestation and the Right to Justification: The Point of Rights-Based Proportionality Review', *Law & Ethics of Human Rights* 4, no. 2 (2010): 142–75.

Kurban, Dilek. 'Forsaking Individual Justice: The Implications of the European Court of Human Rights' Pilot Judgment Procedure for Victims of Gross and Systematic Violations', *Human Rights Law Review* 16, no. 4 (2016): 731–69.

Kurnosov, Dmitry. 'Pragmatic Adjudication of Election Cases in the European Court of Human Rights', *European Journal of International Law* 32, no. 1 (2021): 255–79.

Lacey, Nicola. 'Populism and the Rule of Law', *Annual Review of Law and Social Science* 15, vol. 15 (2019): 79–96.

Landau, David. 'Abusive Constitutionalism' 47, no. 1, *UC Davis Law Review* (2013): 189–260.

Landau, David. 'Populist Constitutions', *The University of Chicago Law Review* 85, no. 2 (2018): 521–43.

Leloup, Mathieu. 'The Concept of Structural Human Rights in the European Convention on Human Rights', *Human Rights Law Review* 20, no. 3 (2020): 480–501.

Letsas, George. 'Two Concepts of the Margin of Appreciation', *Oxford Journal of Legal Studies* 26, no. 4 (2006): 705–32.

Loewenstein, Karl. 'Militant Democracy and Fundamental Rights', *The American Political Science Review* 31, no. 3 (1937): 417–32.

Loewenstein, Karl. 'Militant Democracy and Fundamental Rights, II', *The American Political Science Review* 31, no. 4 (1937): 638–58.

Madsen, Mikael Rask. 'The Narrowing of the European Court of Human Rights? Legal Diplomacy, Situational Self-Restraint, and the New Vision for the Court', *European Convention on Human Rights Law Review* 2, no. 2 (2021): 180–208.

Madsen, Mikael Rask, Cebulak, Pola, and Wiebusch, Micha. 'Backlash against International Courts: Explaining the Forms and Patterns of Resistance to International Courts', *International Journal of Law in Context* 14, no. 2 (2018): 197–220.

Malkopoulou, Anthoula, and Norman, Ludvig. 'Three Models of Democratic Self-Defence: Militant Democracy and Its Alternatives', *Political Studies* 66, no. 2 (2017): 442–58.

Manin, Bernard. 'On Legitimacy and Political Deliberation', *Political Theory* 15, no. 3 (1987): 338–68.

Mansbridge, Jane. 'Rethinking Representation', *The American Political Science Review* 97, no. 4 (2003), 515–26.

Mansbridge, Jane, and Macedo, Stephen. 'Populism and Democratic Theory', *Annual Review of Law and Social Science* 15, no. 1 (2019): 59–77.

Manucci, Luca, and Weber, Edward. 'Why the Big Picture Matters: Political and Media Populism in Western Europe since the 1970s', *Swiss Political Science Review* 24, no. 4 (2017): 313–34.

Marks, Susan. 'The European Convention on Human Rights and Its "Democratic Society"', *British Yearbook of International Law* 66, no. 1 (1996): 209–38.

Misak, Cheryl, and Talisse, Robert B. 'Debate: Pragmatist Epistemology and Democratic Theory: A Reply to Eric Macgilvray', *Journal of Political Philosophy* 22, no. 3 (2014): 366–76.

Möller, Kai. 'Authority and Intent in U.S. Constitutional Culture', *Jerusalem Review of Legal Studies* 10, no. 1 (2014): 125–36.

Möller, Kai. 'Dworkin's Theory of Rights in the Age of Proportionality', *The Law & Ethics of Human Rights* 12, no. 2 (2018): 281–99.

Moravcsik, Andrew. 'The Origins of Human Rights Regimes: Democratic Delegation in Postwar Europe', *International Organization* 54, no. 2 (2000): 271–52.

Mortier, Tobias. 'Reprehensible or Legitimate Aims? A Proposal for a New Approach to Article 18 ECHR in Light of Its Predominance Test', *European Convention on Human Rights Law Review* 4, no. 2 (2023): 133–78.

Mudde, Cas. 'The Populist Zeitgeist', *Government and Opposition* 39, no. 4 (2004): 541–63.

Mudde, Cas, and Kaltwasser, Cristóbal Rovira. 'Studying Populism in Comparative Perspective: Reflections on the Contemporary and Future Research Agenda', *Comparative Political Studies* 51, no. 13 (2018): 1667–93.

Müller, Jan-Werner. 'Should the EU Protect Democracy and the Rule of Law inside Member States?', *European Law Journal* 21, no. 2 (2015): 141–60.

Müller, Jan-Werner. '"The People Must Be Extracted from within the People": Reflections on Populism', *Constellations* 21, no. 4 (2014): 483–93.

Mureinik, Etienne. 'A Bridge to Where? Introducing the Interim Bill of Rights', *South African Journal on Human Rights* 10, no. 1 (1994): 31–48.

Näsström, Sofia. 'Democratic Representation beyond Election', *Constellations* 22, no. 1 (2015): 1–12.

Niesen, Peter. 'Anti-extremism, Negative Republicanism, Civic Society: Three Paradigms for Banning Political Parties', *German Law Journal* 3, no. 7 (2002): 1–32.

Petrov, Jan. 'The Populist Challenge to the European Court of Human Rights', *International Journal of Constitutional Law* 18, no. 2 (2020): 476–508.

Pin, Andrea. 'The Transnational Drivers of Populist Backlash in Europe: The Role of Courts', *German Law Journal* 20, no. 2 (2019): 225–44.

Popelier, Patricia, and Van De Heyning, Catherine. 'Procedural Rationality: Giving Teeth to the Proportionality Analysis', *European Constitutional Law Review* 9, no. 2 (2013): 230–62.

Rostbøll, Christian. 'Second-Order Political Thinking: Compromise versus Populism', *Political Studies* 69, no. 3 (2021): 559–76.

Roznai, Yaniv, and Brandes, Tamar Hostovsky. 'Democratic Erosion, Populist Constitutionalism, and the Unconstitutional Constitutional Amendments Doctrine', *Law & Ethics of Human Rights* 14, no. 1 (2020): 19–48.

Saul, Matthew. 'The European Court of Human Rights' Margin of Appreciation and the Processes of National Parliaments', *Human Rights Law Review* 15, no. 4 (2015): 745–74.

Scheppele, Kim Lane. 'Autocratic Legalism', *University of Chicago Law Review* 85 (2018): 545–83.

Scheppele, Kim Lane. 'How Viktor Orbán Wins', *Journal of Democracy* 33, no. 3 (2022): 45–61.

Scheppele, Kim Lane. 'The Opportunism of Populists and the Defense of Constitutional Liberalism', *German Law Journal* 20, no. 3 (2019): 314–31.

Scheppele, Kim Lane. 'The Rule of Law and the Frankenstate: Why Governance Checklists Do Not Work', *Governance* 26, no. 4 (2013): 559–62.

Sharon, Assaf. 'Populism and Democracy: The Challenge for Deliberative Democracy', *European Journal of Philosophy* 27, no. 2 (2019): 359–76.

Spanó, Robert. 'The Future of the European Court of Human Rights: Subsidiarity, Process-Based Review and the Rule of Law', *Human Rights Law Review* 18, no. 3 (2018): 473–94.

Spanó, Robert. 'The Rule of Law as the Lodestar of the European Convention on Human Rights: The Strasbourg Court and the Independence of the Judiciary', *European Law Journal* 27, nos. 1–3 (2021): 211–27.

Spanó, Robert. 'Universality or Diversity of Human Rights? Strasbourg in the Age of Subsidiarity', *Human Rights Law Review* 14, no. 3 (2014): 487–502.

Stone Sweet, Alec. 'A Cosmopolitan Legal Order: Constitutional Pluralism and Rights Adjudication in Europe', *Global Constitutionalism* 1, no. 1 (2012): 53–90.

Suteu, Silvia. 'The Populist Turn in Central and Eastern Europe: Is Deliberative Democracy Part of the Solution?', *European Constitutional Law Review* 15, no. 3 (2019): 488–518.

Szente, Zoltán. 'The Interpretive Practice of the Hungarian Constitutional Court: A Critical View', *German Law Journal* 14, no. 8 (2013): 1591–614.

Tan, Floris. 'The Dawn of Article 18 ECHR: A Safeguard against European Rule of Law Backsliding?', *Goettingen Journal of International Law* 9, no. 1 (2018): 109–41.

Turkut, Emre. 'The Venice Commission and Rule of Law Backsliding in Turkey, Poland and Hungary', *European Convention on Human Rights Law Review* 2 (2021): 209–40.

Uitz, Renata. 'The Rule of Law at Risk: What Is Next?', *Hague Journal on the Rule of Law* 11, no. 2 (2019): 473–8.

Ulfstein, Geir. 'Transnational Constitutional Aspects of the European Court of Human Rights', *Global Constitutionalism* 10, no. 1 (2021): 151–74.

Umut Orcan, Necdet. 'Legitimate Aims, Illegitimate Aims and the ECtHR: Changing Attitudes and Selective Strictness', *University of Bologna Law Review* 7, no. 1 (2022): 7–40.

Urbinati, Nadia. 'Continuity and Rupture: The Power of Judgment in Democratic Representation', *Constellations* 12, no. 2 (2005): 194–222.

Urbinati, Nadia, and Saffon, Maria Paula. 'Procedural Democracy, the Bulwark of Equal Liberty', *Political Theory* 41, no. 3 (2013): 441–81.

Varol, Ozan O. 'Stealth Authoritarianism', *Iowa Law Review* 100, no. 4 (2014): 1673–742.

Varol, Ozan O. 'Structural Rights', *The Georgetown Law Journal* 105, no. 1001 (2017): 1001–53.

Voeten, Erik. 'Populism and Backlashes against International Courts', *Perspectives on Politics* 18, no. 2 (2020): 407–22.

von Staden, Andreas. 'Subsidiarity, Exhaustion of Domestic Remedies, and the Margin of Appreciation in the Human Rights Jurisprudence of African Sub-Regional Courts', *The International Journal of Human Rights* 20, no. 8 (2016): 1113–31.

Waldron, Jeremy. 'The Rule of Law and the Importance of Procedure', *Nomos* 50 (2011): 3–31.

Wildhaber, Luzius. 'The European Convention on Human Rights and International Law', *International and Comparative Law Quarterly* 56 (2007): 217–32.

Young, Alison. 'Populism and the UK Constitution', *Current Legal Problems* 71, no. 1 (2018): 17–52.

Zysset, Alain. 'Calibrating the Response to Populism at the European Court of Human Rights', *International Journal of Constitutional Law* 20, no. 3 (2022): 976–1005.

Zysset, Alain. 'Freedom of Expression, the Right to Vote, and Proportionality at the European Court of Human Rights: An Internal Critique', *International Journal of Constitutional Law* 17, no. 1 (2019): 230–51.

Zysset, Alain. 'Searching for the Legitimacy of the European Court of Human Rights: The Neglected Role of "Democratic Society"', *Global Constitutionalism* 5, no. 1 (2016): 16–47.

Zysset, Alain, and Çalı, Başak. 'Exhausting Domestic Remedies or Exhausting the Rule of Law? Revisiting the Normative Basis of Procedural Subsidiarity in the European Human Rights System', *Transnational Legal Theory* 14, no. 2 (2023): 157–77.

Zysset, Alain, and Scherz, Antoinette. 'Proportionality as Procedure: Strengthening the Legitimate Authority of the UN Committee on Economic, Social and Cultural Rights', *Global Constitutionalism* 10, no. 3 (2021): 1–23.

Online

Congress of Europe: The Hague, 7–11 May 1948 / Congrés de l'Europe: La Haye, 7-11 Mai 1948 (Council of Europe, 1999), https://book.coe.int/en/books-on-europe/8118-congress-of-europe-the-hague-7-11-may-1948.html.

Eiermann, Martin, Gultchin, Limor, and Mounk, Yascha. 'European Populism: Trends, Threats and Future Prospects', Tony Blair Institute for Global Change, 29 December 2017, https://institute.global/insights/geopolitics-and-security/european-populism-trends-threats-and-future-prospects.

'Hungary: Almost 78% of the Media Are Pro-government', European Federation of Journalists, 9 May 2019, https://europeanjournalists.org/blog/2019/05/09/hungary-almost-78-of-the-media-are-pro-government/.

Koschalka, Ben. 'Polish State Firms Direct Advertising Cash to Government-Friendly Media, Data Show', *Notes from Poland* (blog), 1 April 2022, https://notesfrompoland.com/2022/04/01/polish-state-firms-direct-advertising-cash-to-government-friendly-media-data-show/.

Mertek Media Monitor, 'Centralised Media System: Soft Censorship 2018' (Mertek Booklets 18), 13 December 2019, https://mertek.eu/en/2019/12/13/centralised-media-system-soft-censorship-2018-mertek-booklets-18/.

Mertek Media Monitor, 'Media Landscape after a Long Storm: The Hungarian Media Politics since 2010' (Mertek Booklets 21), 7 December 2021, https://mertek.eu/en/2021/12/10/media-landscape-after-a-long-storm-the-hungarian-media-politics-since-2010-mertek-booklets-25-2/.

Müller, Jan-Werner. 'Rising to the Challenge of Constitutional Capture', 21 March 2014, https://www.eurozine.com/rising-to-the-challenge-of-constitutional-capture/.

O'Boyle, Michael. 'Electoral Disputes and the ECHR: An Overview', https://www.venice.coe.int/webforms/documents/default.aspx?pdffile=CDL-UD(2008)010rev-e.

Pech, Laurent, and Kochenov, Dimitry. 'Respect for the Rule of Law in the Case Law of the European Court of Justice: A Casebook Overview of Key Judgments since the Portuguese Judges Case', SIEPS Report no. 3, September 2021, https://sieps.se/en/publications/2021/respect-for-the-rule-of-law-in-the-case-law-of-the-european-court-of-justice/.

Registry of the European Court of Human Rights, 'Guide on Article 18 of the Convention: Limitation on Use of Restrictions on Rights', ECHR-KS, 28 February 2025 https://ks.echr.coe.int/documents/d/echr-ks/guide_art_18_eng#:~:text=This%20particular%20Guide%20analyses%20and%20sums%20up%20the,principles%20in%20this%20area%20and%20the%20relevant%20precedents.

Silva, Rui. 'Populist Parties Thrive on Discontent: The Data Proves It', The Conversation, 12 November 2024, http://theconversation.com/populist-parties-thrive-on-discontent-the-data-proves-it-242278.

Wójcik, Anna. 'Restoring Poland's Media Freedom', *Verfassungsblog*, 2023, https://verfassungsblog.de/restoring-polands-media-freedom/.

INDEX

Printed by Integrated Books International,
United States of America